Where

Lions Roar

WHERE

LIONS ROAR

Ten more years of African hunting

Craig T. Boddington

Safari Press Inc.

P.O. Box 3095, Long Beach, CA 90803-0095, USA

Boddington, Craig, T.

Second Edition

Safari Press Inc.

1997, Long Beach, California

ISBN 1-57157-069-1

Library of Congress Catalog Card Number: 97-67710

10 9 8 7 6 5 4 3

WHERE LIONS ROAR

CONTENTS

CONTENTS

FOREWORD

Shocking as it seems, a full decade has passed since I chronicled my first decade of African hunting in *From Mount Kenya to the Cape.* At that time ten years seemed a nice milestone and there seemed to be plenty of material. I did not write *Kenya* in the anticipation that our present volume would someday exist–and I'm quite surprised that it does.

Mind you, I'm not the wide-eyed innocent I was when I first hunted in Kenya twenty years ago. Back then I honestly believed that my initial hunt in Kenya would get Africa out of my system once and for all. That plan sure didn't work! Since then I have never claimed–to anyone–that my next African hunt would be my last. I certainly won't make such a claim now. As anyone who has hunted Africa can echo, this huge, magnificent, and greatly troubled continent has a way of grabbing hold–and it does not relinquish that hold. I seriously doubt I will stop going to Africa. The obsession remains as strong now as ever. However, I doubt the conditions will again favor subjecting my readers to a compilation of a decade's worth of African hunting.

This for several reasons. When I wrote *Kenya,* covering the years from 1977 to 1986, I had hunted most of the "standard" African hunting areas, at least from an American perspective–but both my experience and that book were far from complete. I do not claim either that or this volume to be a complete reference on African hunting; both works are nothing more than one man's African hunting experience over a ten-year period. For a more complete picture, one needs to look at H. C. Maydon's *Big Game Shooting in Africa;* James Mellon's *African Hunter;* and perhaps a more current work as yet unpublished.

Even so, when I wrote *Kenya* many African horizons remained to be seen. A decade later I can say exactly the same thing–but it's been a busy ten years. This volume will in-

FOREWORD

clude hunts in Zimbabwe, South Africa, Namibia, Zambia, and Botswana–the countries that dominated *Kenya* and have been dominant in the American safari market as well. In that regard, I can relate from personal experience how these countries and their game and hunting conditions have changed over the past twenty years. Of equal importance, this decade just past has carried me to many of the African destinations that once seemed a distant dream. Mozambique, Ethiopia, Tanzania, the Central African Republic–just the names are the stuff a hunter's dreams are made of.

I'm writing these lines on a rainy afternoon, laptop hooked up to a battery charged by solar panels, in a lovely camp from which I'm trying very hard to shoot a bongo, that wonderful forest antelope that, to many, is the Holy Grail of African hunting. I don't know if we will be successful or not; bongo hunting is neither easy nor simple, and success is hardly ensured. Oddly, it doesn't seem as important as it once might have been. I have long since recognized that I am not a species collector. I have indeed hunted a great variety of African game–but I have no large trophy room and don't particularly covet one. I would like to take a bongo, you bet, and at this moment I still have two weeks of the allocated three to find one. But either way, what I will really have collected from this trip is another of the matchless memories Africa has given me.

Much of the hunting I have done has been an excuse to see new country or to revisit an area that I was particularly enthralled by. In this volume, for instance, you will see that, in 1995, I returned to Lake Bangweulu, using the black lechwe I failed to take back in the 1980s as an excuse. The problem, of course, is that I have yet to see a part of Africa that I wouldn't like to return to! Even so, should both I and my African obsession last another decade, there may be relatively little new to add.

FOREWORD

During the past few years I have become quite fascinated by the remote, difficult areas of central Africa. This is my third trip to the C.A.R., and I would like to hunt Cameroon. I am also fascinated by the opening of the Congo. However, there is some limit to my curiosity.

The forest itself, along with the sub-Saharan savannas and transition zones, are fascinating–but I am simply not enough of a collector to wish to hunt the myriad duikers that constitute the chief game of West Africa proper. One thing I should have learned over the past twenty years is what I like to hunt the most, and I can tell you quite readily. The chess game of serious cat hunting–both lion and leopard–makes hunting them quite fascinating. And of course the danger mustn't be underestimated. I have, however, done my share and I honestly don't expect to do much more hunting of the great cats.

Elephant hunting is also one of Africa's greatest thrills, and, done properly by tracking, it is one of those physically demanding hunts that yield great satisfaction. However, on a writer's income I seriously doubt I will do a great deal more elephant hunting! The other thing, quite honestly, is that, as with cats, I've done my share and can hardly justify doing more. Yes, I will argue endlessly that the future of these species in the real world of Africa–very much a Third World Africa–lies in their having economic value, and that only sport hunting can give them the kind of economic value that will ensure the species' survival. However, I should let someone else enjoy these experiences and accept that I've had mine.

That leaves my two great and lasting passions in African hunting–buffalo and the spiral-horned antelopes. The former because a buffalo hunt has all the elements that make a hunt great: a quarry with keen senses, an element of danger, and physical difficulty. In all ways buffalo are worthy adversaries. The latter, though not dangerous, offer great diversity, extreme difficulty, and unusual beauty. Each and every one, from the numerous varieties of bushbucks through the great prizes–the bongo, mountain nyala, and giant eland–have given me some of my fondest memories of African hunting. The perverseness of human nature is such that, ultimately, the difficulty of the hunt contributes immeasurably to the memory!

I doubt my future will include a great deal more bongo hunting, but just as most Americans never tire of whitetails and Europeans love their roebuck, I suspect I will never tire of hunting bushbucks and greater kudu, either for the pot or for an ultimate trophy. And I will certainly never tire of hunting buffalo. I can't match Ruark's description, when he said that the Cape buffalo "looks like you owe him money." I also can't match Wootters's description of him as "the gunfighter of the African bush, dressed all in black." These are apt. In today's society, I liken hunting buffalo to shooting lawyers: they're dangerous, mean, nasty, ugly, treacherous, smart–and there are lots of them, they are easily replaced, and you don't get too attached to them as individuals.

Hunting buffalo is something I will never tire of, and in the pages that follow you'll join me as I indulge this passion. You will also join me as I hunt elephant, the great cats, and all of the principal spiral-horned antelopes. Sometimes we'll win and sometimes we'll lose–but ultimately, the great prize has been in just being there. Telling about these hunts has brought back some wonderful memories. I wish I could see again and experience again all this decade has brought. This I cannot do, but writing about it has been the next best thing. So turn back the clock to 1987, and join me as we travel from South Africa to Ethiopia and from Kilimanjaro to the Congo for my last ten years of African hunting.

Craig Boddington
South of Yalinga, C.A.R.
May 1996

DEDICATION

To Robert E. "Pete" Petersen, living proof that good hunters make their own luck—and a man who enjoys being afield more than anyone I know; Tom Siatos, the best all-round shot with rifle, handgun, and shotgun that I ever saw; Ken Elliott, a fine shot, especially one heck of a shotgunner, and a great guy to share a camp with; the late Howard E. French, the most knowledgeable gun editor America ever produced; and Gary Sitton, once a great editor and now the most talented gunwriter in the business . . .with thanks to all for giving a chance to a young ex-Marine who thought he could write about the things we all love.

A brilliant African sunrise caught us just as we left the Cape Mountains–cold in July–and passed out onto the endless reaches of the great Karroo, those windswept high plains so much like America's western Great Plains. Our journey was not particularly historic, but in a few hours we would retrace truly historic movements. And, in a microcosmic way, we would trace the amazing development of South Africa's safari industry. We left Lew Tonks's farm deep in the Cape Mountains at some particularly absurd hour, surely before 3:00 A.M. First we passed through Graaf-Reinet, and then we headed northwest, winding our way through dark mountains toward the Karroo.

Tonks's hometown of Graaf-Reinet is one of South Africa's great landmarks. Established some two hundred years ago, it was one of the earliest and most important settlements along the route of the Great Trek. South Africa's cape was settled by hardy Dutchmen fully five hundred years ago, primarily as a refitting stop for ships of the Dutch East India Company. The Cape was as fertile then as it is now, and for generations relatively little incursion was made into the great hinterlands to the north.

1

THE EASTERN CAPE

Then came the English, thanks to a negative result for the Dutch in one of the endless European wars. English oppression, as perceived by the Boer colonists, caused them to inspan their oxen and journey into the wilderness. Theirs was an odyssey lasting several decades, which began with the Great Trek of 1835-1836. This was not one bold move on the part of the Boers but rather a slow, steady migration that eventually saw the founding of the Orange Free State and the Transvaal. Graaf-Reinet was one of the important towns founded along the route.

Of course the Great Trek continued its northern movement, on through the Cape Mountains, spilling out onto the Karroo, then continuing north to find the sweet grass savanna of the Orange Free State, and continuing on for a first blooding with the Zulu nation. The Boers found the Karroo rich in game, with springbok so numerous the herds seemed to writhe like pale smoke on the distant horizon. Most likely it was here, too, that the trekkers first encountered some of South Africa's many indigenous rarities. Except they probably weren't rare then.

Somewhere near the Great Karroo they almost certainly encountered *blaawbok* ("blue buck" in Afrikaans), a bluish-colored, short-horned cousin of the roan and sable, extinct long before the turn of the century. Almost certainly they also encountered the blesbok and its colorful, less common cousin, the bontebok; and of course black wildebeest, vaal rhebok, and so many other species. In those days wildlife was not only free food but also an impediment to the progress of farming and raising domestic livestock. For that matter, the Bushmen that inhabited the region were also an impediment, and were hunted as relentlessly as the game. Though these values are incomprehensible today, remember that North America's wildlife (and her native peoples) suffered similarly throughout the nineteenth century.

The *blaawbok* was a casualty, and what little is known of it comes from a handful of surviving skins and skulls and a paucity of written accounts. Many more species could have been lost, except that a couple of far-thinking farmers saved some of the remnants for posterity. Southern white rhino, bontebok, black wildebeest–all could easily have gone the way of the *blaawbok*, but enough were saved.

We were driving from the Cape Mountains to Phil van der Merwe's farm on the Karroo. *Van der Merwe* is a classic Boer surname (actually, the very surname used for the series of South African jokes, like American Polack jokes, that make fun of supposedly backward Boer farmers), and Phil's farm was one of the places where the bontebok had been saved from extinction.

Just twenty years ago, when I started my African hunting career, South Africa was an almost unheard-of hunting destination. The center was still East Africa, but the sun was setting on the classic East African safari. Uganda was gone, probably never to return. Tanzania was closed but would reopen again in 1981. By then, however, the guard had changed. Twenty years ago things seemed to be business as usual in Kenya, birthplace of safari hunting–but there were already signs of change. Elephant hunting closed in 1973, the same year Tanzania closed hunting. Numerous veteran professional hunters–Dave Ommaney, John Kingsley-Heath, Harry Selby, Tony Henley, Mike Rowbotham–had moved south, seeking new hunting grounds in Botswana and Zambia. And then, in 1977, Kenya closed hunting.

The safari industry was shocked to the core and many of the great Kenya hunters were instantly ruined. Those who had already moved south could chuckle, but many of the rest floundered, some taking years to find new homes and new lives. Finn Aagaard came to America and became one of our best and most knowledgeable gunwriters. My Kenya hunter, Willem van Dyk, did a couple of seasons in the Sudan, then eventually immigrated to the South Africa of his Boer ancestors. Others scattered throughout the continent, wherever hunting remained open—Rhodesia, South West Africa, even Central Africa, where the old Kenya hunter Fred Duckworth now hunts. Still others turned to photographic safaris, and many left Africa forever. Without question, 1977 marked the end of an era.

Zambia and Botswana were prepared to step into the void, but the rest of southern Africa really wasn't. Brush wars had shut down the Portuguese colonies of Angola and Mozambique. In 1965 Rhodesia's Unilateral Declaration of Independence from Great Britain had sparked her own brush war, desultory at first. But by 1977 it was ugly. There was good hunting there, for sure, and a few operators continued in spite of the "terrs," but Rhodesia had to become Zimbabwe before her now-great safari industry could take off. South Africa, too, wasn't ready.

There was some hunting around, to be sure. Thousands of South African hunters had no trouble finding a kudu or springbok for the pot or for biltong. There were even a very few pioneer outfitters–Norman Deane of Zululand Safaris, Bowker and Scott in the Karroo, Peter Knott of Kuduland Safaris, Garry Kelly, and a couple of others. There were also a few pioneer game ranchers like Phil van der Merwe.

In those days, just twenty years ago, South Africa was a very specialized destination. Outfitters like Norman Deane took serious collectors out for vaal rhebok, nyala, and black wildebeest–but virtually no one considered South Africa a prime safari destination. It wasn't, yet.

The greatest modern reference on African hunting is James Mellon's milestone work *African Hunter.* Written in the early 1970s, of several hundred pages in this comprehensive volume, Mellon devotes just ten to South African hunting. Things changed fast.

Beginning sometime in the 1970s, as the sun set on the East African safari, South Africa's game ranching industry took off like a rocket. Thousands upon thousands of acres were converted from livestock to game, and existing game ranchers like van der Merwe and a few dozen more found a bull market for breeding stock. In just a few short years South Africa became a hunting country–and by 1987, when this volume commences, it was hosting more safaris than any other African country.

I saw it happen and saw its hiccups along the way. In the late 1970s I did what most hunters went to South Africa to do: I hunted nyala in Zululand. In the early 1980s I hunted gemsbok and black wildebeest and such in the northern cape, and through the mid-1980s I hunted white rhino in the Transvaal and vaal rhebok in the Cape Mountains. I saw South Africa's safari industry grow and mature. And, yes, I saw some of the banditry that was part of the maturing process—"game ranches" that were little more than pens, put-and-take lion hunting, and worse. Fortunately I also saw PHASA, the Professional Hunters Association of South Africa, mature and grow teeth, and through the 1980s South Africa's safari industry did a fine job of regulating itself and cleaning up its act.

The growth continued, and sturdy Lew Tonks, driving me through the dawn to Phil van der Merwe's farm, was a prime example of that growth. Perhaps a decade or so older than I, Tonks had been a successful electrical contractor in the pretty coastal city of Port Elizabeth, jumping-off spot for most eastern Cape hunting. A lifelong sport hunter, Tonks had acquired a farm in the mountains somewhere along the way. He'd hunted it himself, but he'd mostly raised Angora goats. As the safari industry boomed and wool prices bottomed he'd obtained a professional hunter's license, and–like many farmers–had begun to seriously develop the game on his farm.

In 1986, helping out his old friend and fellow outfitter Lud de Bruijn, Lew had guided me to a super vaal rhebok. This year, in 1987, he was on his own, operating as Camdeboo Safaris. The way things work in South Africa, excepting a few protected species the landowner owns the game found on his land. The game is subject to seasons, but if the land is game-fenced an exclusion to the seasons can be granted, and the game can be hunted or sold at the landowner's discretion. This privatization of wildlife is the primary reason for the wealth of game in South Africa today. Pure and simple, game ranching is good business.

For Lew, as both a landowner and a professional hunter, the best deal going would be to take a client, like me, on his own land–thereby profiting both from the daily safari rate and the trophy fees from his own game. This is the goal for all farmers-cum-outfitters, and the investments made in breeding stock are staggering. Introductions and reintroductions have also radically altered exactly what game is available in various parts of South Africa.

Traditionally, for instance, the northern Transvaal has held the thornbush species also common to Zimbabwe: large southern greater kudu, blue wildebeest, impala, Limpopo bushbuck, zebra. Natal and Zululand were famous for nyala. The northern Cape held Kalahari species such as gemsbok, red Cape hartebeest, and springbok. The Eastern Cape, bounded by mountains, developed its own unique subspecies: Eastern Cape greater kudu, the small black southern bushbuck, Cape eland, Cape grysbok. The Great Karroo on up to the better watered Orange Free State held the plains species: blesbok, bontebok, black wildebeest, springbok, and more.

These days, and increasingly, the lines are blurred. With live-captured breeding stock available, adaptable species such as gemsbok, blesbok, impala, zebra, blue wildebeest, and even black wildebeest are now found discontinuously throughout the country. In the 1970s and 1980s a hunter in South Africa could expect to travel literally the length and breadth of the country to obtain a varied bag. Today, unless he's searching for something special, a hunter could enjoy a much more leisurely safari on one good property–such as Lew Tonks's place–and take a dozen species.

In 1987 Lew's own game was still developing. Plus, to be honest, I did want some special things! Two of those special requests brought us to Phil van der Merwe's farm, and others took us elsewhere. One was the bontebok, close cousin to the blesbok. The latter, a fairly drab and diminutive cousin of the hartebeest clan, is quite common throughout South Africa. The former, similar in size but much more colorful, was originally limited in range and today is quite uncommon. The second reason for our journey into the Karroo was the white color phase of springbok. Both animals provide insight into South African hunting today.

When viewing a head mount it is difficult to distinguish a bontebok from a blesbok. It's said that the base color of the bontebok's horns is white, while the blesbok's are black. Likewise, the bontebok commonly has a continuous white facial blaze, while the blaze of the blesbok is interrupted. These characteristics are not definitive. The brighter body pelage of the bontebok, however, is distinctive. The bontebok has an iridescent saddle over its flanks, making a fairly mundane antelope one of the most colorful in Africa. Bontebok were almost lost during the excesses of the last century, but a remnant few were spared.

Blesbok are slightly larger than bontebok, and the two interbreed freely. As game ranching increased and the hunting industry grew, a great many crossbreeds were sold as bontebok–with the eventual risk that bontebok, saved from ignorance, could be lost due to interbreeding. The game ranching industry regulated itself with the establishment of registered herds, with permits issued for surplus males–echoed by CITES (Convention on International Trade in Endangered Species) permits for exportation of trophies. Tonks had started his own herd, and we saw some dandies on his farm, but he wasn't ready to hunt them yet. So for bontebok we journeyed to Phil van der Merwe's place, which held not only one of the largest, but one of the original, herds.

White springbok are a different story. The common color phase is buff body with white underbody and facial markings, plus black side flashes. Generations ago both black springbok and white springbok (with black horns and black eyes, hooves, and nose, thus not albinos) were identified in certain herds in the Karroo. Through live capture and selective breeding, herds of both black and white springbok were created. Though these animals are typically smaller than common springbok, the color variations are essentially man-made, so I don't agree with their separation into different record-book categories. However, they are both quite beautiful. Some years before, I'd taken an unusually large black springbok–not far from van der Merwe's farm–and of course I'd shot the common variety. I wanted to complete the set with a white springbok, and Phil had one of the best herds.

The white springbok was considered the most difficult of the two, so after coffee and pleasantries we headed out into a vast, treeless paddock. Years before, on another hunt in the Cape, my hunting partner had described white springbok as "those spooky white things." His description was apt. All springbok are much like pronghorn, keen-eyed and wary. For unknown reasons, the white variety seems more spooky than the rest. My .375, the only scoped rifle I had on that trip, was sighted in with fast handloads with 240-grain Trophy Bonded Bearclaws. Even so, I was outclassed on these small, elusive antelope. After several blown stalks and a couple of missed shots we finally got a very fine buck, which I shot badly and then followed up. But it was beautiful, almost pure white with just a shadow of light tan markings.

The bontebok came easier, but not by much. These open-country animals are normally quite visible and vulnerable, but not on this day. We searched high and low, finally finding a small herd up in some hilly country. It was another long shot, not well executed, but just before sundown we got a very fine bontebok.

Phil van der Merwe's place wasn't our first stop during our hunt. South Africa is a good place for two kinds of hunters: the first-time African hunter in search of a good bag of plains game and the experienced hunter looking for South Africa's rarities. The former type of client is much simpler for an outfitter to deal with, especially if that outfitter–like Lew Tonks–happens to own his own game ranch. Unfortunately for Lew, I was in the second group. Thanks to a number of previous trips, I had hunted most of southern Africa's common species and a fair number of South Africa's indigenous prizes as well: nyala, black wildebeest, mountain reedbuck, vaal rhebok, blesbok, and such.

Don't get me wrong; I'm not really a trophy collector. In fact, I don't even have a trophy room. The money that could have gone into taxidermy and trophy rooms has generally gone into more hunting! There are vast differences between the hunting experiences offered by different animals. All the spiral-horned antelopes, for instance, are exceptionally challenging and interesting to hunt–as well as being strikingly beautiful. On the other hand, many of Africa's open-country herd animals are interesting, but bagging them is often more of a collection than a hunt. If I'm in an area that offers greater kudu or bushbuck I'll always hunt them, but it's unlikely that I'll ever shoot another black wildebeest or blesbok.

I am most fortunate to be able to make a living writing about hunting and hunting arms. I dearly love to hunt Africa, and just being there is really excuse enough. However, I've always tried to find a few good reasons to hunt a specific place. While I don't consciously collect trophies, I do collect memories and experiences, so whenever possible I try to broaden my experience by hunting different animals. When Lew and I agreed on a hunt, we went over his game list and picked several specific animals that I hadn't hunted on previous trips. Two of these were the white springbok and bontebok. The rest of our game list comprised Eastern Cape greater kudu, southern bushbuck, Cape grysbok, and bush pig.

The various races of greater kudu differ very little to my eye; I suspect some serious taxonomic splitting was going on when the five races of kudu were subdivided. However, the Eastern Cape kudu does average a good deal smaller in the horn than the southern greater kudu to the north, and also tends to have a much longer and more luxurious black-and-white neck ruff, possibly due to the cool climate of the Cape Mountains. No matter; greater kudu are always worth hunting, and they provided the starting point for my hunt with Lew.

His farm up in the mountains produces pretty good bulls, but he has few bushbuck and no Cape grysbok. I flew into Port Elizabeth on the Indian Ocean coast. "P.E." serves as the jumping-off point for most Eastern Cape safaris, and is one of the prettiest little cities I've ever seen. With a lovely coastline and streets lined with flowering trees, it reminds me of how southern California's coast must have been before millions of people discovered it. Just inland from P.E. is a belt of low, rolling hills covered with dense thorn, not unlike California's impenetrable chaparral. Lew arranged for us to start our hunt here, on a farm owned by Arthur Rudman. Rudman, like Phil van der Merwe, started game ranching long before it was fashionable. His brushy, hilly farm held good numbers of kudu naturally–and most would agree that, after years of careful management, his kudu herd was the best in the Cape. The same type of country is good for bushbuck, and over the years Rudman's place has produced a high percentage of the Cape grysbok taken by visiting sportsmen. Lew knew we could find a good kudu, and felt Rudman's farm offered a good chance for bushbuck and grysbok as well.

It didn't look much like kudu country to me–the brush was as thick as anything I've ever seen. But that thick brush was alive with greater kudu. The obvious problems were seeing and judging horns and getting a shot. We hoped to glass kudu in some of the scattered openings in the early morning, but that didn't happen–plenty of kudu, yes, but only cows and youngsters. As the day wore on we started working along narrow canyons, glassing into the brush and, when that didn't work, tossing rocks to get animals moving. Move they did, often in good-sized herds–but horns we couldn't see as gray forms rustled through the brush.

By midday it was bright and hot and nothing was moving. I had pretty much figured this would take a day or two, and I was looking forward to the afternoon hunt, hoping the cool of evening would get things moving. We didn't have to wait that long. The sun was barely past its zenith when Lew spotted some cows and a fine bull in an oval clearing far up on a brushy ridge. We got a bit closer, but it was still a long shot, and I held the old .375 high on the bull's shoulder and squeezed off just as it walked toward the brushline. It was a hit, but not a good one, and I knew that long before we reached the clearing and found a few drops of blood.

Fortunately kudu are relatively soft for their size; with a similar poor hit I'd have been in for a long day with an American elk or a gemsbok. But this was a kudu, and after a short run it began walking slowly, leaving a good spoor along a narrow game trail through the brush. The trail led us along the ridge toward a saddle, and we moved slowly, expecting to jump the kudu at any moment. We caught it before the saddle, standing behind a thick bush, and finished the job. It was a beautiful kudu with a lovely cape.

In a business in which all too many of us shoot better with our typewriters than with our rifles, I have always tried to tell things honestly the way they happened–though sometimes I'd just as soon not. Along those lines, it might occur to you that my shooting was terrible on this trip–and you'd be correct. There's a good object lesson in this. Not all African hunting is the same, and without making excuses, I had a poor tool for the job at hand. After leaving the Cape I was headed up to Botswana to hunt buffalo and such. I had my open-sighted .470 for buffalo and, mostly for fun, an open-sighted Westley Richards .318. The general-purpose rifle was my old .375 topped with a 1¾-5X scope. This rifle, a left-hand converted Model 70 Winchester, is an old friend and veteran of many safaris. It's a perfectly adequate all-around African rifle, as any scoped .375 is. However, the Cape is a fairly specialized area with most shooting at fairly long range on open plains or from one hill to the next. I got by with the .375, but my shooting was an embarrassment; I'd have been better off with something that shot flatter, kicked less, had a lighter trigger pull, and wore a bigger scope . . . which, as you'll see, is exactly what I carried when I again hunted the Cape a few years later!

But we got the kudu, and the guys made sort of a stretcher like affair and carried it out whole, something I've never seen done with so large an animal. Then, starting with the evening hunt and continuing for the next couple of days, we tried very hard to get a southern bushbuck or a Cape grysbok.

As with kudu, the lines between the various races of bushbuck are extremely blurry. However, unlike kudu, there are significant regional differences in both size and coloration among the various bushbuck subspecies. The southern bushbuck is a midsized bushbuck, but older males are extremely dark, every bit as dark as the nearly black Menelik bushbuck of Ethiopia, at the opposite end of the continent. All bushbucks are difficult to hunt, and the thicker the cover the more difficult they are.

The Cape grysbok is a tiny, straight-horned pygmy antelope, at first glance similar to a steenbok, but smaller, more reddish, and with more rounded ears. Its small size combined with the thick brush it prefers makes it extremely difficult to hunt. In fact, we glassed, we did drives, and we cruised slowly through likely areas early and late, and both animals eluded us completely. With the bushbuck we saw only females, and with the grysbok, well, I can't tell you what we saw for sure. We saw quite a few, but in the brief glimpses we had we were never certain we saw the tiny horns. Lew had set a definite date for our hunt on Phil van der Merwe's place, so we agreed to move on and take a rain check on the grysbok and bushbuck business.

After our successful trip into the Karroo we spent a couple of days looking around Lew's own farm, a beautiful mixture of wooded valleys and open meadows dominated by a significant mountain. He indeed had a fine herd of bontebok coming on, along with plenty of zebra, impala, gemsbok, springbok, black wildebeest, and more. That was a decade ago as I write this, and Lew has long since been hunting all these species and more on his own place.

Then it was time for one of the hunt's main events: a serious try for bush pig. The bush pig is one of those anomalies among African game. It is quite possibly the most widespread of all African game animals, yet it is almost never taken on purpose. Bush pig hang in the heaviest cover available and are almost exclusively nocturnal. Most are taken by accident, when you just happen to bump into one in the daytime, and most African hunters eventually bump into one over the course of a few safaris. I never had. In fact, I'd never seen one, though I'd been in many areas where they occur. For some reason I wanted one very much. I don't think Lew had bush pig on his game list, but as I recall he mentioned casually that there were lots of them in the coastal thorn out of P.E. After much prodding he had agreed to set up a hunt, stating that he thought we could get one. He told me the hunt was set up for Saturday, the next-to-last day of our hunt . . . and then he got very secretive until the evening before.

"Here's the deal on bush pig," he finally said. "You're going to hunt with a couple of local guys who are crazy about bush pig hunting. They've got good dogs and they hunt them every single Saturday. Usually they get a couple, but they don't speak English, only Afrikaans. So they've asked me to give you their ground rules. First, no scopes. It will be close shooting and they don't want any risk to their dogs. That .318 of yours will be fine. Second, no softpoint bullets–solids only. Probably because of the thick brush–you simply won't believe it. Third, you have to keep up with them; if the dogs bay a pig they won't wait for you. Oh, and there's just one more thing." He smiled. "Don't expect me to go with you. I've got this all set up, but I'm not crazy. I'm waiting in the truck." He did, too!

Sometimes the most interesting hunts revolve around the least glamorous animals. What followed was one of the longest and most difficult hunting days I've ever had, and long before it was over I understood why Lew had stayed in the truck. A couple of times I wished I was with him!

We met my South African hosts in the predawn chill at a lonely farmhouse in the thickest coastal thorn not far from Port Elizabeth. They were nice young fellas, although frighteningly trim and fit, and indeed they spoke not a word of English. The farmer gave us some coffee and showed us some wonderful kudu horns, then Lew and I followed their battered truck out into the lands in the gray dawn. This was flatter country than Arthur Rudman's, although we weren't very far from where I'd shot my kudu a week before. I was reminded of South Texas's brush country, with wall-to-wall thornbush about ten feet high cut only by a network of ranch roads much like South Texas's endless *senderos*.

First we went to a couple of known crossings, finding some of the round pig tracks on the second try. Then the dogs were released, fierce-looking mutts of some terrier mixture. They gave voice immediately, heading into the brush. My new friends listened awhile, then we drove around to another road hoping to head them off. So far so good. Except we didn't see the dogs for a long time after that–which is pretty normal stuff for hound hunting everywhere. Either that trail wasn't as fresh as we'd thought, or the pigs outdistanced the dogs, or the dogs and pigs together outdistanced us. But at some point we got the dogs back, and I was given to understand that the easy way, which we'd tried, wasn't going to work.

The hard way commenced––and kept on through most of the day. It consisted of running––not walking, not trotting–along those endless cutlines, trying to keep the dogs in sight or hearing. One of the houndsmen spoke a bit of German, about the same level as my long-forgotten high school German, so we were able to communicate a little bit. Between gasps for air, that is. This man was a lieutenant in the South African Defense Force. At the time I was a major in the Marine Corps Reserve, and I explained to him that mostly meant I was too old for this, but he never broke stride. I run a lot and was in pretty good shape, but I'm not a marathon runner, and I'm sure we ran most of a marathon that day, down one long cutline, up the next, and back again. Somehow the hours slipped past.

It was midafternoon on a blessedly cloudy day, and I don't know how many times we'd lost the dogs and relocated them.

Heck, I didn't even know what direction we were going by then–but in the distance I heard the dogs' barking reach a crescendo. The pace picked up, and even I could figure out they had something. We topped a low rise and the barking was louder, off in the brush to our right. The lieutenant grinned at me and dove into the brush. I followed, every man for himself as we tried to reach the dogs. I was almost there when a single shot rang out, and in moments I crawled through a tangle and saw the dogs worrying the carcass of the first bush pig I had ever seen.

My friends were delighted; this was a normal Saturday outing for them. It wasn't important to them who shot the pig. Yes, I was disappointed–and kicking myself for not pushing harder through the thorn. We dragged the animal, a big sow, through the brush and out to the road . . . and then the dogs tuned up again. One of the guys motioned to me and we took off like a shot, me figuring out a bit belatedly that there had been two pigs; the dogs were now on the boar.

It wasn't a long run. The pig had crossed the road ahead of us and the barking indicated it was bayed up a few hundred yards off to the left. Into the thorn again, this time oblivious of the thorns that literally ripped the clothes from my body. We ran, crawled, and staggered, and finally the barking was close–and the thorn even thicker. My new friend pointed ahead, and I could see dust swirling. I belly-crawled under a low roof of overhanging thorn, right to the edge of what seemed a small room, floored with dust and covered with a slightly higher ceiling of thorn. In that room, in the half-light of perpetual shade and swirling dust, was a scene Dante would have been proud of. The pig, a big boar, whirled and danced while the dogs–one at the nose and one at the heels–stayed just out of reach of its tusks.

I slid the old .318 out from under me, chambered one of the old Kynoch 250-grain solids, and tried to pick a safe shot. The pig whirled to the right, broadside for an instant. At a range of mere feet the bead settled into the vee and I held where the neck joined the skull. The shot crashed in the close cover and the pig dropped, the dogs closing in while thick dust settled over us all.

Fortunately we'd gone in a huge circle, probably several; the trucks weren't terribly far away. I threw my pig over my shoulders, letting someone else carry my camera pack, and we all staggered along. It was sundown when we got back to Tonks, resting comfortably in the truck. I was a wreck, tattered and exhausted–but so were my companions. Lew took one look at us and shook his head. "You see why I stayed in the truck?" I have a feeling he'd been there and done that!

Outside of Maun the ground was baked hard, the grass–and anything else green–long since eaten by cattle and goats. The light plane skimmed over the man-made wasteland for long minutes, then crossed the cattle fence into a different Africa. I couldn't really see the fence, but its trace was clear on the land below. A controversial barrier, the fence was erected to protect domestic livestock from wildlife and their diseases. It blocked the migration of herd animals such as wildebeest and many thousands died, but today it showed up as an obvious blessing. On man's side of the fence was an ocean of smooth red clay, broken only by thatched huts and scraggly trees. On wildlife's side of the fence the grassy savannas, floodplains, and thornbush stretched to the horizon, eventually giving way to the emerald-green mosaic of the Okavango's myriad flowing channels, endless papyrus reedbeds, and palm-studded islands.

It was obvious that anything on the Maun side of the fence must be starving–and equally obvious that animals and herdsmen alike would look across the fence with hunger, and probably anger. When the fence comes down the Okavango will die . . . and you cannot view the dichotomy without wondering how long that will be.

2 THE OKAVANGO DELTA

A couple of years had passed since I'd been in Ronnie MacFarlane's camp, a neat collection of green wall tents and thatched enclosures along the banks of one of the Okavango's myriad lagoons. A huge, spreading *marula* tree shaded the entire camp. It hadn't changed much, if at all. The hippos still called at night, and a camp leopard left tracks near the meat shed. Hunting lions added their distant thunder to the hippos' night music. This was the old Africa, the real Africa that is shrinking so quickly.

We ran into buffalo on the first morning, just a couple of miles from camp. It was a small herd feeding in a meadow of bright green grass, and as our Land Cruiser came around a palm island and into view they faded into the dark thornbush beyond. We took up the tracks on foot, following through open mopane mixed with patches of heavy thorn. They hadn't been spooked badly, at least not yet, and we caught up with them in just a half-mile or so. But they had stood in thick cover, and when we approached we heard only cracking branches and hoofbeats.

Ronnie ran, and I ran with him–not away, but toward the sound. Spooked buffalo will often run just a short distance, then stop to mill and see what disturbed them; charging the herd is often a good way to get a shot. Not this time. Past the thick cover was open woodland, the grass freshly burned, and at the edge of our vision we could see a few black forms trotting away. We ran some more, but the buffalo never stopped. When we ran out of breath we slowed down, checked the tracks to ensure a bull was in this group, and settled in for a long morning afoot.

The bushmen took the tracks, fresh and clear–gray ash in the burned, black grass. They led straight from one patch of brush to another, trotting for a mile, then walking, and then starting to meander. Then they started to circle. Started only, for just a quarter circle off the spoor was enough for them to catch the fickle quartering breeze.

The bush to our left erupted into hooves and cracking branches–they were moving away in flight, not fight. We ran to the sound, clearing the brush just in time to see, once again, broad black backsides and long black tails vanishing into a pall of dust.

Another mile and the tracks showed the buffalo were walking again . . . then another eruption in thick thorn, followed by more tracking. By now the tracks had led away from the dry thornbush and into the floodplains dotted with thick palm islands, surrounded by cracked earth where the waters had long receded. The game of cat and mouse continued here, but the country was such that a shot would be offered sooner or later. We continued.

Some cows had split off long since, and now we followed a small group, just three or four, but with bull tracks clear in the baked earth. These buffalo now understood the game and how to play it; they needn't run far, for the quartering wind was their friend. Again they jumped to our left, unseen, but this time the bush was small enough that, by running like maniacs, we could get clear. The bull was the outrider of the group, on my side. By the time we cleared the grass and brush it was eighty yards away and gaining, and sparse dry bushes still blocked the shot. I sprinted another twenty yards on a converging diagonal, and now the bull was clear.

Some time earlier, when the buffalo had flushed in impossible thorn, Ronnie had said, "If you get a shot, put a solid up his backside." Heeding his words, I went for the rear trigger as I pulled up short and swung the big .470 like a quail gun. I led the bull a bit with the heavy rifle swinging fast, and without my knowing I had pulled the trigger, the 500-grain solid in the left barrel was on its way.

It was a poor opportunity and a lucky shot; I caught the bull just behind the shoulder, quartering forward–almost perfect but a bit high. The bullet hit just high enough to shatter the spine, dropping the bull in full gallop. It slid thirty feet on its nose, raising a rooster tail of fine dust, and never moved. I shot it again, unnecessary this time but my custom on buffalo, and we walked up to admire it.

It wasn't a super buffalo, just a normal Okavango swamp bull with gnarly horns–and it was wonderful. I've missed closer, easier, and slower buffalo, and I'll probably tell you about some of them as these pages progress. But this time it was nice to be a star!

I still had the old .318 Westley Richards with me, hoping to play with it on some plains game. The .318, an example of the common (but inconsistent) convention of naming a cartridge by land rather than groove diameter, used an impossible-to-find .330-inch bullet. Today, with the resurgence of interest in the classic British rounds, I could buy ammo, but just a decade ago it was a problem. I had a good supply of very old Kynoch factory ammo, prewar, Berdan–primed, and corrosive as hell but the only postwar Kynoch I could find was loaded with the wonderful 250-grain steel-jacketed solid. It had done well on that South African bush pig, but wasn't right for antelope. Randy Brooks of Barnes Bullets had swaged down some .338 softpoints, and I shortened and sized .30–06 cases to load them in.

Ian MacFarlane, Ronnie's dad, stopped by camp one day and examined the .318 and my old .470. Ian is a double rifle man and lover of fine old rifles; with his khakis, short haircut, and cartridge belt full of big .475 No. 2 cartridges he seemed straight out of another era . . . and yet totally in place in the Botswana bush. He smiled as he held the .318. "It just makes you feel good to shoot something with a rifle like this!"

He was dead right, but that old .318 was quite a challenge. The stock was a bit long with too much drop, and it had a lot of cast–probably ideal for the right-hander it was built for, but I'm very left-handed! However, it shot those swaged-down bullets amazingly well through its 28-inch barrel: dead-on at 100 with the fixed blade, dead-on at 200 with the second blade. It had three more blades clear out to 500 yards, but I figured that was the gunmaker's optimism. A child of the scope era, I doubted I could *see* anything that far through open sights! I had enough trouble just seeing the tiny front bead, the pre-World War I answer for precision long-range sights. But I wanted to know what it felt like to use a rifle like the ones the great African hunters might have used.

Okay, it's true; I missed a couple of impala, quick tries at something between 100 and 200 yards. I just didn't have the hang of this open sight business. Then we followed a nice ram through some scattered mopane until it made the terrible mistake of standing in front of a tall red antheap at about 125 yards. This time I took more time, burying that tiny bead down into the vee notch. It dropped like a rock–once again demonstrating the theory of bullet weight and frontal area.

In fact, after I figured out that my scope-spoiled eyes needed extra time to properly center that tiny bead, results got monotonous. I've written before about a wildebeest I shot with the .318; I still consider it the best deliberate shot I've ever made. This was a special wildebeest. Like all common game, wildebeest are shot in large numbers, so record-book standards are high and really big ones are scarce. Ronnie had seen it on a previous safari–I think it'd been missed–but he thought we could find it again in the same area, a big flat of short grass dotted with antheaps surrounded by thick thornbush.

We did, and quite easily. In fact, we glassed it from the truck and Ronnie knew him at once. So did I. Virtually all wildebeest are of a type, but even at several hundred yards this one was different. When it looked at us its horns stretched well past its outspread ears, clearly one of the mythical 30-inch wildebeest that I had never seen before. It was with a herd of cows, not spooked but cautious, moving and feeding. We left the truck and moved from clump to clump, gradually closing the distance–except we were running out of both cover and light.

We gained the last antheap, and the wildebeest were bathed pink in the setting sun far out across a wide-open expanse. They were bunched in a low spot of better grass, and the light would be gone long before they moved. We were in a good position, snuggled down on the sun-warmed earth of a termite mound, a good rest and a good spot. Ronnie asked me if I could do it from there. I probably said yes, but I had no idea if I could or not. I raised the second leaf and settled down into a tight sling, checking the sights back and forth and concentrating on that tiny blade while I waited.

Finally the herd became restless and started to line out. When the bull was clear I rode that tiny blade–which now covered a third of the wildebeest–high on its shoulder and squeezed the trigger. It collapsed in midstride, just as the brilliant red sun touched the western horizon.

On my first safari in Kenya I'd shot a very good warthog, but at the time I considered him too ugly to have mounted. I felt the same way when I shot an even better one in Zimbabwe in 1980 or thereabouts. Unlovely as a warthog is, I'd been wanting a nice one to have mounted ever since–but good warthogs are few and far between, especially with the droughts ravaging so much of Africa in the mid-1980s. One hot midday we spied a couple of pigs mud bathing in a low spot on a flat where water had collected. Even through the caked mud we could see pretty good teeth gleaming on the larger of the two, so we crept up behind a brushy antheap about one hundred yards from the pigs. I took a steady rest over a stout branch, settled the bead into its notch, and shot the pig on the center of its shoulder. It dropped in its tracks without a kick. The old-timers were right; the .318 is an amazingly efficient cartridge.

The Okavango is an enchanting place in June. Mornings are cold; middays bright and warm, with a matchless blue sky from dawn to dusk. The scenery changes, too, from the palm islands, lagoons, papyrus beds, and flowing channels of the Okavango Delta to the increasingly dry thornbush beyond. On some starry nights lions roar in the distance. Much closer, the camp leopard coughs and leaves its tracks by your tent. And always there are the hippos with their haunting music . . . especially haunting when it's very close and you have to make a trip in the middle of the night!

During the days the game is always present–herds of lechwe, impala, wildebeest, zebra, and tsessebe. Once in a while you'll spot a sable antelope or the quick flash of a roan.

In a setting like this, time passes too quickly. Ronnie and I spiked out for sitatunga for a few days, moving from island to island in a dugout *makoro* canoe and pitching tents on palm islands. The moon was full and the sitatunga were feeding at night, leaving their Martianlike splayed-toe tracks on the very islands where we slept. One night a very big snake also left its bicycle-tirelike track in front of our tents. Ronnie's only comment was, "Well, there are a lot of mamba on these islands." We'd climb into the tops of big trees and glass through the days, seeing many lechwe and the occasional buffalo, and watching big crocodiles cruise the channels like submarines. We saw a very few female sitatunga, cautious and mouselike as they moved through the reeds, but we never saw a bull.

After we got back and cleaned up, Ronnie decided it was time to get a lechwe. We'd seen dozens of good bulls, but the red lechwe was the one species Botswana offered that I had never hunted, and I wanted a good one. Ronnie knew of a certain lechwe that, like the wildebeest, he'd been saving for a rainy day. This, after our lack of success on sitatunga, was the day.

I couldn't understand how he expected to find one lechwe in thousands of acres of papyrus, but perhaps they're more localized than I had thought. Ronnie had seen it just once, a couple of weeks before, with a client who had already taken his lechwe. It had been with cows in some open, freshly burned bush on the edge of endless, thick papyrus. We cruised the area slowly, and of course didn't see it. I wasn't surprised. And then one of the trackers saw lechwe far back in the brush, at the limit of vision.

We waited patiently, binoculars glued, while the dim forms fed slowly back and forth. There was a bull, and he was big. Ronnie declared it the right one and pointed me in its direction.

The ground was burned flat, but clumps of seared thorn remained. Using them as cover, I crouched over and started to close the distance. Eventually I was crawling on my hands and knees, pushing the .375 in front of me. One last clump, and the lechwe were still 200 yards distant–this time I was very glad I'd chosen the scoped rifle! I took a good rest, waited until the bull was clear, and squeezed the trigger. And yes, this one was as good as Ronnie had thought it would be, a red lechwe with horns as long as a good Kafue Flats lechwe, a fine and beautiful trophy.

That was the second time Ronnie showed clairvoyance on that hunt, but not the last. Or perhaps he just knew his area and his game. A couple of days later he casually announced, "Today we will go get a big kudu." We didn't particularly hurry around camp, leaving well after sunrise. Then we drove endlessly, at least two hours, to a sand river lined with heavy green vegetation. Ronnie mentioned that kudu should be nearby at midday this time of year.

Yes, they were. Up until that day I had never seen a shootable kudu in Botswana, and I considered them sort of an incidental animal that might be occasionally taken. Boy, did I have it wrong–it was just a matter of looking in the right place. There were kudu everywhere along that river–cows, young bulls, mixed herds, and lots and lots of bulls. We shot a fine kudu late in the afternoon, but by that time it was like hunting lechwe at Kafue or Bangweulu; we'd seen so many that we were confused. I lost count, but I think we saw more than fifty mature bulls that afternoon. The one we shot was wonderful, but I don't think it was the biggest we'd seen and passed!

At the tail end I wanted to hunt buffalo once more. Botswana remains the land of the buffalo, but in just a few years I've seen buffalo hunting become increasingly difficult. Botswana is a fine nation, one of the few working democracies on the entire continent. It is also blessed with a huge landmass and a tiny human population. That population, thanks to mineral wealth and plentiful land, enjoys freedoms denied to many Africans elsewhere. Among them is the right to hunt on a citizen's license. Buffalo, providing plentiful meat, are the primary target. As a result, the buffalo have become increasingly wary.

I don't begrudge these citizen hunters, no more than I would the million Pennsylvania whitetail hunters. But think what Pennsylvania would be like with just 10 percent of those hunters, and you have a model for Botswana without the citizen hunters. Some are ill-armed, but some are great hunters. We met a retired game warden one day who was out after buffalo with his .375. Gray-haired and keen-eyed, this old man knew his business. And of course it's his country. But there were a number of citizen hunters around, and the buffalo were scarce and wary.

On the last day we found fresh tracks on the edge of the swamps and followed them from island to island, wading chest deep in the cold water. We caught them on a large island, but as we closed in they caught a whiff of scent. Uncertain where it came from, they came toward us in a rush of pounding hooves and pillaring dust, not charging at all but just blindly stampeding.

Ronnie and I got clear and the herd thundered past, funneling through a narrow gap between two patches of brush. The bulls came last, galloping through thick dust. The shot was much the same as the one that had made me famous a couple of weeks earlier–except much closer. I picked a good bull, swung with it . . . and shot over the entire buffalo, riding the sight too high. I knew instantly and so did Ronnie; no reason to look for blood. Instead he took off running, saying, "Let's go!"

We ran after the vanishing dust, not bothering to track. Once the herd got over the panic they might stop to mill, and this time they did, but not long enough. Just as we pulled up next to them they ran again, raising dust along a long tree line. Ronnie knew the islands, and we cut across the angle, splashing through knee-deep water and watching the pall of dust.

We gained dry land and ran through the tree line, and there the herd stood, chalk-white dust hanging like heavy fog. The biggest bulls were on the right. I knew that; I saw them. Years before, without waiting for the professional hunter's practiced eye, I shot the wrong sable. I had programmed myself never to do it again. So when Ronnie said, "Shoot the one on the left," I did, without hesitation. I hit it well and truly on the point of the shoulder, then again with the second barrel when it turned and cantered, heart-shot, back into the herd. Yep, wrong buffalo, but a great buffalo hunt. And a buffalo hunt is always a fine way to end a safari.

3

THE PALALA RIVER

The Palala River winds its way through deep, brushy canyons, fed by countless streams that leave a network of mopane ridges and rimrocked plateaus. It's a country of big ranches and few game fences, one of the wildest areas remaining in the western Transvaal.

The area was the site of an early white rhino transplant, and I'd had a fine hunt there searching for a particular bull that had a penchant for going through cattle gates. Willem van Dyk, who had introduced me to Africa on my first safari in Kenya, took me there. Together we'd hiked up and down those rugged canyons looking for the right rhino's tracks, and I'd become enthralled by the Palala country.

It was not a well-manicured game ranch. In fact, game was relatively scarce, but what was there was very interesting. There was typical Transvaal game–a few herds of blue wildebeest and zebra, some impala, the odd bushbuck and kudu. A few waterbuck left tracks along the river, and up in the hills there were klipspringer and, surprisingly, southern mountain reedbuck–the northernmost population I'm aware of. Big hyena left tracks in the dust of the trails, as did equally big leopard. It was leopard that drew me back to the Palala, leopard and one more thing.

The Palala hosted big herds of eland, the tan Cape eland without body stripes. We'd run into them several times while searching for my rhino, and I'd vowed to come back and hunt them. The eland and the possibility of leopard, hunted Kenya-style with Willem van Dyk, was plenty enough lure.

We started out combing those deep canyons for leopard sign, and finding it readily enough, big pugs cut deep in the soft dust of the dry season. Then it was time to find some cat food, not always as easily done as said on the Palala. In midafternoon we went to a long, open valley that held one of the few developed water holes; zebra usually came to drink there, sometimes eland, and there were usually a few impala and warthog around. Game was scarce enough that bait animals had to be selected with care; we hoped for zebra, since I wanted the skin and we could get five baits from the carcass–thus finishing all our shopping at once.

Only a few shy impala scattered when we approached the water, but the zebra had been there, leaving their ponylike spoor fresh at the water's edge. We got a line on them, and Willem figured they'd stop to feed on the wooded ridge above the water. We proceeded slowly, and of course he was right; we found a small herd feeding along the ridgetop, their stripes giving them almost perfect camouflage in the dappled shade.

We had the wind, but it was open mopane and we were too close; the herd was suspicious, and there wasn't much time. We were lucky and identified the stallion right away. As usual, it was in the back of the herd, which is where we looked first. Better, it was standing clear and we could see its big neck. I shot it on the point of the shoulder with a 300-grain Bearclaw, and it was down in 40 yards. We quickly skinned and quartered it, finishing the chores in gathering twilight.

Next morning we hung some strategic baits along watercourses, near where we'd seen tracks but close by dense riverine growth so a leopard would feel secure in its approach. Now the game could begin, the chess game of waiting, checking baits, perhaps getting a hit, then building blinds and more waiting.

The best way to hunt leopard is to hunt leopard; you need to be serious about it and stick with it. Lion hunting is much the same, especially over bait. The day you get sidetracked, following buffalo spoor or looking for a big kudu, will always be the day you should have been checking baits or building blinds. I'd learned these lessons the hard way; it took me more than a hundred hunting days to take my first lion, including twenty-one days on that first safari with Willem van Dyk. Leopard hunting, well, so far I was up to only half a hundred days–but at this stage I'd *still* never seen a leopard come to a bait.

I can't say that I'm altogether unlucky on cats; I'd eventually straightened out my lion luck, and I'd called in a nice Botswana leopard with a varmint call. But I still wanted to get a leopard properly, over bait. The Transvaal isn't generally the best place for someone who's unlucky with leopard; they aren't particularly common, although the population is definitely increasing. Worse, South African leopards have been hunted hard for a century, and nowhere are they more clever or more difficult to bait. However, I thought the Palala country was remote enough and wild enough that we would have a good chance. I also wasn't putting all my eggs in the leopard basket; I wanted to track the Palala eland through those rugged hills and canyons just as much as I wanted to hunt leopard. In this regard I wasn't practicing what I preach regarding concentrating on the cat. It's easier said than done; with the wealth and variety of game Africa holds, to this day I have trouble concentrating on just one animal over there–even though I *know* that's the best road to success. And now I was doing it again.

I won't prolong the suspense. We didn't get a leopard. Part of it, perhaps, was because we didn't concentrate on the leopard. There were several days spent tracking eland when we might have been checking baits. Part of it, too, was because

I didn't allow enough time; we had just ten days for the hunt, and that's a bare-bones minimum for leopard even under the best of conditions. Part of it was because the cats just plain beat us.

We had multiple strikes over the ten-day period, and we sat for two different leopard that left tracks big enough to be interesting. The leopard came, both of them, but not while we were in the blind. In this regard we beat ourselves, and I have no regrets. Willem and I both agreed on Kenya rules–natural light only, and when the light was finished, we were finished. This is an altruistic and admirable way to hunt but, after all, a leopard probably doesn't care whether it is shot at night or in the daylight. And when you're hunting leopards that have been hunted hard since Selous's day, the handicap is great when you demand that a leopard come in the daylight.

In those days the landowners were concentrating on building up game numbers and the war on leopards was still in full swing. They were trapped, spotlighted, even poisoned throughout much of the Transvaal. Although leopard hunting was quite legal, baiting per se was not a legal method of take. The Palala, you see, was not a game-fenced area, so the local game laws applied. I had a license to take leopard, eland, zebra, and a few other things. That license specifically stated that we could bait for leopard, so we agreed to do it the old way or not at all. Not at all was the way it worked.

We built elaborate blinds and comfortable seats, using the old truck seat from the back of Willem's Toyota. I added to my tally of nights spent sitting over active baits–adding, as well, to my internal recording of the wonderful sounds heard as night comes to the African bush. But at first one bait and then the other it became obvious the leopard would not return. And then the baits ceased to be active altogether.

By that time it was all right, for the desire to take one of those Palala eland had become a more consuming passion. They were there, plenty of them, but it seemed they knew this game every bit as well as the leopard that were eluding us.

It could have happened early on, before we had a strike on the baits. It didn't, and that was my fault. On the second or third day, after our baits were hung and we had a day or so to concentrate on eland, we found the tracks of a big herd up in the brushy flats above the gorge of the Palala.

We followed them for just a short time before we saw tan forms feeding through the brush ahead of us. Then it turned into a very long morning while we moved from bush to bush, now losing the herd, now catching up again, and every so often catching glimpses of a big, wide-horned bull always screened by drab, thin-horned cows.

The cat and mouse went on for tense hours, with the tan bodies hidden in yellow grass and gray bush. Time and again we almost got a shot, but almost wasn't good enough. It was well past midday when the herd finally made a mistake. There was a long, narrow opening in the brush, and they began to move across the far end. This was the chance we'd waited for, and I was ready with the .375 solidly rested across a stout limb.

Willem watched the herd while I concentrated on the five-yard opening. He knew those widespread horns, and he told me when the bull was coming. I was ready, and I got the cross hairs on it as it entered the opening. Then I flinched, or wobbled, or just plain blew it.

We found a very few drops of blood, something I haven't admitted until this day, and they quickly petered out. We stayed with the herd the rest of the day, but the bull stayed with the cows and never gave us more than the occasional glimpse. Ultimately we concluded what I already knew: that I'd shot high through the withers, missing everything remotely vital. After that, although we played the leopard game as hard as we could, the eland became the more serious quest.

It seemed, too, that the easy pickings were now over. We lost that big herd for several days, but we followed the tracks of several bachelor groups through that thick Palala thorn. As the days wore on the hunt became more serious, but it remained intriguing as well. On the Palala you simply never know what you might run into.

One midmorning a herd led us into a thick grove on the top of a big plateau. We knew from the trotting tracks that the eland weren't close, and yet a herd of big, tawny antelope jumped at close range. Willem and I looked at each other in disbelief, and then we checked the tracks. Yes, they were big, triangular tracks, not the rounded bovinelike tracks of eland. We had jumped a herd of roan, some of the last of the native roan in all of the Transvaal.

On another occasion we were following five bull eland through some thick, hilly country. Unaware of our presence, they were walking slowly, feeding as they went. For once, the wind was in our favor, and there was no reason we shouldn't close the distance. Knowing we were close, we were moving very slowly when movement to our left checked our progress. We slowly dropped to the ground, waiting, and a small herd of bush pigs materialized in front of us.

You'll recall from a previous chapter the lengths I'd gone to see a bush pig, and now I had a whole herd–including a big male–just five yards in front of me. We waited, watching them root and grunt and push at one another. A bird in the hand is worth more than two in the bush; had this happened on so many occasions in the past I wouldn't have hesitated. But now I had taken a bush pig and we were on fresh eland tracks. We waited, motionless, hardly daring to breathe, until the pigs passed. Then we continued on the tracks.

Scarcely a hundred yards farther on we saw tan forms in the mopane just ahead. And then the wind shifted and that was the end of the eland for that day.

The days wore on and we ran out of hits on our leopard baits. Now the eland was the only game in town, and as the hunt neared its end it seemed we were beaten there as well.

By now we had tracked–and spooked–the majority of the eland, and things were getting very difficult. On the last morning we decided to try the big, brushy flats where I'd messed up early on. The herd was there; we found where they'd crossed the road in the early morning hours–the churned up spoor of many eland, with big bull tracks among the smaller hoofprints of cows and calves.

We jumped them several times without getting clear sight of a bull. It was midday, and on a normal day we would have given up. But this was the last day, and the eland enticed us further by running short distances each time, relying on the heavy brush rather than flight.

We jumped them in impossibly heavy cover and sat down to wait awhile, deciding to give it just one more try. After a few minutes we started again, following the tracks cut deep in red earth. I doubt we went a quarter of a mile before we ran smack into the herd, spread out in thick thorn with the nearest cows staring at us across twenty yards of open space. We froze, searching for the bulls.

One was in the clear, but it was a cripple-horned bull we'd seen a couple of times before, not a trophy. Behind it, almost hidden, was another eland. Time stood still while the nervous cows tried to make us out. Yes, we were sure; the hidden animal was a bull.

The cripple-horned bull moved to the left, and even I could see that the bull behind it was a good one, heavy-horned, beautifully shaped, with a thick spiraling ridge. This knowledge came instantaneously while I slowly raised the rifle. The bull was quartering to me, and I shot it on the point of the shoulder.

The glade erupted into motion, and my bull reared like a palomino stallion and swapped ends, running to the left. I stayed with it, working the bolt, and shot it again with a solid, behind the shoulder and quartering forward, the two bullet paths crisscrossing in the heart. It ran into a tree, uprooting it, and collapsed in a cloud of red dust while the herd thundered away. Right then, and to this day, I didn't much care about the leopard we didn't get. That hard-won Palala eland was plenty enough memory to last.

4

BOTSWANA'S CHOBE

While Maun in central Botswana is the primary jumping-off point for safaris into the Okavango region, the Chobe district in the northeast corner is usually reached from the little town of Kasane close by the Zimbabwe border. There's good news and bad news here; one doesn't exactly fly into Kasane, not by commercial means, anyway. However, it's a relatively short ride over good roads from Victoria Falls on the Zimbabwe side, and visiting the Falls is never an unpleasant experience.

We flew into Victoria Falls via London and Harare, myself and Ed and Sherry Weatherby. Ed's goal was to try out his new .416 Weatherby Magnum, the first new Weatherby cartridge in many a year. We were joined by videographer Chip Payne, with the additional goal of capturing the hunt on film. Chip is quite a character; with a wry wit and a cool head, he's not only good with his camera but he's also a good man to have around when the chips (pardon the pun) are down. Chip started his African career as a second cameraman on some of the early Capstick videos. Like all of us, he fell in love with Africa and over the course of a decade has spent months in the field filming.

Surprisingly, Chip doesn't hunt, at least not very much, which makes one of his principal claims to fame in Africa even more dramatic. A couple of years prior to our Chobe safari he was filming one of those dangerous tracking leopard hunts in the Kalahari. The party was following the leopard in two vehicles. As often happens, the leopard charged–but it charged the rear vehicle and came into the truck bed from which Chip was filming. The client's son, who was essentially an observer, was badly mauled. Chip, who had a broken hand from a previous accident, managed to put down his camera, find someone's rifle, and shoot the leopard dead at point-blank range. Even today, years later, he drinks for free at any gathering of Botswana professional hunters.

We were all badly jet-lagged by the time we dragged ourselves into the Victoria Falls Hotel, and we were ready for its old-world luxury. It was early in the year and the Falls were running well; we could see the plume of spray from the green veranda, and it was early enough in the day that we had plenty of time to relax, clean up, and go pay homage to the Falls. The Devil's Cataract was racing, and the spray mixed with the afternoon sun to form a perfect rainbow. Just off the path a couple of bushbuck rams slipped into the brush, surely a good omen of a fine hunt to come.

In the morning cool we motored across into Botswana, arriving at Hunters Africa headquarters. There we had to decide on licenses and of course wait a few more hours for the charter plane. This was essentially a buffalo hunt centered around Ed's .416, but Ed hadn't set foot in Africa for many years. He obtained licenses for a small selection of plains game, and I got a zebra license in addition to the buffalo. Our hunting days were very limited, so we let it go at that.

In the late afternoon our plane was finally ready and we took off, headed west. The Chobe River itself and a few of its major tributaries and flood channels are much like the Okavango, with papyrus reedbeds that are sitatunga haunts and floodplains that hold herds of red lechwe. But away from the river you quickly run into increasingly dry thornbush, until, well to the south, you reach the Kalahari Desert. The game is similar to that of the Okavango, but the buffalo tend to be bigger and there are more sable and roan, and also more eland. Farther south the thornbush game starts to mix with desert game, and you might encounter red Cape hartebeest and the occasional gemsbok. And there are elephant. Lots of elephant. Too many elephant, with evidence of their destruction everywhere.

Historically the area has always held good numbers of elephant, but in recent years the Chobe herds have expanded to some sixty thousand animals, far more than the carrying capacity of the range. Sport hunting, though closed at that time and reopened only in 1996, was never a major influence on Botswana's elephant numbers one way or the other. The increase was partly natural and perhaps partly due to refugee elephant escaping the war in Angola, to the north across the Caprivi Strip. We would see elephant in numbers every day, and we would see countless trees they had bulldozed over in their careless feeding.

It was late afternoon when the plane dropped us at a remote strip a couple of hours from Matsowdi Camp. Professional hunter Steve Liversedge was there to greet us, soft-spoken and competent, veteran of twenty years' hunting in several African countries. Steve had been hunting in Mozambique when Ed and his dad, Roy Weatherby, hunted there, many years earlier.

The next day, taking advantage of needed daylight, we filmed our arrival in camp. Our real arrival was much different. We were tired and dirty and past ready to finally reach our destination. The dark was gathering quickly, and Steve was making the best time he could on the dusty, rutted track. We rounded a curve and drove headlong into a huge pride of lions. The dusk was their time, and they had no reason to give ground. I felt like a Domino Pizza deliveryman who had turned into a blind alley in a bad neighborhood. Chip and I, sitting on the hunting seat in the open bed, uncontrollably shrank inward away from the danger–in particular from one lioness that crouched menacingly a few feet away. I swear it was licking its chops. And then we were past, and in a few minutes we were alighting amid the neat cluster of green wall tents, lit by the warm glow of camp lanterns.

The next morning we did some filming–including our arrival–and we also managed to sight in the rifles. As I was preparing to write this volume, publisher Ludo Wurfbain admonished me to be honest, including things that didn't work as well as those that did. Many of the mistakes I will relate are mine, and I've made a lot of them. But fair is fair, so in the interest of honesty and pleasing my publisher, I'll share the wealth. Ed had provided me with a rifle and ammo a couple of weeks prior to the hunt, so I'd already shot mine a bit and knew what to expect. What to expect is that the .416 Weatherby Magnum has a *lot* of recoil. The muzzle brake helps tremendously–you don't want to shoot this one without a brake. However, even with a muzzle brake, whenever you get more than a hundred foot-pounds of recoil things get exciting.

Now, Ed Weatherby is a truly brilliant rifle shot, one of the best I've seen and absolutely a natural at it. But I *know* he hadn't fired the .416 Weatherby Magnum until the moment of truth when he was obligated to fire sighting shots on camera for the video we were producing. He covered it up extremely well, but taking a close look at his face just after he fires the first shot has become my favorite part of the film!

I think my zebra was the first game to fall to the .416 Weatherby Magnum. After a quick stalk I shot it on the shoulder and was quite shocked when it didn't go right down. But it didn't go far, and the Swift A-Frame bullet performed extremely well. That was a concern that I'd had, since virtually all .416 bullets are designed for .416 Rigby velocities. Before we tackled buffalo I wanted to make sure the bullets would hold together at the much higher velocity. This one did, so we were ready.

Ed was first up on buffalo, and somehow it didn't go well. He and Steve slipped up on a feeding herd, with Chip right behind filming and me trailing a bit. They got their signals crossed and Ed shot the wrong one (as you know, I've done it, too–it isn't hard to do!). Worse, the buffalo moved as he shot, and now we had a wounded buffalo on our hands.

We followed the blood, three abreast when the thorn was open enough, Steve in the lead when the bush closed in around us. We didn't go all that far, but under such conditions a quarter-mile seems very far indeed. We were in a close place, moving single file, and then the green bush parted into a small clearing, not twenty yards across. On the far side was another wall of green, and in that green was a big black patch, too dark and too regular for shadows. Instinctively we fanned out, our two .416s and Steve's .458 trained on that black patch. Agonizing seconds passed, and why we didn't catch a charge I will never understand.

Finally Ed's .416 broke the standoff. The buffalo lurched, took more bullets, and crashed into the brush. Moments later we heard it bellow, and after a few minutes we moved on in.

This was not a good buffalo, so we agreed that Ed must have the one extra buffalo license we'd obtained, but first I'd have a turn.

It was a couple of days later that we drove along a big flat just after daylight. There, across the hunting track, were the sharp-cut tracks and fresh dung of a big buffalo herd. They had been feeding out in the open during the night, and shortly before we arrived they had worked their way back into the sheltering thornbush. You never know what will happen when you take a buffalo track, but these buffalo weren't far ahead and we expected to close.

We found them in an hour or so, and got enough of a glimpse to know there were several bulls in the bunch. But they were extremely nervous and hard to approach, even though the wind was in our favor. As we worked our way back and forth trying to get in close, Steve found the fresh pugs of a lion, and then we knew why they were nervous. We weren't the only hunters.

Knowing it was lions and not us that had made the herd spooky, we could be a bit more bold in our approach, and after a couple more tries we got ahead of them in a grassy swale where the herd had to come through an opening to reach the deeper thorn beyond.

A mass of cows passed first, moving and stopping, and then some bulls. We picked out a big fellow with good bosses, and it stopped right in the middle of the opening. The problem was that high grass obscured the bottom third of its body and most of its shoulder.

Until now I had never tried the behind-the-shoulder lung shot so classic on deer-size game. But a buffalo is no different than any other animal, and I surely had plenty of gun. I held just behind the shoulder halfway up the body, and fired. Even through the heavy recoil I could see it sag and almost go down. Then it gathered itself and ran with the herd. I didn't see it go down, but one of our trackers did. It dropped upright, wedged up by a blackened stump.

We moved in and threw sticks and clods at it, but no movement. It was finished. I do not recommend not firing a finishing shot. In fact, I strongly recommend *always* firing a finishing shot as soon as a downed buffalo is in view. This was, I think, the only time I have failed to do so, so in that context this was probably the only buffalo I have ever killed with a pure one-shot kill. Obviously the .416 Weatherby was awesome, but what I really learned was another extremely deadly shot on buffalo.

As we were admiring my bull a group of three local hunters came up behind us, tracking the same herd from a different angle. Since we'd fired just one shot and since the buffalo were more nervous about lions than us, Steve had already determined that we would proceed and try to get a second bull for Ed. He spoke to these guys and asked them to stay back until we were finished, and they agreed. And so we went on.

It was surprisingly easy. The herd stopped again in some patchy brush perhaps a half-mile ahead, and a good bull peered at us through a thin screen of green leaves. Steve took Ed up to a downed log and he shot the bull perfectly on the point of the shoulder. I could see the impact rock the big animal back onto his haunches, and then it was off.

It went just a short distance, then stood and waited for us, sick but not done. We had it spotted, and Steve and Ed circled him and got in a good finishing shot–thus ending our buffalo hunt.

Again the three local hunters came up to us. We gave them cigarettes, and they followed after the herd. As I recall, they had two .30-06 rifles with them and one old single-barrel shotgun.

It took some doing, but we got the truck in and butchered and loaded our two buffalo, a load so heavy that the Toyota was down on its springs. Then we headed back to camp.

We hadn't been there long when our three local friends drove their battered Land Rover into camp. One of their number, the eldest man, was badly gored in the lower belly, sick with pain and in shock. Apparently, armed with inadequate rifles, they had wounded a buffalo and taken a charge in the follow-up. The old man had taken the horn under his ribs and he was in bad shape.

The external bleeding was contained, so there was little to be done except get him an airplane, which Steve did immediately via our radio. They drove off to the airstrip, a bumpy two-hour ride that must have been unbelievably painful, and the plane was there when they arrived. Later we heard that the old man had lived, an amazing tribute to toughness.

The buffalo business concluded, we finished up our short hunt doing some excellent bird shooting, both dove and francolin, and looking for some antelopes for Ed. He wasn't successful in finding the kudu that he wanted, but he got a fine lechwe with a shot well worth recounting.

There was a big bull in a herd very far off across a grassy floodplain. For me it would have been a very difficult shot, but I've seen Ed do this kind of thing on deer hunts. He simply sat down, rested his .300 across his knees, and flattened the lechwe–quicker than you can read this. It was an amazing display of marksmanship, but that's the kind of shot Ed Weatherby is.

The hunt concluded, we spent a pleasant couple of days at the Chobe Safari Lodge in Chobe National Park. Ed and Sherry and Chip and I took the riverboat up the Chobe, watching the elephant along the banks and the schools of hippo in the channels and the riverine bird life everywhere–and we could look across the river into the high grass that marked the beginning of the Caprivi Strip, still a battleground. We also did some game viewing in the park itself–lots of elephant, and lots of elephant damage. Even then it was obvious that the elephant were eating themselves out of house and home, but eight more seasons would pass before elephant hunting was reopened in Botswana.

From top to bottom Africa is a wonderful place. I'd like to see all of it, but it's too big for any one man in any one lifetime. Worse, much of what I'd like to see is gone. I will never track elephant in the searing heat of Kenya's Northern Frontier District, nor will I see the long-gone herds of scimitar-horned oryx and addax on the fringes of the Sahara, nor will I ever hunt a black rhino anywhere. I have spent most of my African hunting career seeing as much of the continent as I could–but the sadness to this frenetic hunt-and-peck approach is that I have yet to see a place in the African bush that I wouldn't like to see again and again.

By the late 1980s I had seen most of the common hunting areas. Most of these I wanted to hunt again, and in most cases I had left behind some uncollected prize or other to give me a good excuse. In some of the chapters preceding this one, and in some yet to come, I revisit areas I had hunted previously–always with the sense of coming home after a long trip. That is always a great pleasure, even if the changes are bittersweet. But there has remained a burning hunger to see more of it, to see it all before time runs out. And herein lies a great dilemma.

5

THE SIMANJARO PLAIN

By virtue of my occupation I have been fortunate to do a great deal of what I like to do, and let no one think that a day goes by without my counting my blessings. The dilemma is that, by virtue of that same occupation–and because I'm beset by an African obsession that has never diminished with time–much of the Africa that I have hungered for has been beyond my means. One of the places that I wanted very badly to see was Tanzania, that huge country to the south of Kenya. The region was known as German East Africa before World War I; then it was the British colony of Tanganyika until 1961, when Tanganyika gained independence. In 1964 Tanganyika and Zanzibar merged into Tanzania.

This vast country of diverse habitats has always been one of Africa's great game areas, the setting for such African classics as Hemingway's *Green Hills of Africa* and Ruark's *Horn of the Hunter*. Tanzania closed hunting in 1973, reopening in 1981. The reopening should have been great news, but it was tempered by the fact that, at first, only the government-owned Tanzania Wildlife Corporation could conduct safaris. That eased with time, and by the mid-1980s there were several good safari companies in operation. I wanted to see this land of Kilimanjaro, but it seemed an elusive target.

One spring day in 1988 I stopped by Wayne and Inge Daugherty's Bischof's Taxidermy in Burbank to measure some trophies for Bill Baker, a former stockbroker who had recently acquired the famed Pachmayr gun company. Bill met me at the taxidermist's, and while I was admiring nice elephant tusks and a superb selection of plains game he told me he would be going back to Tanzania in late October. Would I care to join him? Yes, I reckon I would!

The hunt was to be with outfitter Luke Samaras, and the plan was to split it in half; the first part in Masailand and the second part in the Selous Reserve. In Masailand we should catch the first of the "short rains," cooling things down but not interfering with hunting. By the time we got to the Selous, in early November, we would be very late and would be pushing the rainy season . . . but this was the time the elephant came out of the thickets in search of new green. For me it was a dream come true, and the reality proved every bit as bright as the dream.

I'm often asked which was my best hunt ever. I can't answer that, for each and every one has been wonderful in its own way. Some, however, do stand out as brighter memories. Sometimes it's hard to say exactly why. It isn't strictly a matter of success, for some of those extra-bright memories came from unsuccessful hunts. But most of the really special memories have several elements in common. One is effort; we tend to appreciate most that which we work for the hardest, and that certainly applies to hunting. The professional hunter himself has much to do with making a safari special. It isn't altogether a matter of performance, but rather of hospitality and teamwork. On reflection, I think that the best safaris result when a team is created between the professional hunter, the client, and the trackers–each with his own job to do. And of course it helps when you throw in beautiful country, diverse and interesting game, and the sense of adventure that should permeate every African hunt. I have been fortunate to have enjoyed a number of safaris when all of these elements were present, and one of them was my first Tanzania safari in 1988.

The logistical problems of hunting multiple areas in Tanzania are enormous, so much so that it is often necessary to break the hunt into safaris within a safari. On a map distances don't look so vast, but the roads are poor enough that a journey of a hundred miles can take a full day. Charter aircraft are the only answer–very expensive in Tanzania–and quite often a camp change means a change in professional hunter as well, with the PHs remaining resident in a given camp while clients are shifted back and forth depending on their game preferences.

Our plan for splitting the hunt between Masailand and the Selous Reserve was a sound one in terms of hunting the greatest variety of game and seeing the most country. When studying Tanzania's incredibly rich game list, it should become immediately apparent that you need to make hard decisions as to what animals are most important *before* you map out the hunt. If you want to hunt the typical East African game–oryx, lesser kudu, the gazelles, gerenuk–then you must hunt Masailand. If you want sable or roan you must go south and west. For elephant your best chance is the Selous Reserve. Virtually the whole country is good for lion and leopard, but hunting cats takes time, and hunting elephant takes time. With luck everything can come together, but I want to say up front that the best way to hunt cats, even in Tanzania, is to spend the entire safari in one area. This applies even more to elephant. Bill and I did not do this, and as a result our successes were mixed with failures, but over all it was a magical and lucky safari.

Since we would end the hunt in the Selous Reserve, we flew into Dar es Salaam, where Luke Samaras met us and instantly whisked us onto a twin-engine charter to Arusha, jumping-off point for all Masailand safaris. We were met there by our professional hunters: veteran hunter Hannes Pretorious, who would hunt with Bill; and my PH, Michel Mantheakis. Like Luke, Michel is a native-born Tanzanian of Greek extraction. He's young, enthusiastic, and has a great sense of humor, and we made a good team.

Luke's Masailand area lay about three hours' drive south of Arusha on the eastern edge of the Simanjaro National Park. On the drive to camp we could see Kilimanjaro's snowy heights gleaming in the distance every time we topped a ridge, proof positive that we were really in Tanzania.

The hunting area itself is mostly dry thornbush cut by a few rivers that, during the dry season, leave only a few scattered pools. Rising out of the Masai Steppe are the occasional isolated mountains, many with hidden springs and catchments, and some with thick forests on their slopes. Along these rivers, in the hills, and in the dry thornbush beyond were small herds of resident buffalo, plus antelope such as lesser kudu, oryx, and Coke hartebeest, preyed upon by wandering lion and more localized leopard. There were a few Grant gazelle, impala, and warthog, and of course, in the heavier growth, bushbuck. However, the bulk of the herd animals–zebra, wildebeest, eland, the big herds of buffalo, Thomson gazelle–were still in the park where there was permanent water. On the edge of the park were vast shortgrass savannas, starting to come green after the first of the short rains. It was our hope that this new green and some additional rain would bring more animals filtering out of the park as our hunt progressed.

Bill had never hunted Masailand before, so his goal was to collect as many of the East African species as possible. I had hunted most of these animals in Kenya, so had no well-defined goals for this part of the hunt. I hoped to take one of those wonderful buffalo Masailand is famous for, but beyond that had no real specifics in mind. Sometimes, in hunting, you try too hard and can't make anything happen. And sometimes, if you sit back and let Nature take its course, it lays a smorgasbord in front of you. But, with two hunters sharing a camp, the results are often the opposite of what was planned or hoped for.

On the very first day, not far from camp, Bill and Hannes ran into a small herd of buffalo, and Bill shot one of the finest Cape buffalo I have ever seen. At a bit over forty-six inches, it isn't the widest, but it had wonderful bosses and horns that dropped well down and curled back around, perfectly matched.

Michel and I, on the other hand, battled and struggled for buffalo. We tracked herds along the rivers and we climbed into the hills. We hunted buffalo at least part of every day. We sorted through a half-dozen small herds and passed up innumerable "normal" bulls in the high thirties and very low forties, and we never fired a shot at a buffalo.

That isn't to say our buffalo hunting was unsuccessful. We had a ball crawling and sneaking around the herds. The special buffalo I sought simply wasn't there, but hunting buffalo on foot brings its own rewards . . . and sometimes a special bonus.

Our camp was a collection of green wall tents that ascended a gentle rise under some shady acacias, unquestionably the most scenic camp I have ever been in. Down the hill a short distance was a river, no longer flowing but with several deep pools. It was the best remaining water for some distance, and during the daytime the Masai villagers would come for water and the herdsmen would bring in their cattle. At night the water belonged to wild Africa, and we saw a wide variety of tracks each morning. One night early in the hunt a big herd of buffalo came to drink, waking us all up with their bovine bellowing and grunting.

In the morning we went far from camp to check game movement along the park boundary, returning at midday. After a rest we drove a short distance from camp, looking for the spoor of that buffalo herd. As Michel expected, we found where they had fed in some clearings in the night and early morning, then moved into some thick bush upriver to sleep through the heat of the day.

We never found the buffalo that day. We had gone just a short distance on their spoor and were crossing a little opening surrounded by dry yellow grass when some sort of unidentified grunt checked our movement. Ramathan, the younger tracker, peered intently into the grass to our left front, then pulled me to him and pointed. "*Simba* (lion)!" was all he said. I stared into the wall of grass, seeing nothing. Then the lion, disturbed from its nap, lifted its head and the image resolved into a fine male, lying broadside, head to the left.

I raised my Dumoulin .416 Rigby, centered the bead on its shoulder, and squeezed the trigger. The dull *click* was sickening and seemed extremely loud. It was loud enough across the few yards that separated us that the lion heard it and stood, uncertain. I'm sure Michel thought that I'd done the unthinkable and forgotten to load the chamber, but I knew the rifle was loaded. It didn't matter; I had to work the bolt and I did so, slowly, but now the lion was fully alerted and it started to slip away. I swung with it ever so slightly and fired–knowing that, now that I'd ejected the single softpoint, I was shooting a solid loaded as backup for buffalo. I saw the bullet go into its shoulder and was grateful when Michel's .458 went off next to me. Then the lion was gone and Michel whispered, urgently, "Reload and be ready!" I already had.

Seconds passed, then there was movement in the grass to the left, fast movement. Through the yellow screen I made out the form of a lion just as the charge began and fired again. The shape disappeared and we backed off, waiting for the shakes to cease before we walked in.

The lion was stretched out in death, a perfect and typical Masai lion with a reddish mane tinged in black, a wonderful and unexpected prize. I hadn't really planned to hunt lion, but I had one on license and Michel likes cat hunting; we had planned to hang a couple of baits just to see what might happen. Now we didn't need to. Bill, on the other hand, was hoping to take a lion somewhere along the trip. He had numerous baits out in both camps but never saw a shootable male–so I got his lion and he got my buffalo, which is the way these things go!

I did plan to hunt leopard, so to that end Michel and I hung several baits in strategic areas. We had one big male feeding for a short time, but after we built a blind and sat for him he never returned, thus adding to my growing tally of evenings spent waiting for leopard. But even our unsuccessful leopard hunting carried its rewards.

Greater kudu are well distributed throughout most of Tanzania, but nowhere are they as common as they are in southern Africa, and in Masailand a good greater kudu is a scarce prize. One theory is they have never recovered from a devastating rinderpest a generation ago, but for whatever reason one cannot count on a greater kudu in East Africa. While hiking in the hills after buffalo and mountain reedbuck we had seen the odd track and occasional female, and late one evening we glassed a big herd of cows and young bulls feeding on a distant hillside, but an East African greater kudu was a trophy I had no expectations of encountering.

One hot, sunny midday we had just checked a leopard bait along a brushy *korango* and were headed back to camp when a young greater kudu bull crossed the track in front of us. In southern Africa such an occurrence would be little cause for remarking, but in East Africa the sight of a greater kudu is a show-stopper. Michel instantly stopped the vehicle, and just as instantly I was out and looking–in time to see the big bull following on the heels of the youngster. It flashed across the road and was gone–but not quite. I stepped around a bush and saw it standing on the edge of the thick stuff, looking back, perhaps sixty yards away. The 7mm came up and the cross hairs found its shoulder just as it bunched for the single, final leap that would carry it to safety. The rifle went off just as it moved, and it collapsed on the spot.

I was excited. Michel was ecstatic. Our young tracker, Ramathan; our old tracker, Salum; and our game scout, Julius, were beside themselves. Over fifty-two inches of ivory-tipped, beautifully spiraling horns were now ours, and the celebration in camp equaled the lion dance I'd been treated to a few days before.

Of course the hunt wasn't all chance encounters and consolation prizes; the lion in lieu of a buffalo, the kudu instead of a leopard. Michel Mantheakis is a great hunter and a real workhorse–also a superb judge of trophy quality. We hunted hard each day, exploring, looking for new buffalo herds, or looking for something special.

On a previous safari he had seen a particularly fine Grant gazelle, and early in the safari we made a special trip looking for it. It was there, and we got it . . . but it started one of the strangest and most severe cases of "miss-itis" I've ever had. I simply can't tell you how many shots I fired before we got that gazelle–a really wonderful specimen.

A day or two later we went up to the shortgrass savanna along the park boundary. Michel admitted that this area was marginal for Thomson gazelle, but if we could find any we would find them here. He was right on both counts–there were a few of the petite, black-sided antelope, but only a few. We finally located a representative male well out across a shortgrass savanna, flat as a billiard table and almost as green. I got it with a perfectly placed shot. But it wasn't the first shot. In fact, had I been counting, I suspect I'd have run out of fingers and might have needed to take a shoe off so I could use my toes.

I don't know what was wrong; I was shooting my David Miller 7mm Remington Magnum, a fine and consistently accurate rifle that fits me like a glove. And of course, when we checked the sights, they were perfect. Once in a while you run into these brick walls, or at least I do, and the only solution is to forget it and go on.

As the safari progressed my shooting straightened out . . . sort of. Although I had taken a lesser kudu in Kenya, he was a very average specimen. Luke's Masailand area is especially good for lesser kudu; we saw bulls nearly every day, and I hoped to take a better one. To that end, and undoubtedly to Michel's frustration, we passed up quite a number of very nice bulls. His frustration no doubt increased when I missed not one but two very good lesser kudu. The first was a snap shot in brush, with no need for apology.

The second came on the day of the lion, shortly before we left the truck and started on the buffalo tracks. We had come through a thick patch of thorn and were looking across a broad, open *dambo* toward the far brushline. On the edge of that brush stood a lone lesser kudu, but *what* a lesser kudu! It had long, deeply spiraled, and extremely widespread horns–unusual for lesser kudu, whose horns tend to be much more parallel than the greater kudu's. It was totally magnificent, and it was standing there waiting for me. The range was about 250 yards, certainly a makable shot, and I had a dead-steady rest. And somehow I just flat missed. Michel was disgusted, but fortunately he's a bit of a mystic. After we got the lion he became convinced that Diana, goddess of the hunt and his personal saint, had caused me to miss the lesser kudu so we could go on to find our lion.

A few days later, while traveling through some dry thornbush cut by deep gullies, a lesser kudu barked and jumped across a gully and ran up a little slope about a hundred yards away. It was running like crazy, dodging through the thorn, and its horns seemed unusually long. As I worked my bolt I asked Michel, "Is he good enough?"

By now we had looked at a *lot* of lesser kudu, and I think he said, "––––, what do you want?"

This time I did it right. I got the rifle swinging ahead of it, and as it straightened out for an instant I swung well ahead of it and the rifle went off. Between recoil and brush the animal was simply gone, and thinking of my really horrible shooting I asked old Salum what had happened.

He grinned. "*Piga, kufa.*" (Hit, dead.)

All of the spiral-horns are wonderful, and all are great prizes, but I think the lesser kudu may be the most beautiful of the bunch. Iron gray with striking white side stripes, petite in size with a pixie face and those beautiful horns, it's pure class all the way–and this was a spectacular bull. Old Salum and I danced a jig around it.

Salum was a character. Probably seventy years old, he had tracked for my uncle, Art Popham, when he hunted with Dave Ommaney back in 1956, a safari that he remembered well because of the full skins taken for museum dioramas. Ramathan, the young tracker, had sharper eyes but was more impetuous. The two of them and Michel made a good team, and our game scout, Julius Sakayo Mahoo and his ever-present Westley Richards .404, was a good addition. It was a pleasure to hunt in the company of all four of them.

Bill and Hannes were staying equally busy. They weren't having much luck baiting in lion, but Bill was doing well on the East African game that was his primary goal. He also took the gazelles, plus a fine fringe-eared oryx. One day they journeyed to the far end of the concession, the only place gerenuk occurred, and came back with a real whopper. On another morning we all went out together and I had the pleasure of

It's not easy to tell blesbok from bontebok. These are the more common blesbok, with less brilliant pelage. Like the bontebok, the blesbok have been saved by game ranching, but they were never as scarce as bontebok.

Lew Tonks and the author with a nice bontebok, taken on Phil van der Merwe's farm in the Great Karroo. The van der Merwe family was one of a small group of Boer farmers who saved the bontebok from extinction.

Phil van der Merwe and Lew Tonks with the author's white springbok. Both black and white springbok herds have been developed through selective breeding. White springbok tend to be smaller, so this is an above average specimen.

The author's Eastern Cape kudu was a fine specimen, taken at long range with a 240-grain Trophy Bonded Bearclaw from a .375. Cape kudu are a good deal smaller than southern greater kudu, but compensate with long, luxurious neck manes.

Crawling after bush pig in coastal thornbush near Port Elizabeth. This is the thickest stuff the author has ever seen! The rifle is butt-forward because there was nobody behind and somebody in front—it was the only way to keep the muzzle in a safe direction.

This is almost the end of a very long day. This photo wasn't posed—the author carried his pig out just like this. To outfitter Lew Tonks's credit, he issued fair warning!

This typical Okavango swamp bull was dropped with a lucky running shot on the first hunting day. By the way, Ronnie MacFarlane and the author are demonstrating the only sane way to approach a buffalo—from behind with rifles ready.

The dugout makoro *canoe is the transportation of choice when penetrating the network of lagoons and islands to hunt sitatunga and other swamp species.*

Fly-camping on the Okavango's palm-studded islands is a wonderful experience. This time sitatunga hunting was unsuccessful, but the islands of the Okavango are worth the visit.

The plains surrounding the Okavango are home to a wide variety of plains game, with herd animals like wildebeest and tsessebe plentiful.

The author hadn't considered Botswana to be good kudu country, but that was because he hadn't hunted the right place. On the day this beautiful bull was taken more than fifty bulls were seen and passed.

The red lechwe is the only Botswana species not readily hunted elsewhere. They're numerous around the edges of the swamps and on the larger islands.

A good warthog surprised at a mud puddle at midday. Really good warthog are also hard to come by—this one was mounted and has a place of honor in the author's office.

Red lechwe are typically much shorter horned than the big Kafue lechwe of Zambia, although coloration is about the same. This one measured just over twenty-eight inches, very good for Botswana lechwe.

The Okavango Delta

It doesn't take long for Africa's cleanup crew to arrive. We skinned, quartered, and caped the lechwe during a midday break, and in just a few moments the vultures dropped in for the rest.

The Palala River

The author with a fine Cape eland taken at the very end of the hunt . . . but only because he blew a good chance early on!

Botswana's sandy soil is ideal for tracking. Buffalo are heavy enough to be tracked under most conditions, but in Botswana tracking is usually fast and easy.

The author and Ed Weatherby with a nice buffalo dropped cleanly by the new .416 Weatherby. This is a very typical Botswana bull, with a good boss but a modest spread.

Chip Payne, the author, and Ed Weatherby with Weatherby's red lechwe, taken with a perfect shot at very long range.

Following the safari a couple of days were spent in the Chobe National Park out of Kasane. Elephant are severely overpopulated in this region and are rapidly destroying the habitat.

Luke Samaras's Masailand camp was a bit of heaven, ascending a gentle rise under some shady acacias–the most scenic camp the author has ever been in.

A nice Masailand lion came early in the hunt–the cat was literally bumped into while tracking buffalo. The rifle is a Dumoulin .416 Rigby, good lion medicine.

Much tradition remains in East African hunting, including serious singing and dancing when a lion is taken.

Michel Mantheakis and the author with a wonderful East African greater kudu taken while checking leopard baits at noon. Greater kudu are scarce in East Africa, making a bull like this a very special prize.

The author had a bad case of "miss-itis" while trying to shoot this Grant gazelle. It wasn't the distance and it wasn't the light—it was just him not shooting very well!

Thomson gazelle on the Simanjaro Plain, a wide-open short grass savanna. This is a very average Tommy, but about all this particular area can produce.

This spectacular lesser kudu may be the author's very best African trophy. Lesser kudu were very common in this area; several were passed and a couple missed before this one came along.

Bill Baker with a fringe-eared oryx, smallest of the oryx tribe and confined to southern Kenya and northern Tanzania.

THE SIMANJARO PLAIN

Chanler mountain reedbuck is found on some of the larger hills in Masailand, an unusual trophy seldom taken in Tanzania.

THE SELOUS RESERVE

The only Selous species that can't be hunted elsewhere is the Nyasa wildebeest, which occurs from below the Rufiji down through Malawi.

Paddy Curtis and crew with a Selous zebra. Like all East African zebra, these are beautiful animals with stark black-and-white skins, with no trace of the shadow stripes of southern zebras.

For some reason hippos in the Selous are often found out in the brush far from water. Hunting a hippo on dry land is an exciting and worthwhile experience. It's also very dangerous.

watching him stalk and shoot a very fine lesser kudu. And so the days passed until the safari was almost over.

It was a long drive to the park boundary, but we headed up there every couple of days to check on game movement. The first time there we stopped by a little mission station and hospital sitting out in the middle of nowhere. The nurse was a very pretty Swedish girl. Michel had been in the bush all season, and it was late in the season; as the hunt progressed I kidded him about the gravitational pull that mission station seemed to exert on our Toyota. But the trip was usually worthwhile, at least for me. I never did figure out if Michel was making any progress!

It was near there that we took both the Grant and Thomson gazelles. It was also near there that we explored one of those big, lonely mountains that jut out of the Masai Steppe. We went up there looking for buffalo and perhaps greater kudu, but Michel had told me that some of these mountains hold Chanler mountain reedbuck.

We climbed up the lower slopes through a fresh burn, then skirted around the top so we could look down a series of lateral ravines. We had crossed two or three of these gullies when the rocks clattered below us and a small herd of reedbuck scampered up the far side. I dropped into a sitting position, and when they stopped on the far lip I was ready. I picked out the male and shot quickly, adding yet another unexpected bonus to our bag.

Although we had received the occasional shower, it wasn't yet enough; the big herds were still far away in the park somewhere. But at the very end of the hunt we could see things starting to change. In the shortgrass savanna along the boundary we now saw the occasional small herd of zebra, more hartebeest, and on the last day we saw a big herd of eland with a typically short-horned Masailand bull. And, finally, we ran into our first herd of white-bearded wildebeest–the first I had ever seen. I shot a nice bull, and then it was time to head back to camp and prepare for departure to the Selous Reserve.

The Masai Steppe is a high plateau of five to six thousand feet elevation. It got hot at midday, especially with the humidity brought on by the coming rains, but it cooled down wonderfully at night. We enjoyed our sundowners that evening around a warm and welcome fire, then retired to our tents where I lay awake for some time listening to the wonderful night sounds. It's no wonder Masailand has spawned some of Africa's best hunting literature, for it is indeed a small slice of heaven.

Southwest of Dar es Salaam, straddling the mighty Rufiji River and running on west into the Kilombero Valley, stretches the vast Selous Reserve, the largest game reserve in the world. It is historic as well as famous; it was here, during World War I, that the German-trained askaris, with Count Lettow-Vorbeck at their helm, led the British forces on a costly and not-so-merry chase that tied up troops and resources so badly needed in France. Of all of Germany's Great War generals, only Lettow-Vorbeck returned to a hero's welcome in Berlin. It was here, too, at the mouth of the Rufiji, that the great ivory hunter Pretorious found and orchestrated the sinking of the *Königsberg*, a German battle cruiser that was damaged and had hidden in the trackless delta for repairs.

It was here, too, that the great Frederick Courteney Selous was killed by a German sniper's bullet. He lies buried under a simple marker in the great reserve that bears his name. Selous, in his sixties then, could have sat out the war in comfort in England. Instead he volunteered for active service, carrying the rank of captain when he was shot in one of the innumerable desultory skirmishes that marked the East African campaign. Earlier, in dispatches, his commanding officer had remarked

6

THE SELOUS RESERVE

on Selous's incredible stamina on the march–a stamina exceeding that of officers and men forty years his junior. Little Old World courtesy survived the hell of Verdun, but on hearing of Selous's death Lettow-Vorbeck sent a personal note of sympathy and regret across the lines.

Selous's spirit must rest happily in his reserve; it is one of the great reservoirs of the African wildlife that he loved. Buffalo roam in herds of a thousand and more, followed by big prides of lion. Leopard are common enough that daylight sightings are routine, and the great cats have a varied menu of plains game to prey upon. Oddly, or perhaps not so oddly, for this is common to other low-lying areas such as the Luangwa Valley, the trophy quality of antelope species in the Selous is rarely remarkable. The exceptions are eland, which roam in big herds and grow huge, and East African greater kudu. The kudu are neither so large nor so plentiful as in southern Africa, but the Selous is easily the best kudu grounds in all of East Africa. There are also numerous Nyasa wildebeest, essentially the only place where this variety may be hunted. There are also good numbers of sable, but bulls over forty inches are very rare. The common game includes Lichtenstein hartebeest, impala, zebra, warthog, and waterbuck; and there are bushbuck, reedbuck, and several varieties of duikers.

What the Selous is most famous for, however, is its elephant. In days gone by the Selous was easily one of the best and easiest places to find a big tusker. These are small-bodied elephant, at least a third smaller than the big Zimbabwe bulls. Because of this, judging ivory is difficult, and assessing which bull tracks are big enough to follow is more difficult yet. The ivory is the long, thin, beautiful East African type, and on such small elephants a fifty-pound tusk seems huge and a seventy-pounder is incredible. The Selous has produced genuine one-hundred-pounders, but such a bull was always incredibly rare. However, until just a few years ago bulls with beautiful tusks in the sixty- to seventy-pound class were relatively common.

6 ......The Selous Reserve

In that year of 1988 there were still many thousands of elephant in the Selous–perhaps as many as seventy thousand, certainly more than forty thousand. This is a great wealth of elephant, but the ivory poachers had taken a terrible toll. In just a decade the Selous elephant had been reduced by half, and the survivors had retreated to the most dense thickets. It was not too late; we would see poachers and we would see the antipoaching teams waging war on poachers. Years later I would return to the Selous and see, with great satisfaction, that dramatic progress had been made. But in 1988 elephant hunting in the Selous was at its lowest ebb.

Luke Samaras had been honest with us; he had told us that our hunt, in early November, came at the very best time, when elephant would start to filter out of the thickets for new green brought by the first rains. But he also said that finding even a fifty-pounder would be very difficult. Luke is a passionate elephant hunter, and he spoke wistfully of the collapse of his elephant hunting back in about 1984. But we were bound and determined to hunt elephant, and Luke was more than happy to give it his best effort.

In retrospect, we played this part of the hunt all wrong. Or at least I did. At this stage I had yet to shoot a good elephant, and my idea of "good" was a sixty-pounder, plus or minus. Luke was very up front in telling me that I probably couldn't find such a bull. He was right; I had a wonderful elephant hunt, but my standards were too high for the Selous at that time. You'll recall that, at this stage, I also hadn't shot a leopard over bait. This I could have easily done in the Selous, even so late in the year. But I wanted to hunt elephant, and in the time we had it was impractical to do both. So we hunted elephant.

We chartered in to the dirt strip at Kingopera, then motored a couple of hours to Luke's camp, essentially on the boundary between his two hunting blocks. The Selous is not as scenic as Masailand, but Luke's camp of many seasons is a neat line of green wall tents that face a broad opening with a little spring-fed water hole. At any time of the day impala, warthog, hartebeest, and sometimes buffalo will come to drink. It's a lovely spot; it felt like home immediately, and it still felt like home when I returned six years later.

Bill Baker hunted with Luke, while I was delighted to find that my professional hunter would be Paddy Curtis. Paddy is a tough, competent Zimbabwe hunter, a wild Irishman during the off-season and a true professional in the bush. In the Luangwa Valley in 1983 he'd guided my good friend Bob Tatsch, and I'd seen him at conventions in the intervening years. I was in good hands.

The Selous is characterized by generally thick woodland, properly *miombo* forest much like Zimbabwe's mopane and Zambia's *Brachystegia* woodland. There are scattered clearings, some very large, and networks of meandering sand rivers with heavy riverine growth. The real difference in the Selous, however, is the incredibly dense thicket lines. These seem to follow almost imperceptible rises in elevation and often go for miles. The thicket lines of the Selous are as thick as the famed *jess* bush of the Zambezi Valley, incredibly dense networks of dry gray thornbush that can be penetrated only along the elephant paths.

The ivory poachers, living off the land and traveling in large groups with one or two shooters and large numbers of porters, had fully penetrated the Selous, leaving a litter of bleached skulls in their wake. They had pushed the elephant into these dense thickets, but now the lure of new green was too much and they were starting to venture out. We would see many elephant herds along the edges of the thickets, but at the sound of a vehicle they would scream in anger and fear and make a beeline for the thick stuff. We never saw a mature bull in the open, although we saw hundreds of cows and calves.

The bulls were coming out, but mostly at night. We would look for tracks along the edges of the thicket; then, if a big enough spoor was found, we would follow them in. This was a somewhat dangerous undertaking. The bulls themselves were no menace; they would run at the slightest hint of man-scent, and it would require more hours of painstaking tracking to come up to them again. The danger came from tracking unawares into cow herds while on bull spoor. The cows had been pushed long enough and far enough, and when pressured in their thicket sanctuary they would inevitably charge. We spent much of our time running from cows!

I said the bulls were no menace, but that's not altogether true. Bill and Luke got in a tight spot with a group of bulls one morning. They might have gotten away without gunfire, but their game scout ended it by shooting a young bull through the throat with his .458.

I also said I might have been better off not hunting elephant, and this is not strictly true; I also might have been more lucky. About three o'clock one afternoon, Bill and Luke found the fresh tracks of a bull that had crossed out of a thicket and into more open woodland. After, as Bill called it, an "elephant walk" of little more than an hour he shot a nice tusker with his beautifully engraved (Pachmayr, of course!) .458 Lott.

Paddy and I tried extremely hard, and we passed up a number of bulls with baseball bat ivory. But we never found anything acceptably close to what I was looking for. I sure did learn a lot about elephant hunting, though! Sometimes we came very close without ever knowing what we were looking at.

One day we started on the track of three bulls shortly after sunrise. We tracked them in the thickets for eight hours, hearing their bellies rumbling and seeing pieces of elephant now and again, but we never saw the ivory of two of the bulls. The last time, in the heat of the day, we came up to them in very thick stuff. At less than ten yards I could see the legs of all three and the curling trunk of the smallest, the one we knew about. And then, as happens so often in the thickets in the heat of the day, the barest puff of breeze kissed the back of my neck. Then came the screams and breaking of branches, and that was the end of those elephant.

On the last morning we found a good, big track and followed it into the thickets. This was a lone bull, and I think we could have closed on it. But after a couple of hours we found where it had lain down, and in the red dust there was the clear imprint of its right tusk. It was impressively long and nicely curved, but very thin. Paddy and I ruefully agreed that it was no more than a thirty-five-pounder, and we walked away and spent the rest of our last day hunting buffalo.

You'll remember that I mentioned earlier that I have trouble concentrating on just one thing when amidst Africa's wealth of game, and that certainly applied in the Selous. We might have put out leopard baits, but Paddy and I agreed we would concentrate on elephant. That certainly doesn't mean we did nothing but hunt elephant.

If we couldn't find an elephant track, or if we tracked up elephant and passed–or failed to catch up–then we would go on to something else for the rest of the day. Quite honestly, I had to be a bit careful; our luck had been so good in Masailand that I had enough license money left to take an elephant . . . and not much else! I would have liked to have taken one of those wonderful Selous eland, but was obligated to leave that for another trip. Likewise I saw a couple of pretty darned good sable, but passed due to declining economy.

Late one afternoon I did take a very nice Nyasa wildebeest, easily the most beautiful of the unbeautiful wildebeest clan. The Nyasa variety, found from the Selous down to Malawi (formerly Nyasaland, hence the name) is Hershey-bar chocolate in color with a prominent white nose chevron. It is the only animal the Selous holds, as far as I'm aware, that is currently huntable nowhere else in Africa. And there are literally hundreds of them. I also shot a beautiful zebra stallion, a worthwhile endeavor since the Tanzanian zebra have beautiful skins, without the shadow striping of the southern zebra.

One day we hunted poachers. We were traveling down a long track through the bush, much like one of South Texas's endless *senderos.* Far ahead I saw some sort of animal crossing the road, but it seemed upright and not at all like a baboon. Then came another, then another. Paddy knew what it was instantly. "Poachers." Then he looked at me and grinned his evil Irish grin. "Well, Major Boddington (my rank at the time), what would you like to do?"

I gulped and said, "You're driving."

He spoke to the game scout and trackers in the back. The game scout was armed, and our tracker, Kalema, took my .416 off the back rack and loaded the chamber. I did likewise with the .375 in my lap. He put the pedal to the metal, saying out of the side of his mouth, "Find the one with the AK-47 and get him first."

We roared into them, a group of about twenty-five–apparently on their way in, since they carried no ivory. There was a lot of gunfire, ending in a few seconds. We captured a couple and took them to Kingopera. One of them had a battered Brno .375 and, in his pack, his reloading equipment. He was shooting homogenous alloy bullets, turned on a lathe, and apparently would dig them out and pound them round enough to use again. For powder and primers he had pliers, punch, and a small sack of AK-47 cartridges! Guys like him have ravaged Africa, but you must respect them as hunters.

An oddity in the Selous, different from my experience elsewhere, is that hippo are often encountered far out in the bush, near small pools but a long way from significant water. I have no patience with shooting hippo in their water sanctuary, but taking a hippo on dry land is an exciting undertaking. A charge is almost certain, and a hippo is a huge animal that quickly becomes a bullet sponge.

Paddy and I tracked a big bull away from a tiny mudhole and found it sleeping in the bush. When it got up I hit it on the shoulder with both barrels from the .470–then reloaded and did it again before we got it stopped. It's amazing how fast you can load a double when you have to!

Mainly, though, if we weren't hunting elephant we were hunting buffalo. Or perhaps it's more appropriate to say we were hunting both at the same time. And while we weren't having much luck with elephant, the Selous is the land of the buffalo. On any given day we would see herds of buffalo, sometimes herds into the many hundreds.

The Selous is not known for huge buffalo, and indeed really big bulls aren't common. But my theory is that, for big trophy buffalo, the first ingredient is lots of buffalo. The Selous has that in spades, and if you're willing to sort through lots of buffalo and you have a bit of luck, you can find monsters. We did not, but, after all, we were hunting buffalo only when elephant hunting didn't work out, and I had a wonderful time sorting through those big herds.

One morning we tracked a big herd for a couple of miles, catching up with it as the buffalo fed through an open glade. I was carrying my double .470, but with so many eyes and in such open country there was no way to get close enough for a sure shot. We had spied an enormous-bodied bull with reasonable spread and huge bosses, and I was determined to take it. I handed the .470 to Kalema and took the scope-sighted .375 he carried. When the bull stepped clear I placed a Swift softpoint behind the shoulder, just as I had in Botswana earlier that year.

It bucked like a rodeo horse, then took off with the herd. There were too many buffalo for a second shot, but it was open enough that we could keep our eyes on it. It went about seventy yards, then turned in a circle and fell over, down and out from a perfect lung shot–just as any deer, elk, antelope, or whatever would have been.

On the last day, shortly after we gave up on the elephant tracks, we found the spoor of a herd of buffalo bulls in the dust of the roadway. There were about a dozen of them, and the tracks appeared very fresh. I suspect we misread their age slightly, for at two o'clock in the afternoon we were *still* following their walking, meandering tracks.

Then we found them. They were all lying down, in a circle, on a little knoll in thick trees. We crawled from bush to bush, checking them out, and there were no monsters. But there was at least one reasonably good and quite mature bull, and it was the last day.

We waited endlessly, and after about an hour they finally got up one at a time. When our chosen bull got up it was in thick bush, and yet again the only shot I had was the lung shot. But now I had total confidence in it. I put an old .470 Kynoch softpoint central on the body right behind the shoulder, and then the bull was off with the rest of the herd. We waited, then followed in their wake.

My bull was down about seventy-five yards ahead, and as soon as it was visible I fired an unneeded solid into its spine. Paddy grinned and said, "Good man." He'd been tossed in Masailand at the beginning of the season, a good story in itself. Apparently his client had wounded a buffalo, and they caught a charge at very close range. The bull put its nose between Paddy's legs and tossed him, then fortunately kept on going. The impact had, well, split Paddy in a rather tender spot. Fortunately (or unfortunately), the client's wife was a nurse, and by lantern light in the dining tent she had stitched up that rather tender spot. To this day they call the place where it happened "Paddy's *Korango.*"

By now we were very far from the truck and it was the middle of a blazing hot afternoon. We backtracked down the little hill to a big clearing and got our bearings, and I volunteered to stay there while the rest of the crew fetched the truck. I'm not sure why I did that; the walk would have been fine, and I was desperately thirsty. I think I just wanted to spend some of the last day alone, watching the perfect African sky and reliving the last few weeks. Despite the thirst, I spent a very pleasant couple of hours . . . but I was ready for the truck and the cold box when they finally arrived.

The short rains were upon us now; that last day was clear and hot, but it had been raining every other afternoon or so and the rivers were filling rapidly. The hunt was at an end, but even had it not been it was time to get out before the roads and rivers became impassable. As it was the airstrip was too soft to take a plane, so we motored back to Dar, taking the ferry across the swelling Rufiji. It was a pretty drive, and a fine end to a truly great safari.

In 1959 globe-trotting trophy hunter Elgin Gates, with the assistance of none other than Jack O'Connor himself, wrote a story titled "The Safari That Opened Mozambique." It was quite a story about quite a place, and in it Gates detailed the taking of not one but three new world-record trophies: southern greater kudu, nyala, and sable antelope.

Elgin Gates is gone now. I knew him reasonably well in later years, and it's fair to say that he was a driven man, always wanting to be the best. He went from motorboat racing to big-game hunting, then to trapshooting, then to handgun silhouette shooting, always excelling. Back in 1971, before I was in the business, a ship I was on put in at Pearl Harbor, and I pulled liberty and went over to the gun club where the Hawaii state trapshoot was being held. Elgin Gates was there, and he loaned me a fine Krieghoff so I could shoot. So I have a soft spot for Elgin Gates and his memory. However, it's only honest to report that in later years those Mozambique records were questioned and eventually pulled from the Rowland Ward records. A world record nyala was certainly possible, likewise a kudu—but a sable exceeding fifty-six inches was very unlikely from Mozambique.

7

INTO MOZAMBIQUE

It didn't matter. Gates's story, needless to say, drove the hunting world nuts, and almost instantly the Portuguese colony of Mozambique emerged as a principal safari destination. Sadly, it didn't last long. By the early 1970s Mozambique became embroiled in its struggle for independence, a bush war that turned into a long, drawn-out civil war after it received independence from Portugal in 1975. Hunting ground to a halt, not by decree but from the risks of being caught in a cross fire. A friend of mine, fellow writer James Fender, made the last safari into Mozambique in mid-1974 and literally had to shoot his way out. For the next fifteen years Mozambique remained a lawless battleground, with little accurate information on the status of her game.

Despite the promise of Elgin Gates's story, in its short heyday Mozambique was known not as a country that produced huge trophies, but rather as one with a variety and abundance of game. There were big kudu, big waterbuck, huge leopard, and a few other things that seemed to grow large, but the area's real claim to fame was a generous bag on a general bag safari. The buffalo weren't normally huge, but their numbers were. There were plenty of lions following the buffalo, and a hunter could expect to take kudu, sable, nyala, and a whole lot more in the course of a normal safari. My colleague and friend John Wootters, together with Jack Carter (founder of Trophy Bonded Bullets and creator of the Trophy Bonded Bearclaw and Sledgehammer Solid bullets) made their first safari there in the early 1970s, shooting the world on a license that seems absurdly cheap by today's standards.

Mozambique was also known for elephant. Lots of elephant. Even today rural Mozambique is wild country, with few inhabitants and fewer roads. It was virtual wilderness just a quarter century ago, and as such was one of the last strongholds of the genuine ivory hunters. Harry Manners and Wally Johnson, Sr., did most of their ivory hunting in Mozambique. So did Ian Nyschens. And so did John Taylor–Pondoro himself. Historically, Mozambique ivory was not heavy, at least not by the standards of a generation ago; however, Harry

Manners did shoot a 180-pounder there. But after fifteen years of bush war between the government forces and the Renamo faction, what could remain?

Over the years the situation stabilized, with Renamo controlling much of the north while government forces controlled most of the south. By the late 1980s it looked like a meaningful cease-fire might finally be achieved, and a few enterprising outfitters started looking at reopening Mozambique. For Zimbabwe operators the most attractive area is the Tete Province, the western bulge of Mozambique along the Zambezi River corridor, since road access from Harare is fairly simple. Piet Hougart obtained a concession in the far west, and my old friends Roger Whittall and Barrie Duckworth secured a huge concession north of Mucumbura, occupying both sides of the huge Cabora Bassa lake and running on east nearly to Tete.

Whittall and Duckworth were primarily interested in the elephant. Roger Whittall is the owner of the vast Humani Ranch in the southeastern lowveld of Zimbabwe; his partner in Hunter's Safaris, Barrie Duckworth, was a game control officer for the Rhodesian Parks department before turning to professional hunting. Back in 1979 I was Barrie's first-ever safari client, and I was one of the first clients on Humani when Roger opened his ranch to sport hunting. During the 1980s their safari business continued to expand, and they had part of the great Chewore concession in Zimbabwe's Zambezi Valley for elephant hunting. Permits, however, were limited; the Mozambique area would more than double their elephant permits.

The Tete Province is very good elephant country; this was the country Pondoro Taylor had hunted in the 1940s, ducking back and forth across the Zambezi to avoid either Rhodesian or Portuguese officials. Its history goes back much farther than that, for Selous himself hunted there a century ago. Roger and Barrie did a couple of experimental safaris in 1988 and found plenty of relatively undisturbed elephant. When I saw them at the 1989 Safari Club convention they were excited about the prospects, and we immediately planned a hunt for September.

I was their last client of the season, and by then they had explored at least part of their concession and pretty well understood what was happening. The elephant had met their expectations, more or less. They had taken no huge bulls, although the odd monster had given them the slip. But the season's tusks, stored in Roger's camp, were all impressive. They ran from the high seventies down to the high forties, with a good, solid average of about sixty pounds per tusk. There was good news and bad news about these tusks. The configuration was more the long, slender, beautiful East African ivory than the typically short, thick Zimbabwe or Botswana ivory, which was good. The bad news was that the nerves had been typically large, so the tusks tended to weigh a bit less than they looked like they should. Which wasn't altogether bad, for even the lighter tusks actually looked very nice.

There weren't vast numbers of elephant in their concession, which was about the size of Vermont, but there were plenty and they had found them relatively undisturbed. The rest of the game had been, well, hammered. Badly hammered. Considering the ravages elephant herds in relatively settled areas like Kenya, Zambia's Luangwa Valley, and Tanzania's Selous Reserve had sustained while anarchy reigned in Mozambique, it's a paradox that the elephants in this area were relatively untouched. The story was that the locals were afraid of elephant . . . but they sure weren't afraid of anything else.

During our three weeks in Mozambique we saw very little other game. There were a few impala along the shores of Cabora Bassa, and of course there were the odd kudu and bushbuck. Once we saw a big herd of roan antelope, and we also saw tracks of sable and the occasional wandering herd of buffalo. There were quite a few grysbok and the occasional bush duiker . . . and not much more. But there were lots of cats. Virtually every *korango* held leopard tracks, and there were a lot of lion. I simply don't know what the cats were finding to eat. Perhaps I'd just as soon not dwell on it.

The game was scarce enough that, as the hunt progressed, if we saw a duiker by midday while tracking or while driving and looking for tracks I'd kid Roger by saying, "Man, this place is stiff with game today." It was a wasteland. But the elephant were there, and we were there to hunt elephant.

We drove into Mozambique at Mucumbura, just a few hours' drive from Harare, then continued north to Roger's camp not far from the two-hundred-mile-long Lake Cabora Bassa. At that time, and probably to this day, you couldn't consider the area totally safe, but Roger and his crew had experienced no problems. There had been no land mine incidents in the area, although one unfortunate local villager had been bayoneted to death for some unknown wrong and left in the middle of the road as an example. We were careful and tried to keep our night movement to a minimum.

Tourism in Mozambique was new enough that problems with visas were continual and frustrating for the pioneering outfitters. I had no trouble in that regard, but I did have my own unique little problem. Lufthansa neglected to put my duffel bag on the plane from Los Angeles to Frankfurt. I knew it in Frankfurt, so I had about three hours in Johannesburg to buy everything I needed for a three-week safari. Shoes, shorts, and a couple of shirts were no problem. Neither was .375 H & H ammo. But finding ammunition for my Heym double in .500 Nitro Express was almost a nightmare. Tony Rogers at Rogers Sporting Arms called a cartridge collector and he brought me eight reasonably fresh Kynoch cartridges–at collector prices, of course!

I would be hunting with Roger, and along with me was cameraman Joe Lee; later Joe produced a really excellent video on the safari. Some distance away, in another camp, were professional hunters Barrie Duckworth and Joe Wright, and farther up the lake they also had a commercial crocodile operation. Roger doesn't go into things part way. Although he had brought his own trackers from Zimbabwe, he had hired a tremendous amount of local labor and camp help; he had the support of the local authorities, such as they were, which is at least partly why he had no difficulties.

Roger's camp was a comfortable cluster of tents alongside a sand river. We wouldn't see much of it in the daylight. An elephant hunt can end quickly, but more often it's a drawn-out affair, one of the most physical of all African hunts, involving countless miles of tracking in ever-increasing heat–and September is a hot month in the Zambezi Valley.

We would leave camp in the relative cool of the morning in search of bull tracks. Sometimes we would cruise the few roads. Other times we would hike down one of the sand rivers feeding into what used to be the Zambezi River and was now Cabora Bassa. Other times we would hike the near shore of the lake itself, looking for elephant or sign of elephant in the reedbeds along the shore. On still other days we would take a motorboat across the huge lake and do the same thing on the opposite shore.

Tony Sanchez-Ariño, perhaps the greatest living elephant hunter, wrote that you "hunt an elephant with your legs; you merely execute him with your rifle." True. If everything works perfectly–and it never does–you can follow one bull elephant or one group of bull elephant on each of your hunting days. You will not see all of the elephant you track. Sometimes they'll outdistance you on their ten-foot legs, and sometimes they'll wind you in heavy cover and crash away unseen. Most of the time, when you do see them, you'll find the ivory not up to your expectations. But if you simply *see* the elephant you're tracking, then you've won on that day. On this hunt, as in most, we won on some days and lost on others.

One day we followed a lone bull in its wanderings through the endless mopane woodland, in and out of *jess* thickets with their wicked buffalo bean, and along the white sand of a riverbed, shimmering in the midday heat. We caught it shortly after midday, sound asleep on its side in the shade of a big tree. It was snoring softly, its knobby back to us; we couldn't see its ivory, and we couldn't circle around lest it get the wind. Slowly we crept this way and that, trying to see what it carried while Joe's camera rolled. Eventually it either heard us or sensed us, and its awakening was the most amazing thing I have seen in the wild.

One instant it was lying down, gurgling and bubbling in its sleep. The next moment it was standing, ears outstretched, fully alert–so fast that its seven-ton bulk seemed to levitate to a standing position. It was a fifty-pounder, with thick, ugly ivory. We stared at each other at less than ten yards, and then it turned and was gone. I think that was also the day we saw the fresh spoor of a black rhino, which was almost like seeing the ghost of a bygone age.

On another day, on the northern shore of Cabora Bassa, we found an old fisherman who said he knew where there were elephant bulls. He was right. We found two sets of very big tracks, fresh from the morning, and we followed them.

The bush was incredibly thick here and the elephant hadn't gone far. The winds were fickle and they knew they were safe. We tracked them slowly and carefully for half a day, but each time they heard us or smelled us before we saw their ivory. That day we lost; when Roger judged we'd bumped them once too often we broke off and headed back to the lake.

On yet another day, also on the north shore of the lake, we found the almost-fresh-enough tracks of three big bulls. These were extremely promising; after a few hours' tracking we found where they had fed in the daylight, the fallen leaves just beginning to turn. A few hours more and we found where a couple of them had lain down and dusted in soft red soil. One of them left the clear impression of a wonderful tusk–perhaps an eighty-pounder, but without question a keeper. We kept on . . . and so did they. Eventually, maintaining that long elephant stride, they turned onto a long-unused colonial road and headed for Zambia. We couldn't go to Zambia, so we turned 'round and left them to their wanderings.

The bush was beautiful and peaceful, but there were many reminders of the long civil war. We found AK-47 hulls on many of the major trails, and human skeletons unburied or in shallow graves. The bush was littered with abandoned villages; most of the people in this area had been resettled to more secure areas during the height of the struggle. But there was very little game. One afternoon we returned to camp just at dark to find a couple of officers from the local garrison awaiting us. They wanted meat for some sort of celebration, and demanded that we go out and spotlight some game for them. Roger took me aside, saying that it was better that we do it; otherwise they would do it with automatic weapons. So we went forth in the middle of the night and shot a few unfortunate impala and a young kudu in the interest of keeping the local peace. At night there was a bit more game in evidence, but not a great deal more.

I did shoot a very fine grysbok one day, and we should have had a fine lion as well. There were a couple of big prides of lion hunting along the lake shores, but out in the dry thornbush far south of camp we had twice seen the tracks of a big, lone male in the dust of a roadway. One late morning, having failed to find elephant tracks, we rounded a bend and there stood a lovely lion about twenty yards away. Roger had unfilled lion on quota, but I had no reason to shoot one; by previous agreement an opportunity like this went straight to Joe Lee. He stepped out of the truck and chambered a round, and as he did so his Dakota .458 discharged into the dirt a few feet in front of him. It scared the hell out of everybody–including the lion.

Accidental discharges are intriguing in that one's initial thought, always, is that the gun just "went off." That can happen, but there must be a mechanical reason for it. Too often what really happened is the safety was off and contact was made with the trigger, and what happened is what is supposed to happen when the trigger is moved far enough–except it wasn't on purpose. Joe is convinced to this day that the rifle went off of its own volition, while I remain convinced that he bumped the trigger. It doesn't much matter–that was a long-gone cat!

There were a few dry-season temporary villages here and there along the lake, populated by fishermen who would dry their catch on long open-air racks by the shore, to best catch the breeze. We often stopped by these little villages, not only to ask about elephant movement but also to trade salt or, if we had any, meat for fish. There is virtually no hard currency in the Mozambique bush, nor any need for it. Salt is the closest thing to money, and a man would work all day at any task for even a small measure.

I suspect many of the villagers we were seeing–especially those under twenty–had never seen a white face. They gathered around in big crowds whenever we came into a village, some aloof, some openly curious, but I never saw any hostility. That's part of elephant hunting, too–talking to the tribesmen, sorting out fact from fancy, and checking out any and all rumors of big-toothed elephant.

It was such a rumor that gave us our bull. One of the fishermen told us of a group of bulls he'd seen feeding along the lake. We were skeptical, for that particular shore of the lake was a broad, grassy opening of reedbeds–it seemed unlikely elephant would stay there. But it was also an isolated spot; our boat landing and the track to it were quite far away. So we checked out this rumor by walking overland three hours, in midday heat, from a village to the lake, guided by one of the locals. These were hungry times in Mozambique, and these poor people would willingly walk all day just on the off chance of some meat.

This time the rumor was true. We found first the fresh tracks of several bulls, then saw gray shapes above the reeds. There were five bulls together, enjoying their afternoon feeding in open grass virtually on the shores of Cabora Bassa. The biggest bull was a sixty-pounder, not up to our wildest expectations but exactly what we'd hoped to find. We backed off and talked about it; there was time remaining in which we might find a bigger bull. On the other hand, this was a beautiful bull, and in a position that should allow good filming. All agreed and ready, we moved in.

We were almost too late. The elephant were starting to move, and the video camera complicated a simple evolution. I had the brain shot, side-on at 25 yards as the bull passed, but Joe wasn't quite ready and stopped me. Then he gave me the signal, but the moment for the brain shot we wanted had passed. I fired both barrels from the .500 just behind its shoulder, angling forward.

At that point we could have left it; no matter what else happened, he was done in two-hundred yards. But in that last bit of confusion before the shot, Roger and I had crossed our signals; he thought I had gone for the brain shot, and since the bull didn't go down he assumed I'd missed the brain. So he fired, and I reloaded and fired again as the herd swapped ends and ran into the thick reeds. Then we compared notes, realized what had happened, and waited a few minutes before moving in on our bull. It had run the prescribed distance and was dead on the lake shore. And it was indeed beautiful.

We took the tail with us as a sign of ownership and hiked back to the village, the last hour in darkness. Next morning we brought the boat in to it so we could collect the ivory and skin, and virtually the entire village converged on us for the meat cutting, the women balancing huge chunks of flesh on their heads for the long walk back.

In the time we had remaining, we tried to bait up a leopard. It should have been easy, but there were two problems. First, game was so scarce that it required as much as a full day of hard hunting to find an impala or duiker. And, second, we couldn't keep the lions away from the leopard baits! We never saw another male lion for Joe, but prides of cheeky lionesses invaded each and every leopard bait, and got to them regardless of where we hung them. So, in due time, we crossed the border once more at Mucumbura and left Mozambique behind.

In October of 1989, just a few weeks later, the CITES meeting was held in Lausanne, Switzerland, and the African elephant was placed on the Appendix I "endangered" list and all trade in ivory was banned. As we know, the elephant was indeed endangered–even extinct–over much of its former range. But in 1989, even by the most conservative estimates, there were more than six hundred thousand wild elephant in Africa–hardly an endangered population. Worse, countries such as Zimbabwe that had done a superb job of managing their elephant were penalized for the excesses of other countries.

Ultimately this has been at least partially recognized, with exclusions for sport-hunted ivory granted to a small but growing list of countries: Zimbabwe, South Africa, Namibia, Tanzania, Cameroon, Botswana. But that 1989 ban finished elephant hunting in Mozambique. As I write this there are indications of a reopening, but now there have been seven more years of neglect and lack of management. Again, one must wonder what might be left.

With elephant hunting banned, Roger Whittall and Barrie Duckworth shut down their Mozambique operation. Piet Hougart and a couple of other outfitters have continued, so at this writing Mozambique remains open to hunting, reasonably productive for buffalo, cats, and the occasional sable and big kudu. But even in the vastness of the Mozambique bush no corner has yet been found that compares with the Mozambique hunting that existed until 1974.

I don't know whether or not my bull was the last Mozambique elephant to be taken, but I do know mine were the last set of Mozambique tusks to reach the United States. Under the provisions of the ban, legally taken ivory had to be in transit before a certain date. My tusks reached Harare exactly one day before that deadline. Knowing I had a mess on my hands, I had Roger hold them there until the U.S. Fish and Wildlife Service concurred that they were in transit before the deadline. It wasn't easy.

Ultimately, I asked for help from anyone I knew who might have influence. The Safari Club helped, but in frustration I finally called Texas Congressman Jack Fields, a serious hunter and great guy. Grudgingly, it was agreed that my tusks had been in transit before the deadline, and about a year later they finally came into the United States. Mr. Fields, I sure wish I lived where I could vote for you! My duffel bag, by the way, followed me into Zimbabwe, but then got misdirected to the Zambezi Valley. Tony Rogers, my friend at the Johannesburg gun shop, finally brought it to the States, about the same time my ivory showed up. To this day I don't know how that duffel bag, eighteen months later with its contents untouched, wound up at Tony's shop in Johannesburg.

8

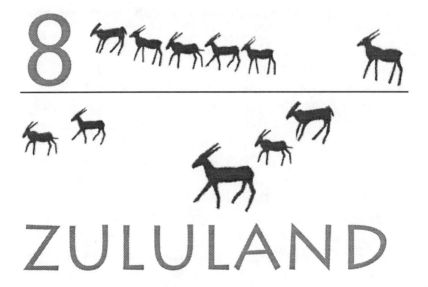

ZULULAND

It's odd how the hunting hot spots for various species can change with shifting times and politics. The nyala, that beautifully marked chocolate-brown member of the spiral-horned tribe, was "discovered" by European science in 1848 near St. Lucia Bay, along South Africa's Indian Ocean coast. It occurs, naturally but discontinuously, from southern Malawi south through Mozambique and west into Zimbabwe, then along South Africa's east coast to Durban or thereabouts. This is not a small range, but for much of this century the nyala has been relatively unavailable to sport hunters. In fact, until safari companies were organized in Mozambique in the late 1950s and early 1960s few sportsmen had taken "the shifty one," as its Zulu name translates.

Nyala were common in Mozambique, and most hunters visiting that country took nyala, so long as Mozambique remained huntable. By the time Mozambique closed, a couple of enterprising hunters had started outfitting foreign sportsmen for South Africa's numerous rarities. Nyala weren't a big draw at first, since they were readily obtained in Mozambique. But when that country closed, nyala hunting shifted almost instantly to Zululand and adjacent Natal. Although some very good heads were taken in Mozambique, this part of South Africa has consistently produced the very best nyala.

Today, however, the picture is muddied considerably. Nyala are not only a beautiful and desirable animal, but due to the high populations along the Indian Ocean coast, breeding stock has long been available. Thanks to game ranching, nyala are available today in darn near every part of South Africa, and there are even a few in Namibia.

They are also much more widely available in Zimbabwe than ever before. There have always been a few; I saw nyala on the Bubi River back in the seventies, and they are on quota in some of the Zambezi Valley concessions. It appears they are slowly extending their range westward along Zimbabwe's river systems, but game ranchers have speeded things up.

Someday I would like to shoot a nyala outside of South African game ranches–perhaps in Zimbabwe or Mozambique, maybe even Malawi, should that country open up. But the truth is that South African game ranches offer not only the best opportunity to take this beautiful spiral-horned antelope, but also far and away the best quality. The best of the best is easily the region known as Zululand.

Zululand occupies South Africa's Indian Ocean coast from north of Durban to the Mozambique border. Politically it's part of the province of Natal, but of course it was not always so. In the early nineteenth century, Shaka created the Zulu's legendary military society, conquering numerous tribes and creating a vast empire. The trekking Boers ran headlong into the Zulus and enough of a standoff resulted to establish boundaries for a half-century. The Boers moved on to the north and northwest, creating the Orange Free State and Transvaal. The country to the south and west of Zululand became the British colony of Natal, and the settlers looked across into Zululand with both fear of the Zulu impis and lust for the fertile land.

In January 1879, a British army under Lord Chelmsford invaded Zululand, splitting his column much as Custer had done against the Sioux just three years earlier. On 24 January, underneath a big, flat-topped mountain called Isandhlwana, the Zulu impis wiped out a major portion of the British force, killing about fifteen hundred British regulars, colonial volunteers, and native levies. It was perhaps the worst defeat the British Empire ever suffered until the fall of Singapore in World War II.

Victory was short-lived; reinforced and regrouped, the British converged on the Zulu capital of Ulundi and the impis died against the British square. Zululand became part of Natal, but perhaps because of that stunning and embarrassing battle at Isandhlwana, Zululand has remained different; joined yet separate. And the Zulus themselves have to this day retained not only their tribal customs, but also their pride. They remain a fascinating people, and their land is a fine place to visit and hunt.

Nyala, of course, is the primary attraction, but there's a goodly selection of other plains game, some occurring naturally and others introduced by game ranchers. It was the nyala that brought us to Windy Ridge, a showpiece of a private game ranch in the heart of Zululand, about an hour's drive inland from the pretty coastal town of Richard's Bay. It's a beautiful, well-watered country of brushy ridges and lush, grassy valleys. Historic country, too. The grave of Cetewayo, the Zulu king who opposed the British, lies nearby, as does the site of Shaka's kraal. To the north is the old Zulu capital of Ulundi, and to the northwest lie Isandhlwana and Rorke's Drift. In the aftermath of their victory at Isandhlwana the Zulu impis flowed west to the little mission station at Rorke's Drift, where about 150 British troops of Company B, 24th Foot, stood them off and garnered the most Victoria Crosses ever awarded in a single engagement.

Our host, Louis-John "L. J." Havemann, was born and raised on Windy Ridge. Fluent in Zulu and steeped in his land's traditions, he would often pause in the hunt to show us Zulu burial mounds and kraal sites along the rivers that water Windy Ridge. In years gone by, long before Windy Ridge became a commercial operation, Havemann and his father had hunted widely throughout southern Africa. His comfortable lodge, thatch-roofed in the local style, contained not only fine examples of Zululand game, but also mounted specimens of darn near every species from Zambia southward. It made a great setting to begin a safari.

Unfortunately, by the time I arrived the safari was already well underway. I was hunting with my old friend Jim Morey, president of Swarovski Optik's American branch. His goal was to produce one segment of a video series on affordable African hunting, so videographer Chip Payne and I would be working together again. But Jim's schedule and mine didn't quite mesh, so I came in a few days after the rest of the crew and picked up the safari in progress.

And progress it had. Jim had already taken a superb nyala, as well as blesbok and impala, all nicely captured on tape by Chip's camera. I had hoped to be there when Jim took his nyala, but it wasn't all that bad a deal–now it was clearly my turn!

I arrived at Windy Ridge about midday and barely had time to change clothes and get my hunting gear together before we headed out for the afternoon hunt. I had two rifles with me, both Weatherby Mark V's–one in .340 Weatherby and the other in .270 Weatherby. We took a few minutes to make sure the sights were on–they were–and we started hunting.

We didn't go far. Hardly a mile from the headquarters, as we dropped off the main ridge that gives the ranch its name, L. J. saw a big kudu bull tending some cows in the valley below. The kudu were in a big, grassy meadow that stretched up from a brushy streambed, making a stalk relatively simple. We dropped off the ridge and were instantly out of sight, hitting the streambed about a quarter-mile downwind from where we'd last seen them.

The streambed was narrow and rocky, but still allowed rapid and quiet movement. With Chip in trace with his heavy camera, L. J. led Jim and me down the streambed at a fast pace, then he slowed and checked the wind. It was swirling here on the low ground, its direction uncertain. Slowly, now we climbed up the bank and crept to the edge of the meadow. We were in the right place, but it was empty.

Then the brush to the right of us erupted as kudu cows streamed out of the riverine bush and trotted across the meadow. I found a tree fork for a rest, knowing the bull would follow. It did, but it came at a dead run, big and beautiful with its horns laid back along its flanks. The distance was close and I'm not afraid of running shots; I should have taken it then, but I didn't. Undoubtedly I was conscious of the camera, and I rationalized that it would surely stop somewhere in the meadow.

In hesitating, I lost the best shot I was likely to get. With the cows in the lead, they ate up the meadow quickly. Worse, for the first fifty yards the bull had been dead broadside, but after that it turned straight away. I had my crosshairs on it the whole time, but all I had was the rump of a very big bull that was getting farther away by the second.

At the far tree line, now 250 yards away, the cows finally slowed to a walk. The bull slowed as well, then angled to the left and finally gave me a bit of a quartering shot. I took it, heard the bullet hit, and then the bull was gone into the trees.

We found its big, heart-shaped tracks readily, but no blood at all. After twenty minutes of painstaking searching we found just a couple of drops, then a bit more. A hundred yards farther on the bull rose to his feet in a patch of dense thorn, and this time I anchored it. It was a great kudu, heavy-horned with deep spirals. The horns were close together, one of those kudu that are actually much longer than they look because of the big curls. For Zululand, it was actually huge, and to this day it is the longest-horned kudu I've ever taken–but it wasn't quite the kind of sequence we'd hoped to get on film, and it was my fault for not shooting when I should have.

A really good nyala, of course, was my main goal. Windy Ridge is famous not only for quality, but for quantity as well; surplus nyala live-trapped there have formed the nucleus of many nyala herds throughout South Africa. There are lots of them, which isn't to say that you see them all over the place. They're cover-loving in the way that a bushbuck is, and they earn their Zulu name. I was looking forward to seeing lots of them, and hoped to find a really superb specimen—perhaps even better than the good bull I'd taken back in '79.

In the next few days we did indeed see plenty of nyala. Often we'd come around a bend in a trail—afoot or in the vehicle—and surprise a dark bull or the much smaller red females with their bright white body stripes. More frequently we'd glass them moving along a distant ridge with the big 30X Swarovski binoculars Jim had brought for the purpose. We saw some great bulls as well. But all of this was an anticlimax for me, because my nyala came very quickly and much too easily.

It was a cool, cloudy afternoon, and we were driving along a track that wound above one of the many brushy, meandering watercourses. Louis-John spied a darker spot in some dark bush on the far side of a little oxbow bend in the stream a few hundred yards ahead. It was a nyala, and L. J. knew instantly that it was a very big one. Of course we wanted to see for ourselves, so he patiently waited while we went through the drill with the big glasses, confirming what he knew at a glance. It wasn't just big but huge, with thick horns in a lovely lyre shape, ending in sharp tips of polished ivory.

It was a stalk in name only; ahead of us enough thornbush grew alongside the road for cover, so all we needed to do was walk slowly up the track until we reached a point adjacent to the nyala. This put us about 150 yards above where it still fed peacefully in that dark patch of bush. I found the crotch of a not-too-thorny tree for a rest, then waited.

At that moment we couldn't see it, but we didn't think it had moved off. It hadn't; in a few moments its head came up and we double-checked those wonderful horns one last time. Up here above we were in a very good spot in that we were looking down on the bull; had we been level with it or below it I doubt we'd have ever seen him. Even as it was I could see only its head and neck, so I waited–seemingly forever but probably just a minute or two. Finally it took a step and I could clearly see its shoulder.

I lost it altogether in the .340's sharp recoil, and when the rifle came back down the nyala was simply gone; I had only the vague impression that it had taken a quick jump to the left and gone down. This was the case, but we had to dig around in the thick bush for several minutes before we could find it. And yes, it was everything I'd hoped for, and a whole lot more.

With both our nyala in the skinning shed we now had the rare luxury of time to enjoy the country. We stalked in close to L. J.'s herd of white rhino and took both film and photos, and Jim and I each shot good blue wildebeest. I hit mine very well with the big .340, but it took off like it had been bitten by a fly. I swung ahead of it and fired again, and this time it somersaulted in a huge cloud of dust. Of course, Chip, great with the camera though he is, didn't quite get that second shot on film. Jim, on the other hand, absolutely flattened his wildebeest with a single Barnes X-Bullet from his little .270 Weatherby!

Jim also shot a really superb waterbuck with the same rifle and load. We'd tried to get it the day before but lost it in some thick stuff. In the early morning we located it in a valley of very tall grass near L. J.'s airstrip, finding it only by his black horn tips sticking up above the grass. The trick to the stalk was finding a spot high enough so we could see it, and we found such a place in a little raised hummock where a couple of thorn trees had grown. It was quartering to us, and Jim shot it very well on the point of the shoulder. It dropped so quickly and so finally that it took us half an hour to find it in the long grass!

Jim's primary remaining goal was a greater kudu, and we searched high and low, seemingly in vain. I was feeling extremely guilty that I'd shot my kudu on our first day, for Jim had never shot one and I'd certainly taken my share. But done was done, and now all we could find were cows and small bulls. Chip and I were due in Namibia to film another portion of the Swarovski series, while Jim would stay with L. J. for a couple more days, then head back to the States. So we left him without his kudu, and of course he shot a big, beautiful bull as soon as the camera was gone.

In 1989 Mozambique's Zambezi Valley was literally a wasteland, with very little game and numerous signs of the long struggle, including many abandoned villages. Surprisingly, the elephant were virtually untouched.

Fishermen on Lake Cabora Bassa were a prime source of information on elephant movement—and since game was so scarce, trading salt for fish supplemented the camp diet.

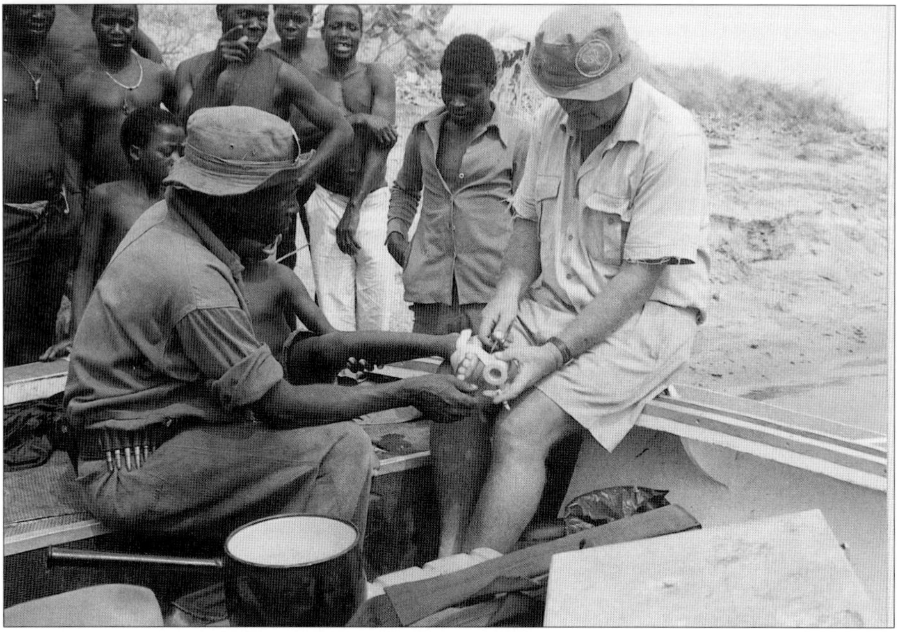

Many of the local children–even teenagers–had never seen a white person. When asking about elephant movement or bartering for fish, Roger Whittall would always break out the first aid kit and do what he could to help.

The great elephant hunter Tony Sanchez Ariño said it best: "You kill an elephant with your legs; you only execute him with the rifle." The only option in elephant hunting is to cover lots of miles.

After days of tracking in thick bush on both sides of the lake, the author's elephant, a nice bull for today, was taken in the high grass literally on the shores of Lake Cabora Bassa.

The little Sharpe grysbok, normally a hard-to-obtain trophy, was one of very few species still common in that part of Mozambique.

"The Ivory Trail." This photo was staged to make a point: This is Roger Whittall and crew's entire take from the 1989 season, from an area the size of Vermont. All good bulls, and no impact on the overall population. The author believes it was a terrible mistake to close down elephant hunting in this region.

Louis-Jean Havemann's Windy Ridge is a classic example of a fine South African game ranch. Converted to game many years ago, it's essentially a private park with a wide range of game for viewing as well as hunting.

The author's greater kudu was his first trophy on Windy Ridge. Parallel-horned kudu are hard to judge; the open spirals on this bull give it a deceptive length of 54 inches, big for Zululand.

Louis-Jean Havemann and the author with a wonderful nyala. Taken easily and early in the hunt, this bull was simply too good to pass.

Like many good game ranches, Windy Ridge has a small herd of white rhino. Without game ranching the white rhino would almost surely still be seriously endangered.

Jim Morey with a really fine common waterbuck. Waterbuck are relatively uncommon in Natal and Zululand, but trophy quality can be spectacular.

Greater kudu are one of the most plentiful of Namibia's antelope, found in virtually all areas. Trophy quality generally isn't quite as good as Zimbabwe, but big bulls are easier to locate in the more open country.

The only real rarity in Namibia is the Hartmann's mountain zebra, a beautifully striped zebra confined to Namibia's rocky hills. This stallion was caught in the open when it led its herd onto the flats to feed.

A good red Cape hartebeest, taken with a .270 Weatherby Magnum. The author looks relieved as much as pleased; the animal was shot at dusk the night before but not found until sunrise.

Gemsbok roam in large herds on Lamprecht's Rooikraal. It's hard enough to tell males from females, but even more difficult to accurately judge trophy quality. Paul Merriman dropped his bull with a perfect shot.

Rooikraal is one of relatively few places in Namibia that has a large population of eland. These are the Cape eland, smallest-bodied of the eland and generally lacking in body stripes.

Professional hunter Joof Lamprecht is also the proprietor of a good gunshop in Windhoek, where end-of-safari business matters are concluded.

The Upper Chinko region of the C.A.R. is a vast wilderness of valleys, ridges, and plateaus. Called "savanna" to differentiate it from the true forest, it's actually a scrub forest with few areas open enough to hunt by glassing.

Having sworn to shoot nothing other than Derby eland, the author did just that, excepting small game for the pot. This is a western bush duiker, smallest of the bush duikers.

Guinea fowl are an important food staple on most C.A.R. hunts. PH Rudy Lubin's scoped Ruger 10/22 is kept handy when driving to and from hunting areas.

Lubin's camp was extremely comfortable, with real mattresses on wicker frames, of course draped with mosquito netting.

Considered a forest duiker, the red-flanked duiker is actually a creature of thicket edges. Beautifully colored with short, thick horns, the red-flanked duiker is a real treat when barbecued whole.

Rudy Lubin at the Trois Rivieres *base camp with several eland taken on earlier safaris. The author wasn't lucky, but the giant eland were certainly there.*

Leopard hunting begins with finding tracks, then trying to figure out where the leopard might be hunting.

Plains game is relatively scarce in the Zambezi Valley, but there are usually enough impala around that locating a bait animal isn't too difficult.

There's an art to finding just the right bait tree, so the cat will feel secure enough to come before dark . . . and so it can be seen against the sky at last light. Once the bait is taken, building a proper blind is yet another art form.

The author and professional hunter/ outfitter Russ Broom taking a break after a long and fruitless job of tracking buffalo. The large herds and thick cover make it very difficult to sort out the best bulls.

The author and Russ Broom approach a forty-four-inch Zambezi Valley buffalo. Zimbabwe buffalo are as good as any in Africa, but the hunting conditions make it time consuming to find the big ones.

The author with a big tom leopard shot on the last night of the safari and recovered while the charter plane was waiting! He's holding Russ Broom's over/under 12 gauge–using it convinced him that buckshot is not the way to go on wounded leopard.

9

BRAND NEW NAMIBIA

I have a tremendous soft spot for the country now called Namibia, a land of dramatic rocky hills and broad valleys under cloudless skies of the deepest blue I have ever seen. It's an arid land with the Kalahari Desert to the northeast and the Namib Desert along the western coast. In between and to the north, depending on rainfall, the vegetation ranges from savanna to thornbush. I consider it the most beautiful country in Africa, somewhat similar to Arizona but with more brush in the valleys. It's a huge country with a tiny human population, and it's one of the best destinations I know of for an enjoyable, trouble-free safari. European hunters, especially Germans, have known this for generations, but for whatever reason, few Americans visit Namibia.

Namibia was colonized by Kaiser Wilhelm's Germany more than a century ago, and it was called German South West Africa until the Treaty of Versailles at the end of World War I. To this day, the ties with Germany remain strong. Many of the ranchers are of German descent, and in many districts German remains the most common language. The country was occupied by South African troops during World War I, and after the war it became officially a protectorate of South Africa. In 1990,

Namibia became the last country on the African continent to achieve full independence.

The transition itself was relatively orderly, but was preceded by years of escalating tension. From the mid-1970s through the 1980s, northern Namibia was a staging ground for South African operations in Angola. During this period, Namibia's own independence movement, the South West Africa People's Organization (SWAPO), began its own low-intensity guerrilla campaign, mostly affecting the northern areas. The United Nations had pressured South Africa to relinquish Namibia for years, and by 1990 it was time and past time. When I hunted there, 1991 was half over; the new country of Namibia was a reality and the general feeling was one of "getting on with business."

Namibia's capital and only major city, Windhoek, bustled with activity as always, and there seemed no shortage of goods of any kind. The city is a fascinating mix of cultures, from German pubs to Herero women in traditional dresses of brilliant colors. But I'm not much of a tourist, and we were there to hunt and make a video, not necessarily in that order. Our stay in town was as short as we could make it.

One of the great things about Namibia is the simplicity of the hunting, but in that simplicity is probably also Namibia's marketing downfall. Although recent game ranching efforts have introduced a few South African species such as blesbok and black wildebeest, Namibia's native game list is not extensive. Most areas offer kudu, Cape hartebeest, gemsbok, and warthog. Springbok and ostrich are found in more open areas, while the only Namibian rarity, the Hartmann's mountain zebra, is found primarily in the rocky hills north of Windhoek. Some areas have blue wildebeest while others have eland. There are duiker and steinbok, and that pretty much rounds out the plains game picture in Namibia.

The country was settled a century ago with Germanic efficiency, with most of the land subdivided into a grid of ranches. Over the course of a century of European-style ranching, most of the dangerous game was eliminated. There are elephant–now reopened to limited hunting–in some of the northern tribal lands and in the Caprivi Strip. These border areas, plus the fringes of Etosha Pan National Park, also hold some lion. Leopard are found throughout the country, although after a century of attrition warfare, they were extremely scarce until fairly recently. Today, thanks to the leopard's great value to sport hunters, most farmers tolerate Old Spots until a safari comes along. Much the same can be said of cheetah, which are also increasing in today's Namibia.

Although Namibia has produced some very good elephant and the odd big cat, for most hunters Namibia is a plains-game safari and a darned good one. I think the limited game list tends to put a lot of hunters off when compared with the twenty or more species a similarly priced plains-game hunt in Zimbabwe or South Africa might offer. That's often a bit of an illusion; there's really only so much that can be accomplished on a typical seven- or ten-day plains-game safari, and Namibia's game list is plenty extensive enough to keep any hunter busy.

Virtually all the hunting is on private land, with landowners charging trophy fees for game taken. However, unlike some countries, a hunting license is required. It's a simple and inexpensive document, and entitles the licensee to two each of every game animal. From there it's a simple matter of a professional hunter's daily rate and trophy fees for game taken.

Back in the 1970s and early eighties, I enjoyed several fine hunts in the Omaruru District, several hours north of Windhoek. As African hunting goes, this, too, was simplicity in itself. The first time I went there, outfitter Ben Nolte picked us up in a mini-van, but thereafter it was just as easy for me (and a lot easier for Ben) to rent a car and drive up, with good highway all the way.

By 1991, things had changed a lot. Ben Nolte had left Omaruru and was out of the safari business, farming in the south of the country. Joof Lamprecht, who had worked with Ben a decade earlier, now had an outfit of his own. We'd corresponded about it for some time, and as the "Affordable Africa" video project took shape, Joof's situation seemed a natural. After looking around for years, Joof and his wife, Marina, had purchased a farm called Rooikraal ("Red Corral," probably after the red clay soil) in the savanna thornbush country northeast of Windhoek.

Like most properties in Namibia where the game has received even a modicum of protection, Rooikraal held good numbers of gemsbok, kudu, and hartebeest, the staples of Namibian hunting. From there, however, Rooikraal was different and well worth the years spent searching for just the right property. Some introductions had been done, with both blue and black wildebeest present, plus both mountain and common zebra. Plus, there were blesbok and impala, and perhaps most valuable of all, a wonderful herd of Cape eland. Joof had essentially everything anyone goes to Namibia to hunt right there on his property, except for springbok, and Rooikraal lay scarcely more than an hour's drive from the Windhoek airport. The net result was that one could be hunting within twenty-four hours of departing home in the States, an unusual and exceptional situation, and extremely pleasant compared with the air charters and long, dusty Land Cruiser rides required to get to most African hunting areas.

Trying to combine filming with hunting is a difficult undertaking, which is why there are so few good videos. The problem is simply that, to make a proper video, you must make a personal commitment that the filming is of primary importance; the hunting must be secondary to getting the best footage possible. I'm much too serious about my hunting to want to do that on a regular basis, especially after I discovered that there is virtually no way to actually make a hunting video show a profit! Videographer Chip Payne and I had just completed a video in Zululand, and now we were in Namibia to do another segment in Swarovski's "Affordable Africa" series. The project seemed sound, and since I'd hunted both areas on previous trips there was no urgency about the hunting. In fact, the video project gave me a good excuse to revisit both Zululand and Namibia.

Of course, there had to be *some* reason for me to be there. In a word, it was gemsbok. The gemsbok, or giant oryx, is one of those classic African animals, and I'd always wanted a really large one, a bull with more than forty inches of horn. The bulls tend to wear their horns down in the rocky Omaruru country I used to hunt, with bulls' horns almost never reaching past the midthirties. I had come very close in northern South Africa a decade before, taking a huge bull of thirty-nine inches. Now, it's absolutely true that an inch worth of horn isn't worth worrying about. But Joof had told me that his country produced very good gemsbok. That would be my main goal. Joining me was my father-in-law, Paul Merriman, who had never hunted in Namibia. Paul, of course, would be trying for a full bag.

Rooikraal was indeed beautiful country, much more gentle than the rugged Orongo Mountains where I'd done most of my southwest African hunting. The rocky hills were there, but they were lower and more isolated, separated by broad grassy valleys cut by fingers of thornbush and studded with flat-topped acacia. We could glass kudu and mountain zebra in the hills, and in the valleys we could find herds of hartebeest, gemsbok, and occasionally, eland.

Chip Payne had extensive experience filming in both Botswana and Zimbabwe, but he'd never seen Namibia before. I knew he'd be enthralled by the video opportunities, and of course he was. He got his camera on big herds of hartebeest and gemsbok right outside of camp, and he was on hand when Paul opened the safari by dropping a fine gemsbok bull in its tracks.

That, of course, was part of the object of the filming: to get a couple of really classic "drop to the shot" scenes for our video. It's easier said than done, especially when you're dealing with tough animals like gemsbok, zebra, and such, but in a hunting area like Rooikraal, where the game was not only plentiful but also undisturbed, the opportunity was unusually good. We got a lot of great footage, but I surely didn't do as well as Paul in the "drop to the shot" department.

Along about the second day, I made a very long shot on a hartebeest with the big .340 Weatherby Magnum. It was a good shot, but it sure didn't drop that hartebeest in its tracks. Later in the hunt, we tried it again with my second hartebeest tag.

We'd made a long stalk on a big herd congregated around a waterhole just at sunset. This time I had the .270 Weatherby Magnum, a fine and underrated cartridge that does a wonderful job on midsize plains game. There were too many eyes to get close, but using tripod shooting sticks, I shot a very big bull as carefully as I could right on the shoulder.

It went off with the herd, but I was certain of a good hit. So certain that we looked in the tall grass beyond for the animal before we went back to look for blood. Big mistake. In that clear Kalahari air, twilight is very short, and suddenly it was too dark to look for spoor. We circled in the direction it had gone, but ultimately had to go back to camp, where I spent a long and sleepless night wondering how I'd messed up the shot.

I hadn't. At first light we found it not seventy-five yards from the waterhole, stone dead from a perfect shoulder shot, the meat still fine after a cold night and, luckily, the cape untouched by scavengers.

As the hunt continued, Paul did a wonderful job performing for the camera. He dropped a fine wildebeest in its tracks–quite a feat on this toughest of all antelope–and did much the same on a lovely mountain zebra. I spent most of my time looking for an extra-special gemsbok.

This was more gentle country than the Orongo Mountains I'd hunted previously. Up there in that rocky country the gemsbok tended to wear their horns down quickly, so that a bull in the midthirties was actually quite good. Here the difference was apparent; there were plenty of bulls in the high thirties, and there were some fabulously long-horned cows. I don't have a problem with hunters who take a cow with inordinately long horns, and of course most of the very best gemsbok in Rowland Ward are well-adorned females.

On close inspection, the difference is obvious in that gemsbok cow horns are not only thinner, but, when they grow to extreme length, are generally not quite straight, growing in slightly wavy lines. For me, however, a real gemsbok trophy is a bull with thick, straight horns. But in a shifting herd in thornbush or tall grass it's extremely difficult to keep them sorted out, and it's even more difficult to be sure of that extra two or three inches of horn you want so badly.

Time and again, Joof and I worked big herds, small herds, and bachelor groups. The goal, of course, was to find a bull that had for-darn-sure horns over forty inches. Sometimes they spooked before we could be sure. More often, after three or four approaches, we waved off because we couldn't be sure. And still more often the length we sought simply wasn't there.

As these things go, when it happened, it happened very quickly. We had just left camp for the afternoon hunt, when somebody spied a herd of gemsbok moving through tall grass off to our right. Joof caught just a glimpse of an obvious bull, a bull with very long and very thick horns, and we bailed out of the truck.

They were moving slowly through some thick stuff a few hundred yards away and we had plenty of bush to give us cover. We moved up behind one thornbush, then another, catching several glimpses of the bull we sought. It would be a great exaggeration to say that it towered above the rest. It didn't. Judging gemsbok is more a matter of subtle finesse than instantaneous revelation. Its horns were thick and straight, and seemed on a par with those of the longest cows–a very good indication. We were sure it had it, and at about two hundred yards we set up the shooting sticks and waited for it to offer a clear shot.

After agonizing seconds, it moved out of the press for just a moment, and in that moment the rifle crashed and I lost it in recoil. The sound of the big bullet hitting was clear, and then the whole herd was off. In those moments I couldn't avoid the feelings of doubt. Did I shoot the right one? Did I hit it well? Did we judge it properly?

This time the common answer was affirmative. A few dozen yards and it was down, and it was everything we'd hoped it would be. Almost. Its horns were wonderfully thick and beautifully straight, and they taped a bit over thirty-nine inches. We hadn't quite reached our goal, but we'd certainly come close enough for celebration.

Late in the hunt, Paul and I both shot beautiful Cape eland, one of Rooikraal's specialties, and on the last evening I took a second gemsbok. This time we were wrong; it was a lone bull, one of the most difficult situations to judge, and its horns were actually a bit shorter than those of the first. It dropped to the shot like a stone . . . but of course Chip wasn't there with his camera, having elected to spend our last night sitting at a waterhole instead!

As much as I hate to face it, chances are I will hunt Africa much less in the next decade than I have in the last two. I'd like to start over, but escalating costs and increasing responsibilities at home mean that I will never again see some of the places I've hunted. Namibia is one place I'm sure I will see again. It's affordable, unusually scenic, and hassle-free to get in and out of. It will be a perfect place to take the kids when they're ready for their first safari . . . and besides, I'm *still* looking for a forty-inch gemsbok bull!

10

THE UPPER CHINKO

It was late in my career, March of 1992 to be exact, that I was introduced to the Central African Republic, which I consider to be one of the finest hunting countries on the continent. The C.A.R. isn't for everybody. It's remote and difficult. There's a lot of red tape involved with getting in and getting out, especially if you don't speak French, and I don't. It's a big, unpopulated country–two and a half times the size of the United Kingdom–with just three million inhabitants. There are few roads, and most of the people are concentrated along the Oubangui River, which separates the C.A.R. from Zaire to the south. Lying just north of the equator, it's a very hot country even during the short winter, and hotter still during the long spring and summer. Hunting is mostly on foot and never easy. Its remoteness also translates to high outfitting costs; C.A.R. is one of the most expensive safari countries in Africa, largely because of the cost of maintaining camps in virtually inaccessible country.

Nothing comes easy in the C.A.R. Rudy Lubin's camp on the Haut Chinko (Upper Chinko) River was fully ten days' hard driving from Bangui–or three hours by very costly charter. The game is hunted on foot, never mind the heat, and every prize is hard-won. The trade-off is that this is the real Africa, an Africa changed but little in the last century. There are no villages, no roads, no signs that mark the border with the Sudan. There are, regrettably, poachers. More of that later.

As I said, it isn't for everybody. In the French tradition, the outfitters do a marvelous job of keeping the camps well supplied, and the cooks are French-trained and wonderful. But all supplies and amenities must be driven in at the beginning of the season, with only sparse resupply available when charter planes bring in clients. Nothing is fancy, and the only guarantee is that you'll hunt harder than anyplace I've been in Africa. For me it was wonderful.

And on that first trip to the C.A.R. I did absolutely everything wrong. In fact, excepting for a couple of duikers, I shot exactly nothing. And it was still wonderful. The fact that I shot nothing was certainly not Rudy Lubin's fault. It was altogether mine; I took my chances and it just didn't work. Rudy is a French professional hunter with some twenty seasons' experience in the C.A.R. His wife is American outdoor writer Brooke Chilvers; both have been good friends for some time, and between us we'd been trying to figure out how my always-stretched budget could get me into the C.A.R. The opportunity arose when Coloradan Dave Liniger and his wife, Gail, had a two-week giant eland hunt planned. A big business deal came up that Dave couldn't miss, so he offered me the second week of his hunt.

I took it knowing a couple of things. First, that I needed luck for one week to be enough time for Derby eland. Second, that March was a particularly unlikely time for Lady Luck to smile. It was spring in the C.A.R.; the leaves would be back on the trees, restricting visibility. Based on this knowledge I made the biggest mistake of all. Since Derby eland was my main goal, and the only thing I really cared about, I made a personal decision to shoot absolutely nothing until the Derby eland was secured. In so doing, I virtually assured myself of a frustrating failure. What I should have done was accept a wonderful opportunity, and I should have made the most of it–but I didn't.

On virtually any map of the C.A.R. you can find, far to the northeast of Bangui and about 150 miles from the Sudan border, a little dot with the inscription *Trois Rivieres.* One might assume that "Three Rivers" is a town or village of some size. It is not. It is the main hunting camp of *Les Safaris du Haut Chinko,* the hunting company owned by Daniel Henriot and for which Rudy Lubin has hunted all these years. Three Rivers also houses the only airstrip in that part of the C.A.R.; it was a four-hour drive from base camp to Rudy's own camp on the Upper Chinko, much closer to the Sudanese border.

Along a main ridge about two-thirds of the way to Rudy's camp we surprised the biggest waterbuck I'd ever seen. He stopped and looked at us from about forty yards off the track, then turned and swaggered this way and that as he gradually increased the distance. I had an open license, and of course I had never before seen, let alone shot, one of these big sing-sing waterbuck. But I let him go. I was there to hunt Lord Derby eland.

The next morning, just after leaving camp, we drove into a big herd of buffalo. It was still almost dark, far too early to judge horns; the buffalo were just a writhing mass of black shapes as they moved into the deeper black of a tree line. All we needed to do was wait ten minutes for it to get a bit lighter, then follow them into the tree line and try to pick out a bull. I had, of course, never before seen, let alone shot, one of these transitional northwestern buffalo. But I was there to hunt Derby eland, so we kept on going.

And so it went. During the next week I had the opportunity to shoot virtually everything that occurs in the terminalia forest/savanna woodland of the eastern C.A.R. That list, by the way, is extensive; not only buffalo and waterbuck, but also western kob, western hartebeest, Nigerian bohor reedbuck, harnessed bushbuck, oribi, and more. But I was there to hunt Derby eland. The only animal that I might have broken my vow over was western roan, and that was one opportunity we did not have. We did see a few roan, small bulls and cow herds–but it was (and has remained) my impression that roan are less plentiful and more difficult to obtain than Derby eland in the eastern C.A.R. I understand the situation is just the reverse in northern Cameroon.

Anyway, I was there on a short hunt with just one goal in mind, namely to hunt Lord Derby eland, named after the Thirteenth Earl of Derby, who was president of the London Zoological Society in 1831, when this wondrous antelope was first "discovered" by Europeans. After much painful experience with the giant eland, I have some definite opinions about them. First, I don't think they're noticeably bigger in the body than Livingstone eland, comparing big bulls to big bulls. Second, I don't think the animals themselves are any more difficult to hunt; eland are eland and none of Africa's antelope are more spooky nor able to distance themselves from pursuers more quickly. The country, with its lack of visibility and lack of roads, does make hunting the giant eland generally more physically demanding and perhaps less successful, but not necessarily more difficult.

If the body size is similar to that of common eland, the horn size simply doesn't compare. A Lord Derby eland is far more colorful in body, cape, and face–more so early in the season, in winter pelage, but even in spring and summer. And the horns of a big bull are simply unbelievable. They sort of start where common eland end, and just keep on going. I'm crazy about all the spiral horns, but I find the giant eland the most dramatic of all of Africa's antelope, and just perhaps the greatest trophy on the continent.

This is what we were after, and this is what we sought to the exclusion of all else. That isn't unusual, nor necessarily a bad call. Americans are typically the "collectors" of the African hunting scene, and when Americans think about the C.A.R.

they are usually thinking either Derby eland or bongo. I was certainly that way on that first trip. What I didn't realize is that the savanna country (technically savanna woodland, or transition from forest to savanna) of the C.A.R. is a fine general bag safari area. Europeans know this and come to the C.A.R. for buffalo, cats, and the various antelope–caring not a whit whether eland are part of the bag or not. Americans play it the way I did–giant eland, bongo, or nothing. There's no right or wrong, but I sure walked away from some great trophies because I didn't want to "interfere" with my chances for a giant eland.

So we hunted eland. They weren't uncommon; in fact, there were plenty of herds around, enough that we followed fresh tracks almost every day. We should have gotten one, really; chances are that if you can follow eland for a half-dozen days you'll get at least one chance sooner or later. We never did. I, of course, had the second half of Dave Liniger's safari. Dave had gotten close to a bull but hadn't gotten it, so technically the odds were even more in my favor.

If you read Africana from a generation ago you get a clear picture that the Derby eland is one of those almost mythical creatures, almost as difficult to obtain as bongo or mountain nyala. I'm living proof that Derby eland are not easy, but hunting for them today is actually quite successful. Part of the reason is that professional hunters like Rudy have learned where to look for them and how to hunt them. Until about fifteen years ago the primary draw in the C.A.R. was big elephant, not just in the forest areas but clear out in the savanna as well. Giant eland and even bongo were hunted primarily as add-ons, but if the client had a hundred-pound elephant, did it really matter whether he got a giant eland or not? Then the poachers moved in and the elephant hunting deteriorated until, ultimately, elephant hunting was closed. Suddenly the primary draw in the savanna areas was giant eland; bongo in the forest. Since the professional hunters had to either concentrate on them or close up shop, they learned how to hunt them.

Today giant eland hunting is extremely successful. So much so that both Dave Liniger and I might have gotten bulls; at least one of us surely should have. As it happened, neither of us did. But certainly not for lack of effort.

Rudy and I tracked eland almost every day. Early in the morning we would drive along the few tracks through known feeding areas, hoping to cut fresh spoor. If that didn't happen we would walk to known salt licks and check for tracks, or make a loop along a ridge or across a plateau that had been a favored movement or feeding corridor. Remember, we had just seven days. I think we tracked eland five of those days. We saw them just twice.

Sometimes the eland just plain outdistanced us. More often the "ides of March" got us. March is not a bad month to hunt the C.A.R.; there may be early showers that will freshen the tracks, but certainly the game will be coming to the rivers to water since the water holes in the bush are mostly dry. These are good things. On the bad side, spring has come and the leaves are back on the terminalia and acacia. This means visibility is limited, so you must be very close to see and judge the eland. Worse, atmospheric conditions are building as the rainy season approaches. The air is hot and dense and heavy, and this means the midday breezes, always fickle, are just plain treacherous.

Time and again we closed on eland only to have the wind shift and come from behind. Then, usually, we would proceed on the tracks to where the eland had stood, then find they had run like hell when our scent hit them. Sometimes we would do this three or four times before breaking contact. The lesson wasn't that March was a bad month, but it was a bad month for a short safari. We needed not only luck but also time, and had neither.

Still, it might have happened. Maybe if I'd been a bit better hunter it *would* have happened. One morning we took the track of two big bulls and followed them endlessly through the terminalia forest. Late in the morning, just as the tracks became fresh and started to wander as the bulls sought a shady place to rest, the cursed wind started to waver. Moments later we found where the bulls had stood under the shade of a big tree–and then deep, splayed tracks showing how they had run when they received our scent. We, too, had stopped to rest when the wind shifted, only a couple hundred yards back. We should have seen them, but somehow we did not.

We waited again, then continued on the tracks. The bulls went scarcely five hundred yards, but this time they heard us approach. And this time, for the first time, we saw them. Or parts of them. I caught brief glimpses of two broad, tan behinds dashing through the bush. Maybe, just maybe, there was a shot I should have taken, but I wanted to see the horns, and of course that wasn't wrong.

Rudy's trackers were wonderful, companions of twenty years and the best I've ever seen. They rarely faltered, and then not for long, and they never gave up until the chase was hopeless. But with the thick cover and the bad winds, two or three strikes was all we could expect. We followed these bulls for a while longer, but now they were eating ground at the trot that eland will maintain for miles. It was time, once again, to start the long journey back to the truck.

A couple of days later we came even closer. This time we had the majority of a big herd spread out in open forest, the closest eland just fifty yards away. This was the first time I actually, truly *saw* giant eland. They were breathtaking, with coats of Hershey-bar chocolate barred with white stripes, and possessing simply amazing horns. But these were all cows. There were a couple of bulls in the herd, but they were somewhere on the far side. Luck could have dictated otherwise, but she did not.

We slithered through the brush alongside them for several hundred yards, trying to maneuver this way and that while the eland fed along unconcerned. Then, of course, the wind shifted and that was the end of that herd. We never saw a bull.

I broke my vow a couple of times in the hunt by shooting both red-flanked and western bush duikers on the way back to camp. And on the last couple of evenings I might have broken it more substantially with a waterbuck or kob. There were literally hundreds of each in the riverine growth close by the Chinko River. But we'd had our chances, and in those last couple of evenings we never saw anything particularly good.

We did see a few Sudanese poachers with their biltong-laden donkeys, and we heard the odd shot along the river. The border with Sudan was fifty miles away, but it meant nothing. Rudy's wife, Brooke, was running the camp that season, and of course the camp staff was there, unarmed, as well. The poachers knew where the camp was, so Rudy had of necessity established a "live and let live" policy with them. At this time there were just a few poachers, working their way down the Chinko River and cleaning out the hippos as they went. It was disturbing, but so far had had little impact on the game and, in any case, there was absolutely nothing Rudy could do about it. Not if he wanted to continue to operate there.

Once in a while a poacher would stop by the camp to cadge tobacco or whatever. Using Swahili, little known in the C.A.R. but relatively common in Sudan, Rudy asked him if he knew he was poaching in the C.A.R. Nonplussed, the man answered, "Man, this is not Sudan or the C.A.R.; this is just the bush."

Over the next two years the trickle of enterprising poachers would turn into an invasion. Once the hippo were gone they turned to the kob, waterbuck, and buffalo. I returned in 1994 and had a wonderful safari, the last safari on the Upper Chinko . . . but in just two years all the common game was gone.

11

THE ZAMBEZI VALLEY

Without question the great Zambezi Valley–especially the Zimbabwe side–is one of the finest game areas in all of Africa. Back when Zambia was Northern Rhodesia, much of the northern bank was settled; the game moved out, or was poached, or was "controlled" in favor of people and crops. The Zimbabwe side, which used to be part of Southern Rhodesia, remained wild and free, and is so to this day.

It is not a general bag area, for during what the old elephant hunter Ian Nyschens calls "the months of the sun," the Zambezi Valley becomes bone-dry from the top of the escarpment all the way to the river. Along the river and on the shores of Lake Kariba are a few exceptional waterbuck and numbers of impala. There are some sable, wildebeest, and zebra here and there, especially along the sand rivers that hold small pools of permanent water. In the hills and riverine thickets you may encounter exceptional kudu and hear bushbuck bark, but if you want to hunt plains game in Zimbabwe go to the ranch country in the interior, where the combination of permanent water, agriculture, and edge habitat has created concentrations of game not dissimilar to whitetail densities in the eastern United States.

My longtime friend, mentor, and hero Jack Atcheson, Sr., said it far better than I ever could: "True wilderness is characterized by the absence of wildlife." Nowhere is this more true than in the vast Zambezi Valley. And yet it is not altogether true. In this paradise of untouched Africa one might go hours–sometimes days–without seeing a living animal. And yet the game is there. One doesn't go to the Zambezi Valley to hunt plains game, but one does go there to hunt the dangerous game. Today the Zambezi Valley hosts the finest elephant hunting remaining in Africa. It is also one of the great strongholds of Cape buffalo. It is fairly unlikely that you will see either animal on a casual drive, but the spoor will be there to follow.

Where there are buffalo there are lion, and good numbers of lion–but the valley is not, never has been, and never will be noted as a great lion area. The low-lying valley is too hot and the bush too dense to produce the luxurious manes trophy hunters crave. You'll find big buffalo-killing lion in the Zambezi, but few MGM manes. You *will* find a real concentration of shockingly big leopards.

I don't know why this is so, for Zambezi leopard have to work hard to earn a living–especially during the long dry season. But there's bushbuck and duiker, impala and baboon, and in most brushy *korangos* you will find a leopard track. Often a big track.

I honestly don't know if I will ever hunt another elephant, but I hope I am a long way from my last buffalo hunt. And although I had taken a leopard, I had never taken a leopard properly, over bait. It was buffalo and leopard that drew me to the Zambezi Valley in June of 1992. Unless one wishes to pursue elephant, I believe these two animals combine to make the perfect Zambezi Valley safari, and to this day I believe the Zambezi is as fine a place as there is in Africa to pursue both species.

Part of the lure was to see the Zambezi, and part was to hunt buffalo and leopard. Part, also, was to hunt with Russ Broom. I'd hunted with Russ and his dad, Geoff Broom, back in 1984. Geoff, of course, was one of Rhodesia's pioneering outfitters; his Matetsi Safaris were famous throughout the seventies and into the eighties. In 1984 Geoff was hunting in Zambia. He arranged for me to spend part of the hunt with his son, Russ, who was just finishing college in the States. Geoff had plans to retire, and he was hoping whatever magazine articles I might write about the trip would help get Russ started in his own right.

I don't know if that part worked or not, but Russ and I hit it off well. We also had a particularly amazing run of luck in Zambia's Namwala and Mumbwa concessions–undoubtedly the luckiest hunting I've ever had. Russ and I (and Geoff as well) had remained good friends, but I hadn't hunted with either of them for eight years. Unable to withstand the Zambian politics of the mideighties, they folded up that operation just a year later. Both hunted in Botswana briefly, then Geoff actually tried to retire. ("I got tired of playing golf after a week or so," he later told me.) Russ made a short-lived attempt to get Malawi open to hunting, then did a couple of seasons in Tanzania, then somehow managed to obtain a huge concession in the Zambezi Valley of his native Zimbabwe.

For him, I suspect it was something of a homecoming–and what a home to come back to. His new area ran from the shores of Lake Kariba to the escarpment and beyond–some twenty thousand square kilometers of the real Africa. At that time he reckoned he had three thousand elephant and over eight thousand buffalo in the area. His game quotas are indicative of the varying densities of game in the Zambezi Valley. These figures are from memory, but it strikes me that he started with a dozen elephant bulls on quota. I *know* he had fully one hundred buffalo and twenty leopards on quota–but just four lion, four waterbuck, and an equally paltry smattering of zebra, sable, and such. That's the Zambezi Valley: a dangerous game area, pure and simple. That suited me just fine.

An American friend of mine named John Sheehan joined me on the hunt. John is a principal in Richard Pascall's Kudu Safaris; they and Russ were trading out some plains game hunting for buffalo. The plan was for me to hunt–successfully hunt, that is–buffalo and leopard with Russ; then John and I would go to Richard's ranch near Bulawayo and hunt plains game, and then go on to the Gwaai River and do a bit more hunting on one of Richard's concessions.

The plan was ambitious. It counted on leopard luck, which I do not have, and did not take into account that I can get downright stubborn at times. I will apologize right now to the people I disappointed, for I never made it to the Gwaai River. I *barely* made it to Richard's ranch–just in time for a half-day's hunt that netted us a very nice kudu bull. Richard is still speaking to me, but I wouldn't much blame him if he didn't. We did get the buffalo, and we got the leopard. But the charter plane, on the last possible day, was sitting on Russ's strip waiting while we brought the cat back to camp . . . .

June is a good month in Zimbabwe, but in the Zambezi Valley it depends on the rainfall. That year June was extremely early; the rains had just stopped and the grass was tall and green, too lush to burn and too high to see into. Everyone says early is a good time for cats, but I think it depends entirely upon whether you're lucky or not. Early is *not* a good time for buffalo, especially not among the big herds in the valley. Shooting a buffalo is not a problem; even shooting a reasonable bull is not a problem. But sorting out and shooting a really good bull is a problem.

That isn't just a problem with being early; it's part and parcel to buffalo hunting in the Zambezi Valley, where there's lots of thick bush and big herds of buffalo. I honestly believe that the Zambezi Valley produces buffalo the equal of any of the so-called top trophy areas, including Masailand, but sorting those big bulls out of the thick bush and from the midst of the big herds is very difficult. Every year a few hunters are fortunate to take bulls in the mid-to high forties, and one or two approach the mythical fifty-inch mark. Most settle for much less, but not because the big ones aren't there.

Every mature buffalo bull is wonderful. On other hunts I've settled for the first hard-bossed bull that came along, and I'll do so again with pleasure. But this time we decided we'd look for a great buffalo. And why not? We could check our leopard baits in the morning, follow buffalo tracks in the midday, and still be in a leopard blind in late afternoon. After all, we weren't going anywhere until we had our leopard!

It was really two separate hunts, though conducted simultaneously. Both became drawn-out affairs, but the leopard business might just as well have ended very quickly. Russ had two young apprentice hunters managing his camp on the shores of Lake Kariba, David Hulme and Ernest Dyason. As soon as we arrived they told us they had a big leopard feeding, and indeed they had–a monstrous leopard with pugs like those of a small lion. It was in a good spot, but the bait hadn't been checked for a couple of days and had gone off.

We quickly shot an impala–fortunately Russ has plenty of them on quota–and built a blind. That very first evening we sat for this monster of a leopard, but like so many evenings on so many safaris our date stood us up. It was black dark and the moon was just coming up when we left the blind.

It came during the night and lolled around the bait until it was light, or nearly so. When we checked the bait early in the morning we found where it had lain beside the bait tree, and its scat was still fresh and warm.

That night we took blankets and a mattress into the blind, hoping we might catch it in the morning. It didn't come back that night, nor the next, nor ever again on that safari. But it was a huge leopard. I know this because Russ's next client shot it from that blind, and was kind enough to send me a photo.

Now we had to start fresh with another leopard, but at least we could hunt buffalo in the meantime. And hunt buffalo we did. Virtually every day we got into at least some buffalo, but the big bull we sought was proving as elusive as our uncooperative leopard. The difficulty wasn't so much the buffalo but the grass; we had to be literally in the middle of the herds to judge the horns, and we just weren't lucky enough to see a great bull. But we saw plenty of bulls, and from plenty close enough.

One hot midday was typical. We'd tracked a big herd for about an hour before we came up to them. This was relatively open mopane forest, and we could see a good number of buffalo from about sixty yards, but nothing good. We crept a bit closer, ticking them off one by one, until a swirl of breeze spooked unseen buffalo on the far right of the herd. They all started to run, but of course only a few knew why they were running. I knew what was next, so when Russ stood up to run I was ready. We ran, not away from the herd, but *toward* them. Under such circumstances you can charge a buffalo herd in relative safety; sometimes they'll circle and sometimes they'll stop, but you can almost always see buffalo you haven't seen before. This time we ran with them for a half-mile or so, stopping when they stopped and choking on their dust as we ran in their wake. Finally, with our eleven pound doubles hanging like barbells on limp forearms and our chests heaving, we let them go—reasonably certain, for once, that there were no big bulls in this herd.

Another time I just plain messed up. I had my Andrews .470, a plain and perfect working double, but John Sheehan had his lovely old John Rigby .450 3¼ inch double. That's both the make and caliber of double I admire most, and he offered to let me use it. We traded doubles for the day, and it was a mistake. We tracked a small herd into an unusually open place, and a really lovely bull stood at about a hundred and ten yards. It had a good boss, deep curls, and a spread of about forty-two inches. And I missed it, shot right over it. No excuse; maybe I would have done the same thing with my own rifle. But I accepted the lesson and took the Andrews back.

Meantime we seemed to be at a standstill in the leopard department. There were plenty of tracks around, but we had absolutely nothing on bait. Russ had another camp up on top of the escarpment, near the boundary with the Chizarira National Park. Professional hunter Ian Lennox was hunting lion up there with Dr. Bob Prokop, and each night over the radio Ian told us he had plenty of leopards feeding on his lion baits. That was our ace in the hole, but we wanted to finish the buffalo business in this camp.

And that, at least, went according to plan. I think it was about the seventh day when we cut the fresh spoor of a small herd on top of a big ridge that rose from the valley floor. This was very thick country, but there were only twenty-some buffalo, a workable herd, and there were big tracks in the red dust of the road.

Perhaps because the cover was so thick and green these buffalo hadn't gone far; I doubt we followed them for a half-mile before Samuel, our tracker, stopped and pointed ahead. Much less than a hundred yards ahead were black forms in the black shadows of some big trees. We shifted this way and that, checking them with binoculars. Cow, another cow, then a bull lying down. This one had a good spread, but its boss was soft on top, not yet mature. Another cow, mostly hidden. Ah, there was a big buffalo mostly hidden behind a tree. Maybe a bull. We stared through the thick brush and finally caught the sweep of a horn when it moved its head. A big horn. He took a step and we could see the boss, fully hard, and the spread was dramatic. This was our buffalo, but we had to get a bit closer.

With Russ in the lead, we left the trackers behind and started crawling up, one bush at a time. We had picked out a tree about forty yards from the buffalo that would give us a good shooting position, but we didn't make it that far. At about sixty yards our bull stepped clear and stood broadside, and that seemed as good as it was going to get. Russ asked me if I could make the shot, and I was sure I could.

I was kneeling to get over a bit of brush, the big .470 steady enough. I buried the front bead in the vee of the rear sight and squeezed the front trigger as carefully as I could.

Through the recoil I could see the bull rock as it received the bullet. Then the little glade erupted with running buffalo. Russ was up and running, too, saying, "Perfect. Let's go!"

The herd quickly outdistanced us, but the bull lagged behind and then stopped. I shot it again–twice. It went down and bellowed, and we walked up on a truly lovely buffalo. It was very wide, more than forty-four inches, with a good shape and reasonable boss–a fine buffalo for anywhere in Africa.

We dug around for another day or so looking for a buffalo for John and hoping one of our baits would hit. We didn't find a buffalo that John wanted, and we seemed out of leopard luck in this area. But Ian was still reporting being inundated by leopards, so we packed up and headed for the top of the Escarpment.

Russ's camp at Kariba was a beautiful place, thatched huts on cement pads that looked out across the flood plain to Lake Kariba. Every morning we could see impala and waterbuck from camp, and once a small herd of buffalo ambled by. The camp at the top of the Escarpment was different, but just as beautiful in its way. This was a tent camp set in a grove of big sausage trees. It was just a few hundred feet higher than the valley floor, but it was much cooler here among the trees and reminded me of Kenya and Tanzania.

It was late afternoon when we arrived. Ian Lennox and Bob Prokop had passed up a big but nearly maneless lion, and they had already left for a leopard blind. Ernest Dyason was there waiting for us, and took us to yet another active bait. Bob's leopard appeared and mine did not; we celebrated his beautiful tom around the campfire that evening.

We didn't get a leopard that night, but we did have an adventure. When Russ and I stepped out of the blind in inky darkness we heard the *whoof* of a black rhino–very close in the darkness. It crashed one way and we crashed the other! We were glad to hear it go the other direction, but then we had to figure out how to get our bearings to get back to the truck. It took awhile.

Ian felt there were a pair of leopards feeding on their lion bait on the park boundary. They had elected to sit on another bait simply because, well, with a feeding pair it's easy to make a mistake. They had their leopard, so they graciously offered us that bait and its already-built blind. Thus began the most bizarre set of circumstances I've ever encountered in hunting.

We checked the bait in the morning, and indeed there were two leopards feeding–a big male and a female. Fortunately the lions had gone on, reducing the complications somewhat. The blind was a ground blind, and we were in it about 3:30. This, by my count, was my sixtieth night sitting over an active leopard bait. And I'd still not seen a leopard come to bait

Not a half-hour later a leopard coughed to our left, close by the blind. It coughed again, closer, and as deaf as I am I heard its soft padding as it passed behind the blind. We waited until dark, but we knew it was pointless. The leopard–or leopards–knew we were there, and they would not feed until they knew we were gone.

Next morning there were tracks all over the place, especially around the blind. The obvious answer was to move the blind, which we did, building a tree blind in a tall, bushy tree another forty yards farther back. In so doing we uncovered a bizarre tragedy. In thick bush behind the new blind, where we were cutting some poles, we found the fresh carcass of a female leopard, obviously dead from a snare wire around its neck, and obviously having suffered terribly. It was an eerie feeling, for it had clearly been alive and in the bush, hurting and angry, when we were in the blind the night before.

This night, my sixty-first night of leopard hunting, was also the last night of this safari. A charter plane would pick us up the next afternoon, and we'd have just a day at Richard Pascall's place before I was due in South Africa.

It started badly. We'd been in the blind just a short time when we heard a rustling in the thick branches above us. Russ turned pale under his tan and whispered, "There's a snake in the tree." I, of course, knew what kind of snake it had to be. I was petrified, and there was absolutely nowhere to go. But it was a mouse.

Later, while we searched in the dark for my leopard, the mouse climbed into the blind and chewed a hole in my leather rucksack. I'd have given it the whole thing in appreciation for it's being a mouse.

It got worse. The leopard came, but we couldn't see it well. This bait was set up as a lion bait, remember, assuming the target would be on the ground reaching up, not on a limb reaching down. We had also moved the blind and changed the angle, and we hadn't done our gardening well at all. The shot felt good, but the leopard sprang from the tree and was gone. Russ told me I'd missed it, but I didn't believe it.

We waited a few minutes, then climbed down to look. Yep, Russ was right. I'd caught a thick and totally unseen branch a good ten feet in front of the leopard; the mark of the bullet was fresh and clean. That, of course, was the end of that leopard. But Russ is as stubborn as I am.

"I don't think there's much chance, but he's been feeding regularly and he might come back. It's the last night. We might as well stay for a while."

So we did. And the leopard did come back. Which is when things went from worse to absolutely terrible. This shot, too, felt good. It was almost good, but not good enough. I'd caught yet another branch, as the morning light revealed . . . but this bullet had hit the leopard.

We found enough sign that evening to know we had a hit leopard, and we knew we didn't have a dead leopard under the tree. That was all we knew until first light. Then Samuel and the bushman, Jack, found the blood trail.

It wasn't a great trail, but there was enough to follow. It led through ever-thickening bush, and all we could hope for was a dead leopard at the end. We soon lost that hope as well.

After a few hundred yards we found where it had lain up for the night, and then moved on just ahead of us. Jack and Samuel stopped when we approached a big, brushy antheap. We spread out in a line and somebody threw a stick. Only one other time have I heard anything so loud. The earth seemed to shake with the leopard's roars, but it was a false charge. Like spotted lightning it took a few steps toward us, then veered to the right and was gone. I was carrying Rusty's SKB over/under loaded with buckshot, and I don't think I got it to my shoulder. Russ got off a shot, but I don't know how.

The trail led on, and now we could see a big, round monolith in the distance, not a kopje but a single massif, rounded and smooth-sided and a hundred feet high. The spoor led us to its base.

At that base, where the water had run off, was a small patch of high grass twenty yards across and fifty yards long. There was fresh blood on the grass right alongside the rock wall. Nobody wanted to go into that grass, so we stood outside and threw sticks. Nothing. We circled, looking for tracks coming out. Nothing. We climbed the rock, looking for sign. Nothing. And from the top of the rock we looked down into that forbidding grass and threw more sticks. Still nothing. So we returned to where the spoor led into the grass.

Russ grinned his evil grin. "Well, somebody with a shotgun get in the grass." I at least had a shotgun. Jack, the little old bushman, had nothing. Without hesitation he stepped into the grass, and I stepped in at his shoulder.

Three steps into the grass I heard the loudest sound I have ever heard. There was a little erosion gully hidden in the grass, and the leopard was hidden in that gully. It erupted at my feet, its deep barking roars pealing like thunder and reverberating off the rock massif. It should have gotten me, or worse, gotten Jack. I think it was trapped by the sheer side of the gully and unable to come straight up. Instead it came up like an outbound quail, but this quail floated and turned.

I hit it with the first load of buckshot, and saw the pattern on it. Then I hit it with the second load and saw that pattern hit. Accounts differ; others think the buckshot made the cat falter. I didn't see it, but in those split seconds two thoughts flashed through my mind. First came the knowledge that I hadn't done anything to the cat. Second came the realization that the shotgun was empty. And then the double boom of Russ's .500 mixed with the sharper crack of John Sheehan's .450, and it was over.

Thanks to the Tarzan movies, my generation's impression of Africa is one of steamy, low-lying jungles. Younger folks–or those who somehow missed Tarzan and Jane–are more likely to visualize the wide-open vistas of *Out of Africa.* Both exist. Maybe it's not jungle in the purest sense, but there is certainly lots of heavy forest, and the savannas of the Serengeti are there as well. But so is a whole lot more–deserts, woodlands, swamps, and thousands of miles of thornbush. Mountains are there as well, serious mountains; both Kilimanjaro and Mount Kenya are among the great mountains of the world, and scattered through the continent are literally dozens of genuine mountain ranges of varying scale.

In bygone eras, Africa's wildlife diversified far more than did animals on any other continent, evolving into life forms ideally suited to the wide variety of habitats. This specialization left Africa with a simply amazing variety of antelopes. Although many are questionable subspecies, hunters' record books list more than one hundred categories for just the African antelopes. There are swamp antelopes and forest antelopes and desert antelopes and more.

12

RETURN TO THE CAPE

Quite a number of these animals can be found in the mountains, but, oddly, Africa has very few true mountain species. Kudu, for instance, are often found in hilly country, and the slopes of both Mount Kenya and Kilimanjaro have historically produced some of the very best buffalo, black rhino, and elephant. Leopard, too, are fond of hilly country. But none of these animals are really mountain species. There are no native true wild sheep at all. The aoudad, or Barbary sheep native to North Africa, taxonomically a bridge between the sheep and goat clans, is the closest there is. There are a couple of wild goats, Ethiopia's walia ibex and the Nubian ibex that ranges from Sudan's Red Sea Hills up into the Middle East. There are varieties of reedbuck and duiker that have adapted to mountain life, and of course there's Ethiopia's mountain nyala, but the list is not extensive. Such a list would not be complete without the vaal rhebok.

In Afrikaans *vaal* means "gray"; the Boers named the animal not after the Vaal River, but because it's a gray-colored antelope, so properly it is not capitalized. "Rhebok" is one of many spellings of the European roebuck, of which this little antelope reminded the early settlers. The vaal rhebok, then, is a small, gray antelope with straight, slender horns. It's well distributed throughout suitable habitat in South Africa, but it is a true mountain antelope; vaal rhebok are rarely seen under fifty-five hundred feet elevation.

This little fellow is a unique animal in many ways and just might be the most challenging hunting trophy in southern Africa. It is sharp-sighted and wary, and prefers high, open basins where it can use its eyes to the best advantage. Young males may occasionally be seen together, but the older males are very territorial and extremely aggressive, and they know how to use those sharp little horns. Male mortality from fighting is believed to be quite high. But relatively little is known about the vaal rhebok. Unlike most of South Africa's antelope, the vaal rhebok has not been successfully reintroduced or propagated by game ranchers. Worse, sheep and Angora goat ranchers traditionally shot them on sight because of an old wives' tale (possibly true!) that rutting males would kill domestic stock that intruded into their territories. So they occur only naturally, and today only in the higher, more remote corners of South Africa.

The vaal rhebok is a beautiful antelope buck with an unusual woolly coat. On top of its forty- or fifty-pound frame, the horns of a good buck–from eight to ten inches in length–appear huge. Having neither the place to display such things nor the budget for taxidermists, I have very few life-size mounts and in the future will probably have fewer, but the vaal rhebok is one antelope that should be done life-size.

I had hunted it several times in years gone by but had been successful just once, with Lew Tonks in the mountains above Graaf-Reinet. That was a fine ram with horns well over eight inches, a wonderful trophy. Unfortunately neither cape nor horns ever arrived in America. That, by the way, is not an indictment against Lew, a fine outfitter. Due to distance, difficulties, customs, hide spoilage, even pilferage by antihunters, sportsmen who journey to Africa simply must understand that there's some chance they will never see all of their trophies. Of course, Murphy being the optimist that he is, the one that goes astray is likely to be the one that was most prized. . . .

So I had beaten the odds and had taken a very fine vaal rhebok. I don't know what the odds are, but there are no sure things with this animal, certainly not if you want a good one. And now I had to try to beat them again.

It wasn't all that much of a hardship. As I've written earlier, South Africa's Eastern Cape is one of the most charming areas on the continent. The country is big and beautiful, the ranches large and still largely unfenced. The Cape Mountains are much like eastern Montana and Wyoming, with the peaks running to seven thousand feet or so and the grassy, open hillsides stretching out forever.

This time I would hunt with Al Spaeth, American-born and living in South Africa for twenty years and more. I had met

Al when I hunted with Lud de Bruijn some years earlier. Al was a buddy of Lew Tonks, and had been in the computer business in Port Elizabeth at that time. Just as Lew had eventually started his own outfitting business, so did Al as South Africa's safari business blossomed.

Al and his wife, Caroline, had made the logical progression over the years. First they were "biltong hunters" who journeyed forth annually to get their kudu and springbok. Then Al studied for and obtained his professional hunter's license. Then they bought a game ranch and improved their herds. And finally they had Thorn Tree Safaris and were full-fledged outfitters.

Al's ranch was a scenic place, nestled in high foothills and combining some heavy riverine growth with bushy hills. A well-appointed ranch-house served as a lodge, and he'd clearly done a fine job with his game. American Ken Jezak was there at the same time as I, enjoying his first safari, and together we looked at impala, blesbok, springbok, black wildebeest, oryx, hartebeest, and kudu. I was with him when he took his first African animal, a fine impala–an important moment for any hunter.

Unfortunately for Al, however, I was a far more difficult client. All I really wanted was a vaal rhebok, and they didn't occur on Al's place; the elevation was too low and the bush too thick for them. If we were successful and had time remaining, a good kudu hunt was always of interest, and we could dig around for a good bushbuck, but first and foremost was the vaal rhebok.

Although I didn't realize it until I arrived, Al had stacked the deck. For vaal rhebok he worked with Noel Ross, a veteran professional hunter who is one of the few experts on vaal rhebok. Noel or his outfit, Belvedere Safaris, are listed with most of the top rhebok that have been taken in the past twenty years.

Noel's place was high up in the mountains, a good hour's drive from Al's place. His farmhouse had some lovely shade trees and there was a bit of brush in the valley, but the ridges above were nothing but rocks, grass, and some low bush that looked for all the world like sagebrush from a distance. Noel agreed that you can't really farm vaal rhebok as you can so many other species, but he'd been working on *managing* the rhebok in his neighborhood for years and he was anxious to show them off. After a quick coffee and a look at some photos of better bucks, we headed to the higher country.

I wouldn't say that we saw a lot of vaal rhebok; as Jack O'Connor once said about Coues whitetails, "Even where there are lots of 'em there aren't very many of 'em." But we sure saw a lot more than I'd ever seen before. And a lot bigger males.

We glassed a small herd with a decent male shortly after climbing out of the brushline, but a long ways before we topped out at the head of Noel's valley. At least it looked good to me; Noel hardly gave it a second glance.

A short while later, as we climbed a switchbacked track to the top of the mesa, a lone ram stood on a little knoll about two hundred yards above us. This was a big ram, well into the record book and darn near as big as the monster I'd taken before. Noel gave it a quick look, then kept on going. I simply didn't know what to say; you just don't pass easy shots at vaal rhebok like that. Or at least nobody else does.

Noel explained that he was looking for a particularly big ram that he knew was in the area. He'd watched it all summer, and a client had missed a long shot at it a couple of weeks before. Vaal rhebok are territorial, and Noel knew that ram was still around–and we would settle for nothing less. At least for a while.

Vaal rhebok are awfully small and their country is awfully big. We were hunting a flat-topped mesa, really more of a big ridge, that ran for several miles with innumerable side canyons. Through the morning we poked into canyon after canyon, finding vantage points and glassing for a time, then moving on. We saw three more males and quite a few females in the process, simply a vast number of vaal rhebok.

I can't imagine a better place to hunt this animal. It existed because Noel watched them carefully and shot very few, only the best. That's probably not as difficult as it sounds, since relatively few hunters who visit South Africa actively pursue the vaal rhebok. Those who don't are missing out.

I was enjoying the clean mountain air and seeing so many of these elusive animals, but I didn't really think we'd find the one Noel was looking for. I wasn't worried, for there were plenty of acceptable rams around just as soon as we tired of looking for this particular one. Noel, on the other hand, was absolutely certain we'd find him. He was right.

We spotted it about noon, far down on a knife-edge with some females. We actually saw them first, then with a spotting scope located the ram lying down in the lee of a boulder. It was huge, with long, sharp horns that seemed completely outsized. It was also in a very bad spot.

The ridge dropped off the mesa in stairsteps; we had a bit of concealment for a time, and then the ridge dropped off and rose again to the little point the ram was on, with no other cover at all. I crawled to a boulder and set my pack atop it; it was almost like a benchrest, and the shot felt perfect. Except we'd misread the distance; we'd called it at 250 yards and it was more like 300. There isn't much leeway on these little things; I hit it a bit low and a bit far back, and it bailed off the ridge with its ewes and was gone into a maze of brushy canyons below.

It took a very long time to find it. I was sick and certain that it was lost. There wasn't enough blood to follow through the jumbled rocks, and of course no tracks. Noel kept at it; we combed the little canyons and cuts one by one, and of course it was in just about the last possible one. I was on one little point when Noel, on another point a hundred yards away, ran right into it. Up close it looked even bigger than it had from a distance, a very special little animal. This one made it home, and Zoe and Stuart Valentine did it life-size for me. It's standing about ten feet from me as I write this, and it's one of my favorite trophies.

After that, Al and I spent a couple of days hunting kudu up in the mountains, with Noel on some outings and just the two of us on others. This was the same beautifully caped Eastern Cape kudu that I'd hunted with Lew Tonks a few years earlier, but the country was altogether different. Instead of the thick coastal brush, we were hunting high ridges and grassy valleys; it was a different kudu hunt than any I've experienced.

Instead of catching glimpses of gray, white-striped hides in heavy brush, we were glassing for kudu across miles of country. There weren't a great many, but more than enough to keep our interest going. One afternoon we glassed a real monster of a bull, good for anywhere but especially huge for an Eastern Cape kudu. It was wide and tall with deep turns, well into the midfifties and thus a potential world record for this subspecies.

It was with a couple of lesser, but perfectly shootable, bulls, all feeding unconcernedly up a little ridge studded with sparse trees. The wind was in our favor and the stalk was a no-brainer; we could even ease along in the truck for part of the way to close the distance more quickly. We dropped out of sight with the kudu still completely unaware and made our approach. The two small bulls were there, but the big bull was simply gone. We never saw it again. For that matter, Al had never seen it before nor did he ever see it again. It was just there and gone.

The bull I shot wasn't that big, not by a long shot. But it was an old bull with great mass and worn-down tips, and we had a perfect hunt and classic stalk for it.

We glassed them from about a half-mile, two cows, a smaller bull that wasn't quite mature, and our boy. We watched them drop out of sight into a little gully, then took off at a trot. We were on an exposed ridge ourselves, and we needed to get down out of sight quickly before the kudu reappeared.

Things always look different up close than from eight hundred yards away, and they sure did once we got there. We'd marked a round knoll with green, leafy cover as the place we'd shoot from, and we made it fairly quickly. But either we'd misread the ground or the kudu had moved–probably both. We finally found them in the deep shade of a little valley, still several hundred yards away.

We planned a new approach, backed off the knoll, and dropped into a convenient gully. This led us around to another ridge that we thought would put us close enough for a shot. This time it worked; we crawled up to the top of the ridge and, by rising to our knees, could see the tops of horns in a little depression below us. Noel motioned me to a stout tree that would make a nice rest, and I crawled up the rest of the way. I made it, but only sort of. Both bulls, their horns lost in leafy branches, saw me and stared. I got the .300 Weatherby steady and ready, but that was as far as I could go; I couldn't tell them apart.

Then one bull stepped out and was clear, and it was the right bull with the wide spread and worn-down tips. It was quartering to me, and I shot it very carefully where the neck joins the shoulder. I expected it to fold, but instead it rocked back, recovered, made a few great leaps up the gully and jumped a cattle fence without hesitation. I was tracking it but couldn't get on it, and then it stopped broadside for a moment. This time I shot it in the shoulder, and it dropped like it was supposed to.

This excellent hunt followed my leopard and buffalo hunt with Russ Broom. By now you should be thinking that I was shooting terribly; I wounded and almost lost a leopard, almost lost a vaal rhebok, and now couldn't even hit a broadside kudu properly. I promised my publisher I wouldn't pull any punches in this book, so I'm telling things the way they happened. But there's one piece of information missing that you might find interesting. Part of the deal of making a living writing about this stuff is getting to (and being obligated to) try out all manner of new guns, scopes, ammunition, and other equipment. Most of it works very well, but it's a real blessing when you can shoot your own familiar rifle and your own familiar loads that have worked for years.

In this case the rifle was just fine, a Mark V .300 Weatherby with a classic-styled stock. The loads were fine, too; the rifle grouped them exceptionally well. But the bullets were experimental, the very first run of Speer Grand Slams in 200-grain .30-caliber persuasion. The Grand Slam is a fine bullet, but this particular recipe needed some refinement; the bullets were blowing up and giving very little penetration. I *did* catch a branch enroute to the leopard, but once the bullet finally got there it left just a minor surface wound. Likewise the rhebok, ditto the first shot on the kudu, which was perfectly placed.

That, of course, is why bullets have to be tested. I dutifully gathered up a little envelope full of bullet fragments and sent them off to Speer. I believe they toughened up the formula, for I've heard nothing but good about that bullet since it's been released to the market. But that first run sure had me talking to myself.

13 THE ARUSI MOUNTAINS

Ernest Hemingway wrote about the green hills of Africa, and so named his book about his 1935 safari. A quarter-century later, in a *Saturday Evening Post* article, Robert Ruark mentioned "the high blue hills of Ethiopia." Well, are Africa's hills green or blue?

I'd seen Hemingway's green hills of Tanzania, and indeed they are emerald green just after the first rains. But Ruark was dead right about Ethiopia's high blue hills, which is strange because I don't think he ever saw them. The sprawling capital city of Addis Ababa sits on a high tableland, the Ethiopian Plateau, which stretches north and south. But as you drive southeast you must drop into and cross the Great Rift Valley. Then you start to climb again, and the real mountains loom ever higher on the horizon. Indeed they are blue, and remain so until you are among them.

East of the Rift Valley you ascend onto yet another high tableland, with the low valleys more than a mile high and the peaks above fourteen thousand feet. Though their heights are abrupt and dramatic, the actual mountain ranges are relatively small and isolated from one another by broad, high valleys that hold some of the most fertile soil I have ever seen. When you see the farmland of central Ethiopia it becomes very hard to understand the famine that wracked this country in the 1980s. The mountain ranges have names: Arusi, Chercher, Din Din, Bale. These are the mountains that hold the bulk of the world's population of mountain nyala.

The mountain nyala is easily one of the great prizes in Africa, generally ranked right along with the bongo and Lord Derby eland but having one of the most restricted ranges of any of that continent's major species. It was identified to Western science in 1908, one of the last mammals on earth to be "discovered." I put that word in quotes because, truly, it's ridiculous to say an animal or, for that matter, a mountain, is only discovered when a European lays eyes on it. The Ethiopians knew the mountain nyala were there, but in the nineteenth century few outsiders ventured into the land of the Queen of Sheba.

Tragelaphus buxtoni is this animal's scientific name, *Tragelaphus* placing it in the same genus as the other true spiral-horned antelopes: greater and lesser kudu, nyala, bongo, sitatunga, and bushbuck (but not eland; they are of the *Taurotragus* genus); *buxtoni* after the English explorer Ivor Buxton, who brought the first known specimens to London. We call it mountain nyala, but it is only vaguely reminiscent of the nyala of southern Africa. In the old days they called it the "mountain bushbuck," which is more apt. Better still is the local Amharic name, *yedaga-agazin,* which means "highland greater kudu." Indeed it is kudu-sized, with big bulls weighing more than five hundred pounds, but it is darker in coloration and with horns that typically curve in as they twist, more like a king-size bushbuck or an extra-large nyala.

Mountain nyala are a beautiful antelope, but also a most elusive prize. They are confined to the high country of Ethiopia, principally south and east of Addis Ababa in those mountain ranges named earlier, but with a few occurring on the west side of the Great Rift Valley. Their total range is barely a thumbprint on the map of Ethiopia, which is itself barely a handprint on the map of Africa. To hunt them one must go to Ethiopia, period. This in itself has been an on-again, off-again project.

Rowland Ward's record book lists several undated mountain nyala trophies, their owners reading like a who's who of African explorers: Buxton, Blaine, Maydon, Powell-Cotton, Rothschild, H. R. H. the Duke of Gloucester; but the earliest dated trophy is Elgin Gates, in 1945. Even for the next twenty years, when the safari industry was booming throughout much of the continent, there are just a handful of entries.

Throughout the first half of this century, outsiders simply couldn't get into Ethiopia except by special invitation. Emperor Haile Selassie came to power in 1930, and toward the end of his reign the phobia against foreigners began to ease. A couple of pioneering outfitters set up shop in the mid-sixties, and quite a few enterprising trophy hunters added mountain nyala to their collections. In 1974 a Marxist revolution ended the Ethiopian monarchy that dated back to biblical times. Hunting was closed during several years of turmoil, then was reopened by the new government in the 1980s.

This period was probably the golden age of Ethiopian hunting; there were several competent outfitters, and they ranged widely throughout the country. The mountain nyala hunting was business as usual–never a sure thing, but reasonably reliable. A pocket of giant elephant bulls was discovered in the southwest, and some of the best elephant in recent decades were taken. Then there were the game-rich Omo Valley and Danakil Depression for plains game, of which Ethiopia offers tremendous variety. These "good old days" were short-lived; another revolution overthrew the Marxist government in 1991, and again hunting was closed for a time.

When it reopened a year or so later the early reports weren't encouraging; success was low on mountain nyala, and there was said to be large-scale poaching. This turned out to be another short window of opportunity; hunting closed again in June 1993. This latest closure was inexplicable, but the given pretext was so game censuses could be conducted. The real rationale remains obscure, but after nearly three years Ethiopia opened hunting again in early 1996 and remains open at this writing. The message should be clear: If anyone reading this has an interest in hunting in Ethiopia, don't put it off.

There is poaching, but there is a far worse problem with habitat loss, especially up in the mountains where the mountain nyala are found. A more fundamental problem is that, despite Ethiopia's great wealth and variety of wildlife, safari hunting has never been big business there. There have never been more than a handful of outfitters, and you don't need to take your shoes off to count every licensed professional hunter in this huge country. In realistic terms, the future of hunting in Ethiopia is uncertain because the loss of the hunting industry would not be significant. This is unfortunate, because I found it one of the most beautiful, charming, and fascinating countries I've hunted.

I had long wanted to see those high blue hills of Ethiopia and to hunt the mountain nyala. When the second revolution came in 1991 I was sure I'd waited too long, and then came a reprieve. Frequent hunting partner Joe Bishop of Denver, Colorado, and I were bear hunting in Russia in 1992 when we started talking about hunting in Ethiopia. To be honest, Joe started talking about it. It seems that, through Bert Klineburger, he had a deposit for a safari with Colonel Negussie Eshete, said safari to be conducted just as soon as Ethiopia reopened and it was practicable. Joe's partner had backed out, and he asked me if I'd care to go along. And so we talked about it.

Veteran Ethiopian outfitter Tom Mattanovich is a good friend of mine, and I always figured I'd hunt Ethiopia with him. I said as much to Joe, but he and gunmaker David Miller had enjoyed a good hunt with Negussie a couple of years earlier, and Joe was real high on him. He also suggested that the way Negussie hunted we could do a two-by-one without either of us being handicapped. In the mountains we could go separate directions, one of us with Negussie and the other with a tracker. Later, if we had time, we could go on to the Danakil and simply hunt together. That decided it. Sharing a professional hunter made it affordable; otherwise, I'd have had to wait a couple more years to hunt Ethiopia. Negussie it would be, and he was a fine choice.

We flew overnight to Frankfurt, spent a restless day in a day room, and then flew overnight again to Addis Ababa. Colonel Negussie Eshete was there to meet us, a smiling, affable, confident man who appeared to be in his early sixties. He'd been a colonel of paratroops under Haile Selassie, imprisoned for a time after the Marxists took over. His English was good, honed at U.S. Army Command and Staff College and our jump school at Fort Benning, Georgia. His vehicles were also in good shape; I started to feel good about the coming safari.

Just prior to departure I'd picked up several negative reports on mountain nyala hunting, not with Negussie but with a couple of other outfitters. I told the colonel this and his smile got broader.

"Mountain nyala are no longer as easy as they used to be. The woodcutters go higher on the mountain every year, and some of the local poachers run them with dogs. But don't worry, Craig; this is the right time of year and the nyala are there. In five days time we will have our nyala and be ready to move to the Danakil."

Of course I didn't believe him, but it was nice to hear that kind of confidence. I relaxed. Joe was already relaxed; he and David Miller had both gotten nyala on their previous hunt, and he expected the same results. That time David had gotten a real monster, but Joe's had been taken with a quick decision that turned out to be *too* quick–his bull hadn't been as big as they'd thought, and now he was back looking for a bigger one.

We checked in at the Addis Hilton and stowed our gear, then drove to the game department to purchase licenses. Addis Ababa is a huge, sprawling city sitting at 7,000 feet elevation–it gets warm during the day, but cools wonderfully at night. The city is generally bustling and seems fairly prosperous, but there are more beggars in the streets of Addis than I have ever seen in any other African city. That's the down side, and it's extremely depressing. The up side is that all of the stories you've heard about the beauty of Ethiopian women are absolutely true; from the streets of Addis to small villages in the countryside, count on your head turning constantly!

Ethiopia is one of few African countries that requires purchase of specific hunting licenses prior to the safari. It is unthinkable to go deer hunting in Colorado without purchasing a deer tag, but imagine Colorado with twenty-five different varieties of deer. Which licenses should you buy? Countries such as Tanzania and Zimbabwe that work on a "trophy fee for game taken" system make life easy, but countries such as Ethiopia and Zambia that require up-front license decisions make things very difficult, and of course mistakes will be made.

There is a general license that entitles you to two dikdiks, three warthog, and perhaps some birds, but everything else is *à la carte.* Joe and I each bought mountain nyala and Menelik bushbuck licenses. Then choices got harder. What else was in the mountains? Joe wanted a klipspringer, and I asked about the variety of reedbuck we might encounter. "Mountain reedbuck" was the answer. I mistakenly assumed this meant Chanler mountain reedbuck, which I had taken in Tanzania and which occur in some Ethiopian ranges. So I didn't purchase that license (maybe $100 as I recall!). Nope. The reedbuck we saw, and we saw some dandies, were Abyssinian bohor reedbuck–but there was nothing I could do about it.

Would we actually make it to the Danakil? Negussie was sure that we would. I was skeptical, and Joe didn't care since he'd already taken most of the game we might find there. We each bought gerenuk licenses, and I bought Soemmerring gazelle and beisa oryx licenses. Joe had taken those animals previously. Joe, at my urging, bought a greater kudu license–I was counting pennies and couldn't afford one. Joe would have bought an ostrich license; he'd never shot one and wanted the skin. But we didn't know we'd see ostrich all over the Danakil, and nobody thought to mention it. Neither one of us bought lesser kudu licenses–at $275, one of Africa's great bargains then–and of course we saw not one but several superb lesser kudu. If I'd really been counting pennies I'd have gambled that much against what the cape alone was worth! But we made our purchases and our mistakes, enjoyed some fine native dancing at the hotel, and in the morning we headed southeast, bound for the Arusi Mountains.

In those days there were few exclusive concessions in Ethiopia, but Mount Kakka was Negussie's nyala area. The main peak towers above fourteen thousand feet–measured by Joe's altimeter–and it loomed in the distance hours before we reached camp at its base. En route the road took us through an endless series of ascending valleys. The soil was black and fertile, and even though farmed by hand, it was clear this ground could grow anything. But by the time we reached camp the plight of the mountain nyala was no great mystery. The mountains were already cleared, stripped for farmland, right up to the lower slopes. The Arusi Mountains were no longer a mountain range, but a collection of isolated peaks.

Mount Kakka was one such peak. Camp was at 9,800 feet, and our camp sat between cultivated fields in a bare valley. It was a very pretty spot and a beautifully sited tent camp, but the remaining brushline was still a good way above camp, and only some four thousand vertical feet of mountain remained above us. If every mountain in Ethiopia was being stripped like this one–and we had driven past many that were in worse shape–then the mountain nyala was doomed.

The drive from Addis was beautiful every step of the way, but it had been a long journey and we were still jet-lagged. Negussie's son, Danny, had driven up from Addis with us, along with our game scout from the game department, Koli Bee. The rest of Negussie's crew were there to meet us, trackers Mammo Michael and Deribie Bulcha, Negussie's camp manager, Sissai

Shoamene, and all the rest. They were a pleasant, friendly, and competent crew. None except Negussie and Danny spoke a lot of English, but all had enough to get by. Ethiopia is one of the more literate countries in Africa, and since Amharic is spoken nowhere else in Africa or the world, English is taught as a second language in all schools, even in the local villages. Ethiopia is different from the rest of Africa, and the Ethiopians are different; they have a proud history and a civilization that predates that of Western Europe. They're a people with plenty to be proud of, and hunters will have a far better experience if they keep this in mind.

We were greeted royally when we rolled into camp at sundown, but Joe and I were too tired to enjoy the scenery or worry about the next day's hunt. All we wanted was a quick dinner and those inviting camp beds . . . and that was what we got.

Our camp was in the last little valley that could be reached by vehicle. From there travel was by foot or horseback. We were roused hours before dawn, and it was near freezing at the high elevation. We had coffee and a small breakfast close by a roaring fire, and then we were introduced to the small, tough Ethiopian ponies that would get us at least part of the way up the mountain. I was grateful for them; I could already feel the elevation and it was only going to get higher.

That first morning we stayed together and worked our way up, glassing as we went, to a jumble of high rocks we called Negussie's Fort. From there, arranging things like a military operation, the colonel placed his trackers and spotters like the spokes of a wheel. Except for all the additional help, it was obviously a glassing hunt just like any mountain hunt. On the way up we'd seen a big hyena skulking off into the brush and we surprised some reedbuck and klipspringer, but we saw no mountain nyala. That didn't surprise me, but I was surprised at how quickly we did see some.

We'd hardly been at the Fort for a half an hour when one of the trackers pointed to a draw opposite our vantage point. Three females were picking their way along, looking for all the world like greater kudu cows except they were brown instead of gray. Our team dismissed them immediately, but I kept my binoculars glued to them until they ambled out of sight; I simply couldn't believe that I was actually seeing these legendary creatures.

Those three were the first, but hardly the last. Throughout the day, in this draw or that brushy hillside, we watched nyala rise from their beds and feed for a while until they vanished back into the tall heather. I'm sure we saw thirty nyala that day, but no big bulls at all.

To this day I don't know why the older males were so invisible during our time on the mountain. It was full moon, which certainly didn't help. There was also some poaching pressure. A couple of days later we surprised a lone spear-armed poacher. He had three or four dogs with him, and he had just speared a female reedbuck. Our game scout arrested him, took his name, and–something I'd just as soon forget–at the point of my rifle we made him spear his dogs. Although he had surely speared the reedbuck, I simply didn't understand what damage a lone spearman could cause in the grand scheme of things.

A couple of days after that I understood completely. I was hunting with Danny and Deribie that day while Negussie, Mammo, and Joe hunted elsewhere. We were high up on a ridge, glassing, when my binoculars picked up movement far below. I put the spotting scope on it–and it was a horse! A saddled horse, and there were others in the shade nearby. Then I picked up several men sitting in a group. Fascinated, I watched while the men broke up and went to their horses.

They had apparently planned a drive, just as Pennsylvania deer hunters would. Except there were no guns, only spears, and they were in platoon strength. I counted twenty-two men, about two-thirds of them mounted, and too many dogs to count. The horsemen made a line and drove some cover toward waiting spearmen. Perhaps they had seen tracks and knew game was present, for a half-dozen mountain nyala females broke in front of the horses and ran toward the spearmen. Through the

20X Leupold spotting scope it was like watching *Zulu Dawn* through a microscope. I saw the spears flash in the sun, but apparently they missed–this time. A few months later Ethiopia closed again, locking out legally licensed hunters but giving the spearmen with their horses and dogs free rein.

But these meat poachers were hardly trophy hunters, and in spite of them we saw plenty of females and young males. I expect I saw more than two hundred mountain nyala, though there's no way to guess at the percentage of multiple sightings. There was no shortage, but I never saw a really large male. Deribie was sure he saw a good one on about the fourth day. It was still very gray dawn and we were working our way up a long, narrow canyon. Deribie spotted nyala crossing the canyon far ahead of us and was sure there was a big male with long ivory horn tips. We circled around and tried to get in front of them. The wind was good and they shouldn't have seen us, but either we somehow spooked them or they just outdistanced us. We never saw them.

We were seeing plenty of nyala, more than enough to keep our interest up. It seemed just a matter of time, and indeed it was. Joe got his on the fourth day. Like us, they had seen dozens upon dozens of females and a few young males, but the bigger bulls were eluding them. On the fourth day they rode far around to the back side of Mount Kakka, and when they rode into a little basin they saw a very nice bull on a grassy slope far above them, well above the brushline. They stalked to the limit of the brush, and then Joe dropped the bull with a single shot from his Sako 7mm Remington–at a measured 430 yards.

They had gone far that day, and we were already in camp when Joe, Negussie, and company returned. As is Negussie's custom they fired a couple of shots from the top of the ridge, letting the world know they had taken their nyala. And then the dancing and singing commenced. Joe dismounted with the trackers, and they danced and sang all the way down the long slope and into camp.

It was the next day, far around the mountain but in the opposite direction from where Joe had taken his bull, that I watched the mounted spearmen at work. It was past midday, and it had taken us half a day to reach that point. We headed back and had hardly gone a mile when Deribie jumped off his pony and grabbed me, pointing.

We had just topped out on a side canyon. On the far side, to our right and well below us, a nyala bull was working his way up through the brush. He was in thick heather, and I had a hard time seeing him, but Deribie had spotted the bull instantly with his naked eyes. The bull wasn't getting farther away, which was good because he was plenty far away at the start, but he was threading his way along on the far hillside. My crew was urging me to shoot, but long seconds passed before I found him . . . and then I'd lose him and find him again as he ambled along through the thick heather. Here I take full responsibility. My guys wanted me to shoot, but I didn't expect them to understand trophy quality. I got the binoculars on the bull, and he looked good. I knew he wasn't huge, but after just seeing that huge group of poachers–and after days of seeing females and baby bulls–I decided he was good enough.

I lay down over a rock with the .340 Weatherby over my day pack, and I shot him. The big gun should have flattened him, but it didn't. I heard the bullet hit, and then he moved farther up the hill. I shot him again, and then he was gone into the cover.

Forgetting the 13,000 feet of elevation, we ran across the canyon, found the spoor, and ran along it. I was sure the bull would be down and dead. I was wrong. He jumped again at close range, and despite heaving lungs I swung with him and shot him yet again. And finally, after dreaming about it for so many years, I could admire my mountain nyala.

He wasn't big. Not as big as I'd thought he was, and far short of what I'd hoped to take. But he was a mountain nyala, and he was a nice bull with a good shape to his horns. I didn't feel bad about it then and I don't feel bad about it now. In fact, I felt pretty darn good about it when Ethiopia closed yet again a few months later. Now that it's reopened, perhaps that's something I can do again someday. But that day I felt pretty happy. And, just like Joe, I got off my horse and sang and danced my way into camp after we'd topped the last ridge.

Joe came back with a good klipspringer that night, so our business in the mountains was almost finished. Negussie broke camp the next morning, sending Sissai and the big truck on ahead to the Danakil to make a new camp. His plan was for us to drive to Asela, a big town on the northern edge of the Arusis, where we could hunt Menelik bushbuck for a day or two while camp was being set up.

The Menelik bushbuck is a midsize, very dark bushbuck also found only in the Ethiopian highlands. They occur in most of the same areas as the mountain nyala but seem relatively uncommon up in the high country; their real habitat is the foothills and lower slopes and, due to the deforestation in these areas, they remain plentiful in few places. In fact, the chances of obtaining Menelik bushbuck today are generally poorer than for mountain nyala.

But again Negussie was confident. He should have been; he'd predicted five days for two nyala, and on the morning of the sixth day we were breaking camp. "By tomorrow," he said, "we'll have two bushbuck and be headed for the Danakil."

He wasn't quite right, but close. It was well past midday when we reached Asela, checking into a spartan but clean Italian-owned hotel on the main drag. After a quick rest we drove to a cooperative farm literally on the outskirts of town. There was big Russian-made machinery everywhere, and very little cover. I simply couldn't believe even a bushbuck could hang on under these conditions, but Negussie assured us there were plenty.

You couldn't have proven it that night. Going different directions, we hiked through some groves of eucalyptus and pine forests, and along a reasonably brushy streambed that at least looked like bushbuck habitat, but at dark Joe and I had seen just a couple of females between us. Which proved, at least, there were bushbuck present.

In the morning Danny and I worked along the same streambed, while Joe and Negussie walked out some cover elsewhere. I saw absolutely nothing, but Joe got a glimpse of a pretty good ram. In the afternoon Negussie and Joe hunted the other side of town and saw another good ram just at dark, too dark to shoot. By then my bushbuck was completely skinned. We had gone back to the same co-op, and had just left the truck when a local herdboy came up and said he could take us to a nice ram. Why not?

We followed him into a pine forest, a grove of big trees with relatively sparse underbrush. Just a hundred yards into the grove the herdboy pointed into a little swale. There, hidden behind a tree with just its neck and shoulder exposed and slanted sunlight glinting off its dark hide, was a very nice bushbuck ram. I raised the rifle and shot it offhand and we carried it out into the open. It was a really nice Menelik bushbuck, almost coal black and extremely pretty.

Joe had taken a good bushbuck on his previous safari with Negussie, so he voted to head on to the Danakil at first light. Negussie wouldn't hear of it. My ram was good, he said, but not one of the big ones. We had to try again. So we did.

And we found it. On the advice of one of the farmers, we still-hunted into the same pine grove where I'd shot mine, keeping the morning sun behind us and the wind in our faces. Shortly somebody saw a bushbuck slipping through the trees ahead. I dropped back while Negussie and Joe slipped ahead after it. They followed him for quite a distance before I heard a single shot from Joe's Sako.

When I came up to them they were standing around a bushbuck with grins on their faces, and when I saw it I understood why. What a bushbuck! It had more than sixteen inches of thick, twisted horns–a superb length for any bushbuck, but almost unheard of with the small Menelik. Joe has hunted darn near everything, but that big little ram is one of his very best trophies.

Now, finally, we were ready to leave the mountains behind and head to the hot, low Danakil Depression. And whatever Negussie had in store for us, I wasn't about to question him ever again.

14 THE DANAKIL DEPRESSION

After leaving Asela we quickly dropped down into the Great Rift Valley, then headed northeast. The country was more arid, but still hilly and mostly green; the actual Danakil Depression, a natural basin lying largely below sea level, is far to the north and runs all the way to Eritrea and the Red Sea. We found our camp on the Awash River, within Awash National Park. This was another new experience; at Negussie's orders Sissai had rented a campsite within the park much as you or I might take a campsite within Yellowstone or Yosemite. Except, in this case, when we left to go hunting every morning we would drive past the ranger station with rifles visible and get nothing more than a friendly wave.

The Awash flowed past, dirty and brown, within ten yards of our tents. On the far side, on a little mud bank, a big crocodile napped. Driving through the park to and from hunts we would always see lesser kudu and beisa oryx and smaller antelopes. This was my first experience with a black professional hunter, and it was totally positive. Negussie was a good outfitter, and his equipment and camps were sound. He had a competent staff and exceptional trackers, but perhaps the most important element was that Negussie was well known and idolized by all the local people in all the areas we visited. He had no trouble figuring out where we should hunt, and no trouble getting truthful information from any locals we encountered, a good example being that he could produce Menelik's bushbuck when most of the other Ethiopian outfitters had thrown in the towel on this species. But there was one thing even Negussie could not do, and that was hunt in the park itself.

To find the game we sought–Soemmering gazelle, beisa oryx, gerenuk, Cordeaux dikdik, and Joe's greater kudu–we had to travel a long distance from our campsite in the park. That first afternoon we drove north to Awash Station, a frontier town that reminded me of the way Dodge City must have looked a century ago. But north of town, instead of Boot Hill, there are a number of burned-out Soviet tanks from the various civil wars. At Awash Station the hard-surface road forks; an easterly road leads eventually to Djibouti and Somalia, while a northerly fork leads up through the Danakil and eventually to the Red Sea.

That first afternoon we drove east, then back south into the foothills of the Ahmar Mountains. Here, from a couple of Negussie's favorite vantage points, we spent the evening glassing for greater kudu. This animal we did not see, but along the way we used Negussie's worn but accurate .22 Brno to take a couple of the pretty little Cordeaux dikdik, distinctive with their crest of long hair between the horns. From his lookouts, a couple of prominent ridges that gave good visibility down into the surrounding thornbush, we saw no greater kudu that day. We did see several lesser kudu bulls. One particularly good bull fed his way across our front at long shooting distance; I don't know about Joe, but I sure kicked myself for not buying the cheapest lesser kudu license in all Africa at that time.

From his lookouts Negussie pointed to places where he'd taken greater and lesser kudu, and where he'd baited in lions on past safaris. I didn't doubt him; although just an hour from Awash Station and a half-hour off the hard-surface road, this was already wild Africa and good game country.

The next morning, long before light, we set out for our expedition into the Danakil. Here Negussie did something very intelligent that rated him high points as an outfitter, at least in my estimation. To get beyond the park and closed tribal lands and into the heart of the oryx, gazelle, and gerenuk country we would have to drive to Awash Station, then more than two hours north on the hard-surface road. Negussie took two vehicles, his Land Cruiser and the old Land Rover which Danny drove. In Africa professional hunters constantly set out beyond the point of no return, so I asked him about this. His reply was simple, as if I was stupid to ask. "It's a long way up there, and if we have a breakdown we don't want to walk back!"

Daylight found us well north of Awash Station, and I quickly saw one of the strange anomalies of hunting in Ethiopia. I had been told that the Danakil was shot out, witnessed by the fact that each and every herdsman carried an AK-47. Indeed every herdsman did carry an AK while they tended their herds of camels and goats along the road. I asked Negussie about this and he smiled his wonderful smile. "The AK-47 has replaced the spear as a symbol of manhood. But you will see from the game that these people don't poach; eating wild game is not part of their ethic. They might poach the occasional zebra for fat, and certainly they'll shoot a lion if it comes into their herds, but they leave the antelope alone. You'll see."

I saw. When it got light I could see that we'd left the hills behind and the brush had thinned out considerably. And there was game everywhere. In thornbush draws and groves of low acacia we could see gerenuk and lesser kudu. Across big, open short grass savannas we saw great numbers of Soemmering gazelle and beisa oryx–plus numbers of wild ostrich and more than a few small herds of the beautiful pinstriped Grevy zebra. This was still tribal land, no hunting allowed–and obviously no significant poaching, either. In twenty years of bumming around Africa I have never seen so much game from any hard-surface road.

Shortly we crossed some undefined line and were in open hunting country, and now we began to look at gerenuk in earnest. Possibly feeling guilty about his huge bushbuck, Joe had given me first shot. I blew it, big time.

We spotted a very nice male in a big herd quite some distance away and made a long and circuitous stalk on foot. The herd was feeding in some low brush on the far side of a clearing, and the situation was perfect. We stalked up behind a single bushy tree, and the ram stood with its herd less than two hundred yards away. I stepped in front, picked a stout chest-high limb for a rest, slipped off the safety and raised the rifle.

It went off with a terrible crash, scaring hell out of all of us and sending the gerenuk off to Somalia. I was embarrassed and Negussie was mad as hell. I didn't blame him. My first thought, of course, was that the rifle was bewitched and had simply fired on its own. It hadn't. I found the fresh scar on an unseen twig, a twig that had caught the trigger and fired the rifle before I got it into position. A stupid mistake and a good lesson worth relearning: You don't take the safety off until you're ready to fire. More important, and at least this was done correctly, never trust a safety and always point the muzzle in a safe direction. Other than losing a shot at a fine gerenuk, there was no harm done except to my ego.

A while later Joe missed a very good gerenuk. This is the only shot I have ever seen Joe Bishop miss; he's the finest field rifle shot I know. So far it simply wasn't our day. A little while later I made a long shot on a very big gerenuk, and this time we got it. Mind you, all of this was done right off the main highway, which is the best proof I can offer that plenty of game remains in Ethiopia.

With one gerenuk secured we turned west off the main road and bumped our way along a winding track that led through low hills and scattered thornbush. We still saw a number of gerenuk–but not what we were looking for–plus several lesser kudu. This was another area that was possible for greater kudu, and there were fresh lion tracks in the dust of the road.

Our destination was a big shortgrass savanna that Negussie was certain would hold both oryx and gazelle. I'm not sure what creates these dry lakes of shortgrass in the thornbush; perhaps the alkali content of the soil. But this one opened out of the thornbush and stretched a couple of miles across and a dozen miles in length. We skirted the edges carefully, and indeed there was a big herd of beisa oryx at the far end.

This was my first experience with beisa oryx. They're big animals, larger than fringe-eared oryx in both body and horn and, to my eye, as large in the body as the giant oryx of the south. Just like all oryx, it's the very devil to pick out the bull in a herd. Perhaps even more difficult than with gemsbok, for I couldn't see as noticeable a difference between the circumference of horns of a male and female. This herd slipped into the brush when we were far away. They weren't spooked, so we followed on foot for quite a distance. Shooting an oryx with long horns would not have been a problem, but in the thornbush we simply couldn't be sure we had a male, so after an hour or so of hot work we gave up and returned to the savanna.

Then we turned to a big herd of Soemmering gazelle that had fed out into the open during our absence. This, too, was a failure; they were spooky and there was no cover, and we never had a chance.

By now it was midday, and Negussie suggested we take a break under some shady trees below a rocky ridge on the north side of the plain. We had lunch and a welcome cold drink and then organized vehicle cushions and whatever padding we had for as comfortable a nap as possible. It was very hot now, perhaps as hot a day as I've spent in Africa. Negussie pointed to his tracker, Mammo, who was scrambling up the ridge above us. "Mammo never sleeps during the day. He will keep watch. The last time I slept here Mammo woke us up and pointed out a big, lone oryx bull right in the middle of the savanna. We got him, and he was the biggest bull of my career, 36½ inches on each horn. Perhaps we will be lucky again."

An hour of fitful, sweaty, fly-slapping rest later we were roused by Mammo's low whistle. We climbed up to him and he pointed through the shimmering mirage out onto the plain. Feeding across and perhaps a half-mile out was a lone animal that, in the heat waves, I first took to be a gazelle. It was not; it was a lone oryx bull and clearly a big one. It was moving slowly and we sat and watched it for an hour while, almost imperceptibly, it worked its way ever closer–appearing larger all the time.

There was very little cover, but the wind was fine. We waited in agony until it finally passed us, now perhaps 500 yards out, and then we made our move. We closed to about 250 yards before he turned to face us, and then we shot it. He was just shy of thirty-seven inches, a wonderful oryx. And, yes, I think Colonel Negussie Eshete is some kind of magician.

It was still very hot and we were low on water, so we decided to call it a day and return to camp. En route we stopped at Awash Station and found very welcome ice-cold Cokes at a local coffeehouse. And then we were treated to the traditional Ethiopian coffee ceremony. Never have I been in a friendlier country. Part of that, of course, was due to Negussie's magic, not our own.

The next morning we retraced our steps until we found Joe a superb gerenuk. This one was up on its hind legs, using its long neck to browse far up into an acacia. It was in this position, upright but broadside to us, when Joe shot it–it was truly spectacular to watch. Then we moved off into a short grass savanna and found great numbers of Soemmering gazelle. For the record, there were also great numbers of Grevy zebra, which have been closed to hunting for several years.

Joe Bishop has a gun collection that, though modest in numbers, contains some of the finest sporting rifles I have ever seen. When he goes hunting, however, he uses only a pair of battered fiberglass-stocked Sakos, one in 7mm Remington Magnum and the other in .375. On this trip he had just the 7mm, and it's Mag-Na-Ported. He's long extolled the Mag-Na-Porting on his 7mm not for the recoil reduction, but because of the reduced muzzle lift, which allows him to call his shots. He suggested I try it on a gazelle, and I was only too happy to do so–my .340 Weatherby, from the rested positions I was shooting from, was kicking hell out of me.

We found a ram on the edge of a big herd and had to wait some time for him to clear. When it did it was facing me at some distance. I held just under its chin and squeezed the trigger. Instantly there was pandemonium in the herd. A good ram showed clear for a moment, and Negussie urged me to shoot again. I didn't. Joe had been right; thanks to the Mag-Na-Porting, I alone saw what nobody else could see. My ram had dropped to the shot, penetrated from chest to ham by a Barnes X-Bullet, and this was a different ram. Skeptical, Negussie drove up to the spot and there lay a fine Soemmering gazelle.

Now we were down to just Joe's Abyssinian greater kudu license, plus perhaps a warthog or two on our general licenses, and we had about four days left. We spent that evening in the mountains close by Awash Station glassing, and a couple of herdsmen–friendly despite their ever-present AK's–told us of a big bull they'd seen the day before. We made plans to hunt for it in the morning.

That night Joe came out of the shower saying, "I screwed up. I took in a mouthful of water." It was midmorning the next day before we knew the extent of the disaster.

In the morning Joe wasn't feeling well, but we tried it anyway. We left the vehicle and began hiking into some hills where the kudu bull had been sighted. By ten o'clock Joe was feeling terrible; we called it a day and headed back to camp.

Negussie thought it was malaria, but by now Joe's stomach was starting to swell. We put him to bed, hoping it would pass, and I lay down for a nap myself. It was a blistering hot noon when I got up to check on him. He was very feverish, nearly delirious, and his belly was as distended as if he'd swallowed a watermelon. He had a good thermometer in his kit and I took his temperature–105 degrees and climbing!

We carried his cot out of the hot tent and into the best shade we could find and stripped him to his underwear. Using half the staff to fan him with blankets and the other half as a bucket brigade, we doused him with water and fanned him, while Negussie organized for a fast run into Addis. In this country there is no charter service readily available, so our only option was to break the fever and stabilize Joe as best we could, then make a break for town.

Miraculously, our air-conditioning apparatus worked. In a couple of hours the fever was down to a survivable level. I packed everything up and we drove straight through to a clinic in Addis. An Ethiopian doctor there took a culture, almost instantaneously diagnosed a stomach parasite, and gave Joe a couple of shots and some pills. We got him to the hotel, and just in time as whatever had been the problem started to work through his system.

That was the end of our Ethiopian safari. We had a couple of days left and Negussie was more than willing to try for kudu closer to town, but in the aftermath Joe was shaky and ready to go home. So we left that greater kudu as unfinished business, and I hope the politics allow us to try again. As an interesting aside, once he got home Joe went to his own doctor to make sure the pills he had gotten in Ethiopia were the right thing. After a week of tests his doctor came up with the same parasite–and the same treatment–that the Ethiopian doctor had offered in less than thirty minutes.

15 THE GREAT RIFT VALLEY

Russ Broom had been hunting in Tanzania for several seasons before he latched onto his fabulous Zambezi Valley concession in his native Zimbabwe. After a few years of hunting for a couple of other Tanzanian outfitters he'd organized his own company with an African partner. His dad, Geoff Broom, was getting increasingly bored with retired life on South Africa's scenic Indian Ocean coastline, so when Russ took the plunge and organized the Zambezi Valley operation Geoff and his wife, Sue, came up to Tanzania to take over that operation. Neither Russ nor they knew what a mess they were walking into.

It would be unfair and dishonest to say that everything went smoothly. There were massive partnership and employee problems, and there were lost trophies and, even worse, trophy fee payments that went astray and had to be made good. On top of that, there were deposits kited by unscrupulous agents. In his early sixties, Geoff Broom suddenly switched from a leisurely break from retirement to a fight for his family's future and reputation. This was several years ago, and that was a messy season. My trophies, and those of both partners and friends, arrived very late and, yes, there were skins missing and other skins ruined.

I relate this for two reasons. First, it was whispered but common knowledge at the time that "Geoff Broom had problems." Yes, he did–just about every serious problem an outfitter could have save one: He had great areas teeming with marvelous game. Second, where many a lesser man would have (and has) walked away, Geoff Broom made it good. He paid trophy fees a second time and salvaged all that was humanly possible of his clients' trophies. He found new Tanzanian partners and, as needed, he acquired new areas. He stayed in Tanzania, for a time risking jail there, and he still has great areas teeming with game. I've known Geoff Broom a long time and I expected nothing different. Neither did the Atchesons, longtime friends and agents. Neither did the vast majority of his clients. But he and Sue went through a couple of lean years getting it sorted out.

I didn't know anything about all this when I hunted with Geoff in Tanzania. In fact, I didn't know anything about it until nearly a year later, when the bulk of the problems were resolved. Knowing about them did nothing but add to the respect I hold for Geoff Broom, one of the all-time great professional hunters in Africa.

Professional hunting is, in general, a game for a man in his middle years. Especially today, with shorter seasons and smaller quotas, genuine experience with the dangerous game comes slowly. Many of the young hunters have the recklessness of youth and, although I find it a frightening and sobering thought, at this stage in my own career I have more experience than most younger professionals. I suppose that's a natural evolution for someone as addicted to Africa as I am, but I'd just as soon be with somebody who knows a lot more than I do!

Unfortunately, while age brings wisdom and caution, it also has its price. At a certain point the tracking jobs become too long and the reflexes begin to slow. Worse, however, is burnout. At some point, for too many professional hunters, it just becomes a job and a paycheck, not the passion it once was. These things happen to different people at different ages. Everyone slows down a bit, but experience compensates with the ability to hunt smarter, not faster or harder. Burnout, when the PH is just going through the motions of finding game for his client, is far more insidious. I have hunted with PH's younger than I who, though competent enough, are badly burned out. Some take a break for a season or two and come back strong. Others have rare flashes of insight and turn to managing camps or outfits, or leave the industry. Still others turn to drink, and a few get careless and get hammered by one or another of the Big Five. Oddly enough, the real legends in African hunting, and there are very few, never lose the passion that drove them to the profession in the first place.

Harry Selby, now seventy years of age and in his fifty-second consecutive season, has never lost it. Robin Hurt, much younger but certainly entitled to "legend" status, has never lost it. There are others, undoubtedly some I don't know, but Geoff Broom is among this select company.

Geoff Broom was always a hunter. He tells a wonderful story of how, as a boy, he went out to shoot guinea fowl with his .22 and shot a marvelous greater kudu–and was soundly thrashed by his father for taking such a shot with so small a rifle. As a young man he hunted ivory in Mozambique and other countries bordering his native Rhodesia. As an adult he founded Matetsi Safaris; he, Ian Henderson, Brian Marsh, and Peter Johnstone (still of Rosslyn Safaris) were the outfitters who started what is now Zimbabwe's huge and important safari industry.

In the 1980s he and his then-young son, Russ, hunted Zambia. Then the new government nationalized his home and concession at Matetsi. Shortly thereafter Zambian politics made continuation as a noncitizen impractical. A short season in Botswana, and Geoff Broom retired to the Indian Ocean coast to play golf. Perhaps it was this break that made him know how much he missed it, for when I hunted with Geoff Broom in the early nineties there was nothing missing, nothing at all. We started early and ended late, and we walked all day after buffalo. And when we saw something really good, Geoff's eyes would sparkle like a little boy's and he'd say, "Lovely, simply lovely." That's exactly what hunting with a legend should be like.

I was interested in western Tanzania, where I hoped to hunt East African sitatunga, roan, and such. Geoff had never been there, but he had an interest in adding western Tanzania to his Masailand and Rungwa operation. He proposed an exploratory hunt, sharing Tanzania's astronomical air charter costs and using a temporary camp. It sounded good to me, but he insisted that we first spend a few days in Masailand.

That year he was hunting Mto Wa Mbu, a block made famous by Robert Ruark forty years ago. Sitting to the north of Lake Manyara and straddling the Great Rift Valley, Mto Wa Mbu is a broad, open valley of savanna grasslands interspersed with thornbush. On the west side are the high hills of the Rift Valley wall that eventually rise to Ngorongoro Crater far above; on the east side are other hills, more isolated but still significant landmarks.

The crater itself, a protected reserve for many decades, holds some of the biggest buffalo and best-maned lions in all Africa. And sometimes outsized specimens go on walkabout into the nearest hunting area, which happens to be Mto Wa Mbu. But like all Masailand areas, the hills on both sides of the Rift Valley hold resident buffalo, and there are usually a few lions around. The *korangos* and small forests hold big leopards, and the thick cover holds lesser kudu, bushbuck, and the occasional greater kudu. The savanna and savanna woodland on the valley floor hold the greatest numbers of game: big herds of zebra, white-bearded wildebeest, and Coke hartebeest; small but resident herds of Grant gazelle and Thomson gazelle; occasional herds of gerenuk, fringe-eared oryx, and eland. In short, it's a paradise for wildlife, and I can't imagine that it was better when Robert Ruark visited it in 1952, the year I was born.

15 .... The Great Rift Valley

When Geoff planned the hunt I wasn't sure why it was necessary for me to visit Masailand; I'd hunted the Kenya side on my first African hunt, and the Tanzanian side in 1988. There wasn't any Masailand game that I hadn't hunted, and since the animals I hoped to find in the west–sitatunga, roan, perhaps sable–are high-ticket items in Tanzania, I had to watch my budget pretty carefully. Part of it was sheer practicality. My good friend Tom Bulloch and his wife, Roberta, would be in camp with me. Tom had not hunted Masailand, so he wanted to collect some of the classic East African species before heading south to the Rungwa area to concentrate on hunting lion and leopard. You have to use creative planning for air charters in Tanzania; a single airplane could drop Tom and Roberta in the Rungwa and take the rest of us on to Mpanda in western Tanzania. That gave us a good excuse, but the main reason was that Geoff wanted me to see it, and I'm glad he did.

The Great Rift Valley of Mto Wa Mbu is the kind of Africa you always dream of. Most of the water holes in the hills had dried up now, but there were both natural water holes and Masai wells scattered here and there along the valley floor. The Masai used them for their cattle, of course, but the game used them as well. Early in the morning we'd see big herds of oryx, hartebeest, wildebeest, and zebra moving from the valley floor back into the sanctuary of heavier brush. Later we'd see gazelles, gerenuk, bohor reedbuck, steinbok, and duiker. The bird life was fantastic, too–not only brilliantly colored songbirds, but also gamebirds in incredible profusion. One flock of guinea fowl stretched for a quarter-mile, and francolin were constantly running across the road or flushing at the Toyota's approach.

During our few days in Masailand we mostly just looked around. I shot a nice Grant gazelle and a particularly exceptional Tommy, of which there were many; and we hunted extremely hard for an East African bohor reedbuck, of which there was no shortage, but the big males eluded us. The reason I did not shoot the entire list of Masailand species was mostly that I didn't try. Tom, of course, was doing a lot more hunting than looking. He got a super gerenuk, along with the dik-dik, gazelles, and such. But as luck would have it–bad luck, that is–I jumped a fine lesser kudu bull at about ten yards and watched it trot off through scrub thorn. That was the Masailand animal Tom wanted the most, and of course that was the only bull seen while we were there.

The one animal I was really interested in, no great surprise here, is one of those monstrous buffalo Masailand is famous for. I didn't get a buffalo on the Kenya side years ago, and I didn't get a buffalo in Tanzania's Masailand, either, back in 1988. The idea that there are lots of buffalo, let alone *big* buffalo, in Masailand is bunk. There are lots of areas with more buffalo than most Masailand blocks. But that high, cool plateau produces superb trophies in most horned species, just like higher, cooler country throughout the continent–Matetsi, Kafue, Mount Kenya, etc.

The Masailand bush is also open enough that you can often sort through the herds and see all the bulls; if there's a big one you have a good chance of seeing it and getting a shot. This is usually not the case in the heavier, more uniform thornbush of southern Africa. Given my poor track record on East African buffalo, I didn't hold out much hope, but I never tire of hunting buffalo. And besides, I needed first and foremost a buffalo for the magazine story I intended to write. Geoff wasn't sure how plentiful they would be in the west, so he suggested we try to find a reasonable bull at Mto Wa Mbu. Business is business. . .

Early in the season there had been some big herds of buffalo in the valley, but they had vanished as the watercourses dried and the grass yellowed. Now there were just a few resident herds up in the hills on each side. Geoff had the bulls more or less named, or thought he did.

Late one afternoon we took a drive up into the hills on the west side, hoping to find tracks crossing the road. We did better than that; two ridges away, perhaps six hundred yards, a herd of buffalo fed along contentedly. The wind was perfect and we had no trouble closing most of the gap–until we got caught on an open hillside with the herd on the next hill, not two hundred yards away. All we needed to do was wait until the buffalo fed over the ridge, then we'd drop into the gully, run up the far hill, and we'd be among them–but they were moving too slowly and it was too late. So we sat there, pinned down, and watched them until nearly dark.

The agonizing part of it is that there was one of those legendary Masailand bulls in this herd. We saw him several times as he fed in and out among his cows. Geoff didn't know this bull–this bull had a spread of a solid forty-four inches, a great bull. We never saw his bosses clearly, but he was extremely distinctive in that his horns had very tall, straight tips. Geoff knew generally where the herd would be in the morning, so we left them in the gathering dusk and went back to the Toyota.

I would have started where we left off, but Geoff figured the herd would water during the night, either at some seeps at the base of the hills or even out on the valley floor. We did it his way, glassing the slopes from below, and of course we found the herd in about twenty minutes. The wind was okay, so rather than make any elaborate circles we simply climbed up the steep hillside to them. It took a good while, but we had the buffalo herd in view and more or less in shooting range well before nine o'clock.

We *still* had them in view at two in the afternoon, and we still hadn't seen the big bull. I think he was there all the time. Geoff thought so, too, which is why we'd stayed with them through a long morning and a hot midday that was getting awfully thirsty. At first they'd fed along the hilltops, from one patch of cover to the next, and we never quite saw all of them. Then, at midmorning, they'd retired into a dense patch of brush. We spent the next few hours crawling first one way, then another, trying to find the bull in the herd.

It was unusual in that it wasn't all that thick, and there weren't all that many buffalo, maybe fifty or so. Also unusual was that we played with them for that long without spooking them. Several times we crawled within ten yards of one buffalo or another, but there were always little knots of unseen buffalo somewhere ahead in the deep shade. The night before we had seen the one big bull and two or three other very reasonable bulls in the herd, and this morning we saw no bulls that were even marginal. Somehow we were missing them, so we stuck with it.

Eventually we'd exhausted ourselves as well as all options for crawling in close without spooking them. So we backed off, lay down in the shade, and waited. Sooner or later they'd move, and then we'd have them. Our problem was that, excited at seeing the herd so quickly and anticipating a quick stalk in the cool morning, we'd forgotten to carry water. Geoff, twenty years older than I, was just fine–but I was hot and thirsty, so I suggested we charge the herd, get them to stand, and just maybe we'd get a shot.

So we worked in as close as we possibly could, until we were literally among them. Then we stood up. Instantly there were buffalo everywhere. They milled for a moment, then rushed out of the little grove. We rushed with them, and they did what good buffalo–or at least, buffalo that haven't been harassed–will do: They drew up in company formation and stared at us. In the seconds we had we ticked off the front few ranks. There were bulls, but they were immature with soft bosses. Either the big boy wasn't there, or he was in the back somewhere. Then they were off, across the ridge and gone into the brush.

Geoff figured they wouldn't go far and he wanted to look at them one more time. So we followed in their direction, not really on the tracks but just taking their general line. After a couple of hundred yards the ridge dropped into a deep, brushy *korango,* a side canyon that led to the bottom of the hills and on out into the valley itself. On the far side was a ridge similar to the one we were on, relatively open with scattered trees and small patches of thornbush. The buffalo were nowhere in sight; the herd must have either crossed the canyon and kept going, or dropped into the bottom and turned left or right.

Then someone saw a couple of black forms to our left, on the far lip of the *korango* but several hundred yards farther down. It might have been the herd, but it wasn't. Only one buffalo was visible, and it was a spectacular bull. "I've never seen that bull before," said Geoff in wonderment.

Staying on our side of the canyon, we simply sauntered down the ridge. If we could have gotten opposite the bull, we would have had a 50-yard shot. But we ran out of cover at about 125 yards, with a steep, noisy gully to our right, an open gravel slope to our front, and the biggest buffalo I have ever seen staring up at us from between two trees.

This time Geoff didn't say, "Lovely." He doesn't swear much, either, so I think he just said, "Oh, my!"

The buffalo wasn't alerted; he had seen movement, but I think we were out of his danger zone. The shot was a bit far for buffalo, but I was carrying a scope-sighted Dakota .416 Rigby, so there was no problem. I sat down and wrapped the sling around my arm and put the cross hairs under his chin. But the angle was very bad, so I waited. He seemed to calm down; he dropped his head and took a single step forward. Now I had the cross hairs on his spine between the shoulder blades. Still I waited. Another step or two and he would turn broadside and give me the shot I really wanted. He took the two steps forward without turning, which put him behind a little bush. And that was the last we ever saw of him.

From our vantage point, it looked as though he had absolutely nowhere to go, but over there the ground was a little different. Judging from the tracks, he had stepped into a tiny low spot and walked on down into the *korango* and out of our lives.

For long moments I kept the rifle trained on the bush he had stepped behind, knowing he would step out any second. But as the seconds got longer, I knew I'd made a terrible mistake.

Then another bull stepped into the opening and stood exactly where his big brother had stood. Geoff, like me, knew intuitively that we'd goofed. Rather, I had goofed–the shot had been perfectly acceptable, but I'd wanted it perfect. This buffalo was clearly not as big as the first, but he was also, just as clearly, the second biggest buffalo I had ever seen. "This one is also very good," said Geoff. "You'd better shoot him."

So I did. After the frontal chest shot, he turned and ran up the slope, then he ran in a semicircle back into the *korango.* I had to stand to see him, then run to my right a few steps, but I hit him twice more, hard. Then he was in the *korango*'s thick bush.

We waited a bit, and I switched from the .416 to my double .470 that a tracker had carried. Then we circled up the draw a couple hundred yards and went in after him.

Geoff has tremendous experience with buffalo, but I was shocked at the way he had pinpointed this unseen bull. Just a couple dozen steps into the thick bush, he rose in front of us, whether for flight or fight I don't know. I threw up the .470 like a shotgun and shot him as if he were a big black quail. He dropped at the shot, rolled once down into the gully, and I shot him again with the solid in the left barrel. Then he bellowed, and we walked up on, by far, the best buffalo I have ever shot, 47 inches wide with good bosses and a perfect shape.

He is a perfect example of what Masailand buffalo can be, or for that matter what great buffalo anywhere can be. I was delighted with him then and still am today . . . but I know his partner was four inches wider! Geoff and his young associate, Keith Hendry (who'd been guiding Tom Bulloch), had been in Mto Wa Mbu for four months, and they'd never seen these buffalo. Geoff theorized that they were Ngorongoro bulls that had wandered in. While Geoff and I were in western Tanzania, Keith saw the big bull twice and confirmed his size . . . but of course they never found him when they had clients. This bull was, perhaps still is, one of those legendary, almost-mythical fifty-inch buffalo–and I'll never forget him.

We dropped Tom and Roberta Bulloch off at the strip at Rungwa Game Reserve, where professional hunter Brian Johnson met them for the rest of their safari, then the plane took us on to Mpanda, a little outpost of a town in far western Tanzania. At that time Mpanda was an open block, meaning it was not held as an exclusive concession by any outfitter. Geoff had never been there, but Brian Johnson and apprentice hunter Sam Wyche had scouted the Ugalla River country far to the north before the season and reported good potential for sitatunga, sable, and perhaps lion, along with a reasonable assortment of other game.

There was no camp and no equipment in Mpanda. The plan, confirmed by radio, was for Sam Wyche and Brian Johnson to convoy from Geoff's Selous Reserve area to the Rungwa with the equipment for both the Bulloch safari and our own. Then Sam would continue on with a Land Cruiser and a truck and meet us in Mpanda on the appointed day. We spent a long and very nervous day–and well into the night–sitting on the dirt strip at Mpanda hoping Sam would show. He did; his headlights appeared about ten o'clock at night.

16

THE UGALLA RIVER

All things considered, that was pretty good coordination. Tanzania is a huge country, and the road network ranges from horrible to nonexistent. Western Tanzania, especially, is truly the back of beyond. Under the best of circumstances just a hundred kilometers is a long day's drive. Under the worst of circumstances–which describes the roads in western Tanzania–Sam's journey of several hundred kilometers took several days. There are relatively few charter aircraft available, so hunters who wish to hunt multiple areas incur shocking charter fees. But there isn't any other sensible option; given the value of hunting days, not to mention wear and tear on your body and psyche, you simply can't spend four or five days on the road switching areas. But somebody has to, and in this case poor Sam was elected.

We spent a quiet night under the stars on the Mpanda strip, then in the morning bought some vegetables and a couple of miraculously available spare parts. We also picked up a game scout, a required ingredient for any Tanzanian safari, and struck off to the north toward the Ugalla River.

Shortly after leaving the cultivated area near town we were in sand forest, relatively sterile habitat that typically holds little wildlife. The sandy soil, however, yields roadways that erode but little. It wasn't a bad trip, but we saw no game and few tracks, and it was still a full day's drive. It was late afternoon when we reached Ugalla Station, a tiny settlement along the railroad. Then we struck west on a smaller track to a campsite Sam and Brian had picked out along some unnamed tributary of the Ugalla. By nightfall we had a reasonable camp set up and were ready to start exploring.

Which is exactly what we had to do. The game scout knew the area a little bit, and Brian had hired a couple of locals to show us around. But before we could even begin seriously hunting we had to learn the area and find the game.

Some of it was easy. Our little tributary led through low hills for several miles, then dropped into an ever-broadening floodplain until it eventually reached the Ugalla. There were always fresh tracks of buffalo and Lichtenstein hartebeest, and we never passed through without seeing at least a few defassa waterbuck. Sable tracks were everywhere; sable antelope were perhaps the most common large antelope in the area. The first day or so we concluded that we could get a good waterbuck just about any time we felt like it, and locating a good sable was simply a matter of time.

On to the west our little river led us to slightly higher, drier country. Here there was some concentration of roan sign, plus more hartebeest. There were some bushbuck around, but game that should have been present but was never seen included topi, zebra, and impala. And there were surprises.

One midmorning, while scouting farther up the Ugalla for sitatunga haunts, we were driving through a grassy floodplain studded with brushy palm islands. We needed camp meat badly, and I had rushed an easy shot at a warthog and missed it clean. We came around an island and a reedbuck, the first of that species we'd seen, jumped up and ran a hundred yards or so, then stopped to stare at us. I got out, took a quick rest and a bit more time, and shot it. Our "camp meat," which we had perceived to be a mediocre common reedbuck, was actually a very good East African bohor reedbuck–the animal we'd spent a couple of days trying to find in Masailand.

Sitatunga was the main event, and we put most of our time into figuring out where they were and how to hunt them. Brian had gotten some fishermen to put up a couple of *machans* where they had seen sitatunga. One was on the edge of some big papyrus beds near the confluence of our tributary and the broad, winding Ugalla. It seemed a likely place, exactly the kind of reedbed Geoff and I had hunted in Zambia's Bangweulu and Botswana's Okavango. We saw sitatunga from it, too–enough that we probably spent too much time there.

On both morning and evening hunts we saw females and short-horned youngsters picking their way through the papyrus, but a long way out. We reasoned that there had to be big bulls around, so after a couple of days we moved the *machan* deeper into the papyrus where we could see a bit more country. After a couple of days of this we were still seeing just females and young males, and it finally occurred to us that we might not be in the right place.

We had driven past the other *machan*. It was out on the floodplain a quarter-mile from the river, and it overlooked a long, narrow strip of low papyrus along the river. It wasn't the kind of sitatunga haunt either of us was used to, and we'd blown it off. In a "now you tell me" sort of scenario, one of the fishermen insisted that he had often seen a big sitatunga here. We walked along the edge of the papyrus, and sure enough there were the fresh tracks of both a male and a female sitatunga.

So we sat there for a couple of nights and mornings, but by now the full moon had arrived; we found fresh tracks made during the night, but dusk and dawn came and went with no sitatunga ambling past. That stand did yield a fine bonus, though. Shortly after dawn we glassed a big herd of sable coming to drink several hundred yards downriver. After drinking they stayed and grazed on the plain, and the herd bull looked really fine. Eventually it was late enough to conclude that the sitatunga weren't going to show, but the sable were still there.

I climbed out of the blind and stalked them alone, catching them just as they started toward the brushline. The bull was moving and I hit it a bit far back with the first shot. Then he was into the herd as they ran into a clump of palm islands that preceded the actual thornbush. I came around a corner and the bull was standing, quartering away and looking back. This time I shot it very carefully behind the on-shoulder and in line with the opposite shoulder. The herd went into the brush and stopped again. I was sure the bull would go down, but I could catch glimpses of it milling among the cows and he did not. Eventually they moved off into thicker bush, and I waited for Geoff and the trackers. I was confused and needed some help!

There was only a drop of blood outside the brush where I'd shot it the second time–and then nothing. Thanks to a very good piece of tracking we found where it had left the cows and gone deeper into the bush on its own. Then, a quarter-mile later, it rejoined the cows. There was never another drop of blood.

A few hundred yards farther on, in some open *miombo* forest, we saw the cows and a couple of young bulls stopped among some trees. The big bull wasn't there. Then one of the trackers saw it, off to our right and about the same distance from the cows as we were. I shot it in the spine, and this time it went down to stay.

The first shot had been too far back, as I'd called it. The second shot had gone in behind the on-shoulder and *exited* the off-shoulder, as I'd called it. It had missed the heart by an inch or so. This is another test-bullet story, just the opposite of the blowup problem I had a bit earlier. These bullets were a first run of the Winchester Fail Safe, and they were acting just like solids; the sable was not the only animal that required multiple shots regardless of placement. This was duly reported to Winchester, and they must have changed the formula. I've used them since and they work wonderfully, but that first batch was too hard.

A day or two later the fresh sitatunga tracks in front of our *machan* weren't funny any longer. The strip of papyrus was long and narrow, and somebody came up with the bright idea of driving it. We spread out, Geoff staying on the outside and me forty yards in, with the rest of the crew between me and the river. Once in, the papyrus was both higher and thicker than it looked. I realized almost immediately that I wasn't in a good place for a shot, but I didn't do anything about it. After all, you can't drive sitatunga, so we were just killing time, weren't we?

The bull came up almost at my feet, just a brown blur in the papyrus with dimly seen horns. It streaked forward, then broke to the right, while I flailed through the papyrus trying to get clear for a shot. I never made it; I was still fighting head-high reeds while the sitatunga, a very nice male, dashed right in front of Geoff, made it to the tree line, and then stopped for a moment before walking gracefully into the brush. We kicked ourselves for several more days.

With that sitatunga blown out to who-knows-where, we had a problem. Our game scout's solution was to drive to Ugalla Station and hunt some big reedbeds nearby. It was a good solution. From the railroad station we could walk down the tracks a couple of miles, then cut across a short stretch of thornbush to a backwater of the river that was wall-to-wall papyrus. It was perfect, and our game scout told us Robin Hurt had shot a very good sitatunga there not long before.

We hunted it several times and we saw sitatunga. We even saw a very nice bull–but he was six hundred yards away on the far bank, and there was no way to get closer. It was also a major undertaking to get there; we had to drive an hour and a half from camp, then walk for the best part of an hour.

One morning we hit upon the bright idea of blazing a trail through the brush, so we brought Sam and crew with us so they could work on it while we hunted. Somehow Sam got in some uneven ground in thick bush where he could go neither forward nor backward, so he made his way out to the railroad right-of-way to get his bearings. You don't drive on railroad rights-of-way in Tanzania, and you especially don't get caught doing it. Sam got caught. When we eventually drove out of the bush a deputation of angry people, including the local headman and the local station keeper, was waiting for us.

They grabbed Sam and we all went down to the station to sort it out. And there we were, in the office of the railroad station–Sam, Geoff, me, and our game scout on one side of the table; the headman and the station keeper on the other. Sam was scared; the idea was to take him to Tabora to face charges. I was mad; it was absurd, and I was inches away from trying my "angry American" act. The game scout was sort of on our side, but waiting to see how things developed. Geoff was masterful; it was one of the most brilliant performances I've ever seen. He knew Sam wasn't going to Tabora; before we went into the office I'd slipped him all the *shillingi* I had on me. Unfortunately it wasn't much, so Geoff needed to palaver long enough to get the bribe down to a level our budget could stand.

Over and over, we were told that we–especially Sam, for they'd watched him drive the truck and knew we weren't there–had broken Tanzanian law and that it was a very serious violation. Geoff would counter, with amazing patience and sincerity, that we knew we had made a mistake, we felt terrible about it, we understood it was wrong, and so forth. And eventually he got to the punch line: Since, after all, there was no damage done, wasn't there something we could do to make it right? It took a couple of hours, but we walked out with Sam and without my *shillingi*–and I understood why Geoff Broom has been such a successful outfitter for so many years.

At this stage we figured we'd best stay clear of Ugalla Station, which put us just about out of options for sitatunga. We were also just about out of time, so it looked like we were going bust on sitatunga. We had taken a very fine waterbuck along our little camp river, but the roan were also giving us the slip. We'd seen some youngsters and we'd seen some huge bull tracks, but we couldn't seem to find the bulls making those tracks. On the morning of our last full day we went back to our original *machan,* staying late because so little time remained. At about nine o'clock a glint of something caught my eye out in the papyrus. It was a bull, but a short-horned youngster. I watched him for a long time, thinking he was as close as I was going to get. Then we called it a morning.

On the way back to camp we stopped at the fishing village to buy a chicken (yes, times were getting tough!). The fisherman told us he could take us to a sitatunga bull, right now if we liked. Geoff and I looked at one another and shrugged. Why not?

He led us to that palm-studded peninsula where I'd shot my reedbuck. Out on the point, and around the point, was a very thin stand of tall, green papyrus. Ten days earlier it hadn't looked like a sitatunga haunt, but after our experience with driven sitatunga hunting it suddenly didn't look so bad. In fact, it was even more drivable than the other stand had been.

This time I stayed on the outside while our new friend and our trackers dove into the papyrus and made a line. Geoff, amused by the whole thing, stayed on the edge behind me. And so we began.

I doubt we'd gone fifty yards before the female jumped in front of someone. I saw her for only an instant, just a dark blur streaking through the papyrus, and then she was gone. I was sure the male would follow, and equally sure such a shot would be totally impossible. But long minutes passed and nothing happened. We rounded the point, with me moving a bit ahead and staying in clear spots that offered all the visibility I could find.

So it was that, with just a hundred yards of papyrus remaining, I was ahead of the drivers when the bull jumped. Jump is the right word. It didn't sneak, it didn't scurry, and it didn't run–it bounded over the papyrus in twenty-foot leaps. The drivers shouted when they saw it and I turned. On the first leap it was behind me, broadside in midair, and I saw its horns. It wasn't huge, but it was mature with ivory tips, and it was all the sitatunga I was likely to see on this trip. On the second leap it was still behind me, but it had turned my way. The third jump carried it past me and seemingly over me, but it was probably twenty yards out in the papyrus. I had the Dakota .300 up and swinging, and the rifle went off with the field of view a blur of brown.

It had passed me when the rifle went off, but I swear the barrel was pointed high in the air! It was an impossible shot, but I knew I'd hit it. Then it touched down and was gone into tall green grass. Geoff was beside me in an instant; he had seen the bullet hit. The trackers came to us and I pointed out where he'd touched down. There on the grass were bright crimson splashes, and the sitatunga was just a little farther on.

We'd worked extremely hard for this animal, but part of that was the fact that we'd started with little knowledge of the area. If we'd known as much on the first day as we knew on the last, things might have happened more quickly. My sitatunga was "normal" for East African sitatunga, smaller in body and horn than the Zambezi variety–but there have been a couple of very large sitatunga taken in western Tanzania. I'm not convinced they're necessarily smaller; rather, I don't think a lot is known about them. My impression is they are far from scarce.

Geoff wound up not outfitting this area; he obtained a concession much farther down the Ugalla that was better for cats, buffalo, and roan–and a lot more accessible. But I enjoyed that remote corner of Tanzania, and I'll always remember it as a part of the real Africa of which so little remains.

17

THE LAST SAFARI ON THE UPPER CHINKO

Just two years had passed, but the Upper Chinko had changed. The Sudanese poachers with their donkey caravans had long since finished the hippo and turned to whatever else they could convert to biltong for the long haul back to the Sudan. Where there had been hundreds of waterbuck and kob there were now just scattered survivors; where there had been herds of buffalo there were no longer even tracks. The devastation wasn't total, not yet; the game that ranged far from the rivers wasn't affected much. Derby eland, roan, and hartebeest numbers were relatively unchanged, and the game unworthy of a poacher's bullet–bushbuck, duiker, oribi, warthog–still roamed the riverine growth. But in just a day we could see this area was in trouble.

Rudy knew it; never a big talker, especially while hunting, he was unusually subdued while we drove through the empty landscape. After twenty-two years this would be his last season on the Upper Chinko. By hunting hard and covering lots of ground he could still pull out the great prize, Derby eland, along with some of the lesser game . . . but for how much longer? At the end of the season he would burn his camp and move farther west, hoping to stay ahead of the poachers for a few more seasons.

The burning was still some weeks in the future. We hunted early that year, in late January and early February, during what passes for a brief winter in the Central African Republic and before the full extent of the damage done by the poachers that had flocked in during the rainy season was known. This time I had come early when the weather would be cooler (a comparative term in Equatorial Africa), the winds more stable, and when the Derby eland would have their most colorful winter capes. Perhaps most important, this time I had two full weeks to hunt.

Sharing the camp was my buddy Joe Bishop. Like me, Joe had hunted Derby eland once before unsuccessfully, though his hunt had been in another part of the C.A.R. some years before. If he was successful, the Derby eland would complete Joe's collection of the African spiral-horned antelopes, to me one of the great feats in the hunting world. Joe would hunt with Jacques Lemaux, a longtime partner of Rudy's and a good match for Joe–both were always laughing and joking, just as Rudy and I were mostly serious.

Other than a visible reduction in game, little had changed in two years. We caught a night flight from Paris into Bangui and sped through customs with little delay. A charter plane took us to *Trois Rivieres,* where Jacques and Rudy were on hand to greet us. After a quick lunch and cold drinks, we made the hard four-hour drive to Rudy's camp on the Upper Chinko, stopping to sight in our rifles along the way.

Camp had changed but little, a comfortable collection of thatched huts on packed dirt floors; I'd been there only once before, yet it felt like home. To Rudy it *was* home; he'd spent much of his life there for the past twenty-two seasons.

This time I was confident we would get the Derby eland; we had more time in better weather, and I understood the country better. I told Rudy that, once again, I wanted to concentrate on the Derby eland . . . but this time we wouldn't look gift horses in the mouth if they came our way. The difference, of course, was that gift horses were getting scarce on the Upper Chinko.

As I wrote earlier, I don't believe Lord Derby eland is much different from the other varieties. More colorful, yes, and certainly more impressive in the horn, but all eland are wary and elusive, and they cover tremendous amounts of country. In the C.A.R., where there are so few roads, there aren't a lot of shortcuts available.

It is always possible to simply run into a herd. I never would have believed it, but at the conclusion of this safari, on the "main road" back to *Trois Rivieres,* we drove into a herd of eland, and a perfectly acceptable bull stood at fifty yards and watched us. Over two safaris in good Derby eland country, that is the best look I ever got at a Derby eland bull–including the one I shot.

One feature of the C.A.R., and I suppose neighboring areas, that I haven't seen much in southern or East Africa, is the presence of natural salt licks. These "salines" aren't all over the place but are common enough that most camps are sited within striking distance of several. A tremendous variety of wildlife visits these licks on a regular basis; there's always a chance of surprising a herd of eland at a saline, and it could happen at any time of the day.

But these are anomalies; when you're out in the bush after Derby eland you aren't looking for eland, but rather for fresh tracks, and if you happen to see the animal standing in them, count your blessings. The Derby eland are great wanderers–not necessarily more so than other eland, but their country is very big and there's no grid system of roads that can be cross-checked for tracks. In winter, when most of the ground water has dried, the eland will typically drift to the major rivers during the night or early morning, then feed their way back onto higher plateaus or ridges where they can catch a light breeze as they rest through the midday heat. This could be a daily journey of twenty miles and more, so to have a chance at an eland the sign must be fresh and must be found early in the day.

After two decades in the area, Rudy knew where to look for sign. Perhaps at a saline, or along a road that paralleled the river, or simply by making a cast on foot through good country. We did all these things the first few days. One morning we drove to the end of one of Rudy's few hunting tracks, then walked for a couple of miles along the base of a big linear ridge that dominates that part of the concession. Bingo–fresh eland tracks below a little spring.

Rudy's trackers are some of the best I've ever seen, but this herd had been in the area for a couple of days and it took much time to sort yesterday's spoor from today's. Eventually they worked it out, and we followed the herd along the ridge and through a saddle to the far side. Here we jumped a herd of buffalo and I was sorely tempted; had I known this would be the only herd of buffalo we would see I'd have called off the eland business without hesitation. But the eland tracks were fresh and the wind was still good, so we continued.

Although still late January it was very hot that week, and heat makes for unstable midday breezes. An hour later the wind shifted . . . and a few hundred yards farther on we found where the eland had scented us and run. This happened twice more, with no actual sighting of eland, and then we gave it up and made the long walk back to the truck.

Another morning we drove an hour or so back toward *Trois Rivieres,* then walked to the west to a big flat-topped plateau. I remembered this place from two years before; it's a particularly beautiful spot with rimrock along the edges of the plateau. From the top you can look out for miles and see nothing but rolling hills and woodlands. Over the course of the previous hunt, and during this one, I think we made this walk five or six times; it's my favorite place in that area. We never shot anything there, but we might have. This day the eland spoor was all old, but it's also a particularly good area for roan. There are always roan tracks somewhere on the plateau. This time we saw a nice herd of a dozen or so, but the bull was small.

If a morning hunt fails to turn up eland tracks–or if you attempt a track and wave off before midday–the game plan changes. Unless you luck onto smoking-hot tracks–unlikely past midmorning–there's no point in attempting to track eland in the afternoon. So we spent such afternoons still-hunting the riverines for bushbuck or looking for waterbuck, kob, and such.

Joe and Jacques were doing much the same, and we were all chagrined at how little game we were seeing. But Joe came back with a fine warthog one evening, and a day or so later, he took a truly spectacular Nigerian bohor reedbuck. A day later I shot a reedbuck as well, a good one, but nothing like Joe's. So far, though, all hands were concentrating on eland.

On the fifth or sixth day we left camp well ahead of daylight, gray dawn finding us on the main road–a road Rudy had built twenty years before when he pioneered this area–driving slowly along a high ridge that paralleled the Chinko several miles to the east. Patrice, Rudy's great tracker, signaled a halt. There in the road dust were the clear, fresh tracks of two eland bulls. It was six o'clock in the morning.

Five hours later we were still on the tracks, except by now one bull had split off and we were following a lone bull with huge tracks. It was very hot by now, pushing one hundred degrees, and the tracks meandered as the bull looked for a place to lie down. The tracks crossed a little streambed and turned into thicker cover. Patrice signaled that it would be in there, and Rudy called a halt so we could rest and be ready.

I drank some water and checked the rifle for the hundredth time, and then we took up the tracks again. The eland was walking, taking a bite now and again–fresh-cut, unwilted leaves showed he was very close. Long minutes passed, then more minutes, and still the tracks continued.

Then Patrice pointed ahead. There it was, maybe seventy-five yards in front of us, walking slowly from right to left. The brush was miraculously clear and the quartering angle perfectly acceptable. I shot it through the ribs, aiming for the off shoulder. We heard the bullet hit, and the bull catapulted into a gallop, right to left. I tried a fruitless second shot through the trees, and then it was gone. It was 11:30 in the morning.

This was the midpoint of the longest day of my hunting career. Later we would find I'd had the line of the shot just right, but the 300-grain Nosler Partition had failed to penetrate. Right then all we knew was that we had a problem.

Patrice and the rest of the crew held those tracks for the next five hours. There was some blood, but never enough to be encouraging. What was encouraging was that the bull stopped frequently. We jumped it a half-dozen times in cover too thick for a shot, and each time it would run only a short distance before slowing to a walk. Sooner or later we must get it . . . unless we ran out of daylight.

We had taken its tracks very far and now the shadows were getting long. Ahead of us was a long, grassy valley that led to a saddle in a major ridge–the same ridge we'd crossed a few days earlier, but many miles from where this day had started. I knew without Rudy telling me that we were at our limit; if it crossed the saddle we'd have to leave it and hope we could still follow its tracks in the morning.

As we entered the valley we all saw movement at the far end. It was there, walking slowly through the grass. We gained a bit of height and it turned broadside. I shot, heard the bullet hit. Rudy shot as well, and that bullet hit as well. The bull ran and we ran, and then it stood between two trees, up above the valley and just below the saddle itself. We shot again, and this time, finally, it dropped. It was almost half past five.

It was a huge bull, very old, with bases as thick as my calves and tips that had started to wear down. The winter cape was in full color, with jet-black collar and big dewlap. It is my most prized African trophy, and to me the most impressive and imposing animal on the continent. Among the great prizes–the bongo, Derby eland, and mountain nyala–there is always much discussion as to which is the most difficult to hunt. It all depends upon your experience. Later, as you will read, I hunted bongo unsuccessfully for twenty-one days. I rate the bongo, hunted without dogs, the most difficult; the mountain nyala the easiest of the three. Joe Bishop, on the other hand, took his bongo on the first day of his first bongo safari. I suspect he'd put the Derby eland at the top of the list. Whichever, Lord Derby eland is a fabulous trophy.

It was Joe's turn the next day. He and Jacques left camp very early and walked–partly in the dark–to a very remote saline. There were fresh tracks at the salt, and they followed them through another very long, hot morning. When the winds got fickle they waved off and headed back. But somewhere along the way Jacques decided they should check the saline one more time rather than make a direct line for the vehicle. Two years later I hunted bongo with Jacques, and I know this was not a flash of intuition. If at all possible, Jacques Lemaux *always* checks the saline on the way back. And I know how he checks it.

Well short of the area I know he checked the wind carefully, then circled so it would be in their favor. They moved up close, slowly and quietly, and then, long before the saline was in view, they left the trackers behind while he and Joe crept up alone. This saline was in a depression below a little bluff, and the wind enabled them to approach from behind that bluff. Jacques would have crept forward on hands and knees those last few yards, letting the saline become visible a few yards at a time. He would have made sure Joe was right behind him.

This time there was a herd of eland in the saline, and among them was a huge bull. The bull was facing them, but its head was down as it licked the saline. Joe crept forward, rested his Sako .375 over Jacques's shoulder, and shot down between those monstrous horns into the spine at the top of the shoulders.

It was well past dark before we heard deep voices singing the eland song above the grind of Jacques's engine. They stopped well outside the circle of light and Joe danced in with his trackers. "Just an eland," said Joe when I asked him how big. I was disappointed, but I should know Joe Bishop better than that.

His "just an eland" was, and is, the most spectacular creature I have ever seen. Mine was fine, and I wouldn't trade, but his had perfectly matched horns that flared out in a vee–and each horn was more than fifty-two inches long. Joe has it all, from the great sheep of Asia to a fabulous bongo, but he agrees with me that his Lord Derby eland is his finest trophy.

Suddenly we had the luxury of time, time to explore, time to hunt as hard or as lazily as we liked, and time to savor our success. Rudy and I spent our mornings looking for a big roan and buffalo tracks we could follow, and in both endeavors we failed. We saw some roan here and there, but in general Derby eland are more common than roan in that part of the C.A.R. The buffalo had apparently been hammered by poachers and most of the survivors had moved on. We devoted the afternoons to hunting bushbuck, waterbuck, and kob along the riverines.

One afternoon, not far from camp, we still-hunted along a river, slipping through the brush until we could get a view of the dry channel. We had seen a couple of bushbuck females, and then, far up and on the far side, we saw a bushbuck ram feeding among some driftwood logs. I had to slide down the bank to get clear of overhanging branches, and then I got into a sitting position with tight sling. The old .375 came through for me; the ram dropped at the shot and we had secured a very fine harnessed bushbuck, unquestionably the most beautiful of all the bushbuck subspecies.

A couple of days later we got a nice sing sing waterbuck along the same river, and Joe took a superb harnessed bushbuck as well. Although there were now very few in the area, somewhere along the way I got a very fine western kob as well.

The last few evenings we devoted to calling duikers. This is a most interesting exercise; they call the duikers by pinching the nose and making a nasal, mewing sound. In this area the common duiker is the red-flanked in the more open areas, while there are numbers of blue duiker in heavier bush. There are also a very few yellow-backed duiker. When calling you simply don't know what might come in.

One afternoon we called in a beautiful harnessed bushbuck; it came and stood broadside for an instant, not twenty feet away. A few moments later, a yellow-backed duiker crashed in and was almost in view when a puff of wind gave the show away. On another afternoon–while I sat with Rudy's .22 expecting a blue duiker–a very big leopard crept within bayonet range, then realized we weren't duikers and was gone in a spotted flash.

We took a fine red-flanked duiker and called in several blue duikers, an animal I wanted very badly, but I had a lot of trouble closing the deal. I was carrying Rudy's scoped Ruger .22, and either there was too much brush–if I could see the darned thing–or the animal dashed in and dashed out. For the last couple of outings I switched to Rudy's shotgun with SSG, and on the last evening, just at dark, I heard the tiny hoofbeats on the dry leaves and could just make out the dim form.

It was a fine and successful safari all around; both of us did well, and better than might be expected under the circumstances. But long before it was over Rudy knew this was his last season on the Chinko. During the break between the ideal eland hunting and the beginning of his bongo season he took off with some supplies and his GPS and found new country to the west, country the Sudanese poachers haven't reached. So far he's done well there, but unless the rainy-season invasion is stopped it's just a matter of time–and likewise for all of the wildlife in the uncharted bush that is the eastern C.A.R.

18

RETURN TO THE SELOUS

I had no plans to return to Africa any time soon and, for the first time in years, wasn't looking for any. I'd been to the C.A.R. in February and to Tanzania the previous October. I was licking my financial wounds. Moreover, I was living in Colorado and had put my preference points into a super archery elk tag for the September season. Then Paul Roberts called.

Besides being a good friend, Paul is the current owner of Rigby's, the old-line English gunmaker. And besides all that, Paul is one of few people in the English gun trade today who's a serious hunter. The poor guy has the African bug as bad as I do and has spent about the same amount of time over there trying to find a cure. We had never hunted together, but a few seconds into the conversation I realized we were about to–and that my elk permit and the preference points I'd used to get it were going to waste.

It seemed that Paul had come up with a new cartridge, Rigby's first new big bore since 1912 when John Rigby brought out his beloved .416. This new boomer was called the .450 Rigby Rimless Magnum, essentially the .416 Rigby case necked up to take a .458-inch bullet. Paul and his partner, Patty Pugh, were taking a couple of rifles out to Africa on a test run, and he'd appreciate it if I could join them for a buffalo hunt in Tanzania. I was hooked, instantly, for several reasons.

First, Paul is a good guy. Second, we'd be hunting with Luke Samaras, who is also a good guy and good friend. There was a time, I'll admit, when I would have hunted with the devil himself to get to Africa, but not anymore. These folks had nothing satanic about them–it would be a fun group. Third, Paul said the "B" word, meaning buffalo. When all is said and done they remain my greatest hunting passion. I think. Had the scheduling conflict been with a really good whitetail permit, I'm not sure what the answer would have been, but for me a choice between buffalo and elk was simple.

My fourth reason was pure unadulterated ego. I was, and am, unabashedly flattered that an English firm like Rigby's would call on an American writer like me for such a project. It's taken a lifetime to reach a point in my career where I might receive such a call, and I wasn't about to be too busy!

Paul and Patty were hunting–oops, in proper English, "stalking"–in Zimbabwe and showing off their new cartridge before coming to Tanzania, so all I had to do was show up in Dar es Salaam. As we surely all know by now, I'm a rifle freak. Between North America and all the rest of the continents I can't tell you how many times I've lugged gun cases around airports and sweated out waiting for them in baggage areas, nor how many bizarre gun permit and customs rituals I've observed. I can tell you that this trip, with one duffel bag and one carry-on, was pure pleasure.

Luke Samaras, of course, was in his home-away-from-home in the Selous. His wife, Jane, saw me through a simplified, firearms-free version of Tanzanian customs, and I slept blissfully while Paul and Patty flew in from "Zim" and underwent the full treatment.

I'd arrived in the early morning, they at midday. By late afternoon our charter was carrying us over the Rufiji and on to the dirt strip at Kingopera. Luke and his son, Jasper, were there to meet us, and at nightfall we could see the cheery glow of camp lanterns through the trees ahead.

The camp, roughly a line of green wall tents facing a long, narrow *dambo,* was like a time warp. Nearly six years had passed since I'd set foot in it, and yet it was like coming home. Six years can be a long time in Africa, but Luke's camp and his operation had changed but little–a most unusual island of stability on that turbulent continent. As we caught up on things around the campfire and over dinner, I learned that Luke was still using this camp as a base to hunt his two adjoining Selous Reserve blocks; and that he still had his Simanjaro area in Masailand where I'd hunted with Michel Mantheakis. As Paul and Luke relived old times I also learned that this current stability had been hard-won–and I learned a bit more about Paul Roberts and Luke Samaras.

Paul had first come out to Africa as a very young man, more than a quarter-century earlier. By sheer chance he hooked up with an equally young farmer and part-time professional hunter named Luke Samaras. They'd hunted together often over the next few years, but things had begun to change. The Samaras farm was nationalized, and suddenly Luke was a full-time professional hunter. Then Tanzania closed and Luke hunted in Kenya. Paul hunted with him there; that evening he recounted a great story.

When they went to the game department to buy licenses the official mentioned that there was a problem rhino in their hunting block and he could have a rhino permit, waiving the thirty-five-day-safari restriction. By then Paul's passion had become elephant hunting, as mine is buffalo but even more so. Paul was in the process of saying he didn't want a rhino when Luke elbowed him in the ribs. They got the rhino, a fine bull. Though black rhino have been closed (and rightfully so) for less than twenty years, this makes Paul Roberts one of just two hunters of my generation who has taken black rhino. Times change quickly!

In 1977 Kenya closed and Luke Samaras, with a young family, was in trouble. So were all the Kenya hunters, but Samaras was luckier than many in having a friend like Paul Roberts. Paul and his father, now deceased, had acquired Rigby's a few years earlier. Samaras and his family came to England and he worked for Rigby's until Tanzania reopened in 1981. Since then Luke Samaras Safaris has been much as it is today: small, low profile, and solid, with good country in both Masailand and the Selous Reserve.

I knew that Luke much preferred the Selous, spending less and less time elsewhere as the seasons passed. Until this trip I didn't understand why.

We'd had a fine hunt there in 1988, but not an easy one. We had tried to hunt severely harassed elephant, and evidence of poaching was everywhere. Hunting elephant means doing little else, so other than buffalo we had seen relatively little other game in '88 and this was compounded by the time of year. That was a November hunt, the end of the season and the start of the rains. The perfect time for elephant, if there was one then, but a poor time for all else, with plenty of water around and the game widely scattered.

It was now September, an ideal month to see the Selous in its glory. And we did. Oddly, we didn't see the huge herds of buffalo I'd seen in '88; undoubtedly they were elsewhere in the vast reserve, along flowing rivers. But we saw old bulls and medium-size herds every day, and we saw everything else as well. In spite of our own tough slogging, I had recognized the Selous as a great hunting area on our previous safari. Now I recognized it as one of the two best general-bag areas I'd ever seen.

The Selous is not known for sable, but we saw sable every day. Most of the bulls were typical Selous sable, topping out at thirty-eight inches or so, but we saw an eye-popper of a bull pushing the midforties. The Selous is not known for kudu, but we saw kudu every day, and I saw three bulls over fifty inches, super stuff for East Africa. And of course we saw plenty of

Lichtenstein hartebeest, Nyasa wildebeest, impala, reedbuck, warthog, zebra, and such. The Selous *is* known for eland, as it should be. More about that later.

It's also mostly known for its dangerous game, which is also as it should be. We were there mainly to hunt buffalo, and I know of no place where you can see more buffalo. We weren't there to hunt lion, but we saw lion, and I know of no place that has more lion. The problem is that few Selous lions grow big manes–the country is too hot and thorny. There are well-maned lion in the Selous if you work at it, but you must expect to turn some down looking for the right one. Leopards are endemic. Daylight sightings are common, and baiting is reasonably certain, at least until late in the season when the antelope and warthogs have dropped their young. Patty proved this by hanging a duiker first thing and shooting a big leopard off of it second thing.

The Selous is perhaps best known for elephant, but in recent years this has been past history. Luke admits that his elephant, and his elephant hunting, collapsed due to poaching pressure by about 1985. Things were probably at their nadir when I hunted there three years later. The best news is how much better things were in 1994. Thanks to the ivory ban and greatly improved antipoaching efforts, elephant poaching has stopped. Luke hadn't seen a poacher's track or a fresh kill all season. It didn't stop because they got all the elephant; something like forty thousand elephant remain in the Selous, less than half the peak population but still a great many elephant. In 1994 the elephant were much more visible and immeasurably calmer. Often we drove or walked into herds, and instead of screaming in rage and stampeding in panic–or charging–they would give way with dignity and fade slowly into the bush. It takes years to grow good ivory, and those long, beautiful tusks the Selous is famous for are scarce today–but if the status quo continues the Selous will only get better.

Initially I teamed up with Jasper, while Luke hunted with Patty and Paul. Later, after Patty's leopard and a buffalo or two each, we would all hunt together. This was fine with me and, as it happened, a great honor: I was to be Jasper's first-ever solo buffalo client.

This was something of a rite of passage, for me as much as for Jasper Samaras. Throughout my career I'd looked up to and tried to learn from my professional hunters, and I'd been with many good ones. Most, historically, had been older than I, and always much more experienced. Even my buddy Russ Broom, ten years younger than I and Jasper's age when we first hunted together, had already shot many buffalo and guided many clients when I met him. Now, suddenly, I had the unfamiliar experience of hunting with a man twenty-odd years younger than I who was taking someone out for buffalo for the first time.

It was daunting. Not because of Jasper, either. He knew the country well and he knew buffalo. But instead of being the bumbling client, I was expected to be the old pro. I felt old and inadequate!

We spent half the first day playing with Paul's rifles. I was as impressed as I expected to be. In his new .450 Rigby Rimless Magnum Paul had combined the .416 case with the traditional 480-grain bullet of the .450-3¼" Nitro Express. This cartridge, introduced by John Rigby in 1898, established the 2,150 fps and 5,000 foot-pounds of energy that became the stopping rifle formula for virtually all the Nitro Expresses and even the .458 Winchester Magnum. Of course, the large .416 case made possible much greater velocity–the new .450 was loaded to 2,378 fps for a much more powerful 6,288 foot-pounds of energy. Although the bullet weight was traditional, its construction was brand new; Paul had selected the bonded-core Woodleigh softpoints and steel-jacketed solids. I didn't think there was much question about whether it would work.

I was more interested in the current Rigby rifles. There were two, both based on much-reworked Brno magnum Mauser actions. Both were simply lovely British rifles: relatively plain but elegant; beautifully inletted and finished walnut; good met-

Noel Ross and the author with an exceptional vaal rhebok. Generally hunted at elevations from five to seven thousand feet, the vaal rhebok is one of Africa's few true mountain species.

Noel Ross and the author approach a big-bodied Eastern Cape kudu bull. These kudu tend to have long hair and extremely prominent markings, possibly due to the cool climate of the Cape mountains they call home.

Joe Bishop and friends with the best trophy of the safari, a monstrous Menelik bushbuck measuring more than 16 inches.

Joe Bishop in Colonel Negussie's camp below Mount Kakka, Negussie's hunting area in the Arusi Mountains. Camp isn't above tree line; the lower slopes and high valleys have been stripped of vegetation, and the brushline starts a few hundred feet higher.

Ruark's "blue highlands of Ethiopia" are indeed blue from a distance. Sturdy mountain ponies were used to gain elevation each morning.

Mountain nyala are hunted like most other mountain game: by intensive glassing. Negussie likes to get up high on known vantage points and put several spotters out like the spokes of a wheel.

The author and crew with one of the tough little Ethiopian ponies. The mountains look gentle from a distance, but at 13,000 feet elevation the ponies are a real blessing.

The author's mountain nyala was smaller than he'd realized, a below-average trophy. When Ethiopia closed two months after the safari, this nyala started to look a whole lot better!

The Menelik bushbuck is a small, dark, and very beautiful bushbuck, and a difficult prize to obtain in Ethiopia today. This is a nice ram, taken near the town of Asela.

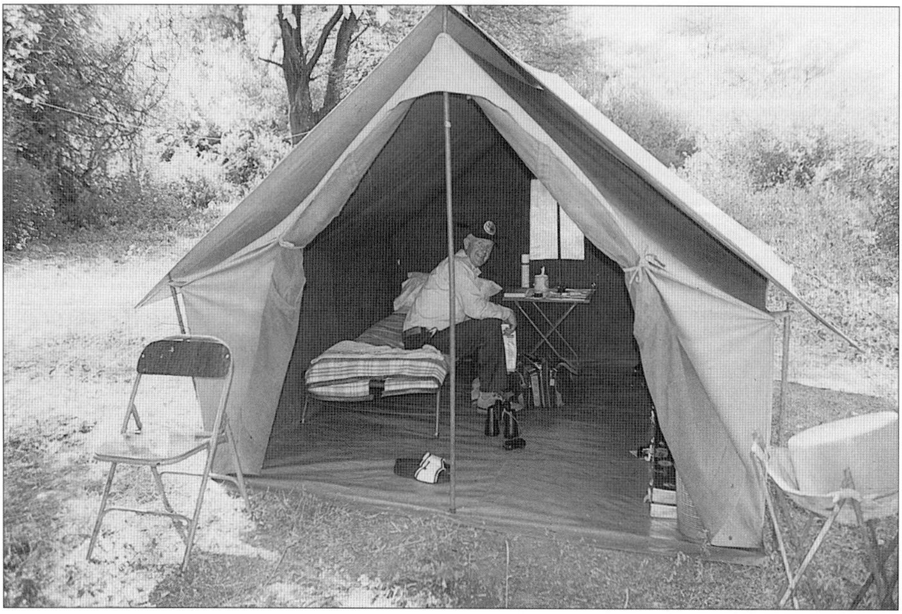

Camp in the Danakil was a simple tented affair set up in a campground in Awash National Park—much as you might rent a campsite in Yosemite.

The Cordeaux dik-dik, distinguished by the feather like crest between the ears, is extremely plentiful in the hills near Awash Station.

The hunters awoke from a nap to find this superb beisa oryx bull feeding his way across the savanna in front of us. This was the second time, in the exact same place, that this has happened to Colonel Negussie.

Joe Bishop with a fine gerenuk. These long-necked "giraffe antelope" are extremely common in the Danakil.

The Dankil Depression

The author and Colonel Negussie with a good Soemmering gazelle, a very large bodied gazelle found primarily in the Danakil.

The Great Rift Valley

The author and Geoff Broom look out across the Great Rift Valley in Tanzania's Mto Wa Mbu concession, made famous by Robert Ruark forty years previously. The savanna and dry bush of the valley are home to the full range of Masailand species.

Stately giraffes were extremely plentiful and could usually be seen browsing on acacia, their favorite food.

Geoff Broom and the author with the kind of buffalo Masailand is famous for. There aren't a lot of bulls like this anywhere, but Masailand is one of the most likely areas to produce buffalo of this quality.

The drying rack at Geoff Broom's camp. In any discussion of African hunting it's important to note that the meat is always *utilized. Lacking refrigeration, what can't be readily used is cut into strips and dried in the shade.*

A nice Grant gazelle from the Mto Wa Mbu area. Grant gazelle weren't exceedingly common, but trophy quality was very good.

This is an outstanding Thomson gazelle. The area held more Tommies than the author has ever seen, with superb specimens available if you looked carefully.

End of safari paperwork at Geoff Broom's camp. Tanzania has a system of a relatively inexpensive basic license, with additional trophy fees for animals taken—an ideal system for a country with such a diversity of game.

The Ugalla River camp was an exploration for outfitter Geoff Broom, so a minimal tent camp was brought in by truck from the far-off Selous Reserve—a long and brutal trek over Tanzania's rutted roads.

Geoff Broom congratulates the author on a nice sable. This is a fine and pretty bull, but the impression was that these sable are smaller in the body than sable from Zambia and Zimbabwe, hence a bit shorter in the horn than they appear.

Some local fishermen had built a couple of sitatunga machans. *This one overlooked a patch of papyrus that looked too small to hold sitatunga . . . but there were fresh tracks nearby.*

The rains were starting, and the trails got very slick. They got the vehicle winched out with little difficulty, but in just a few more days the area would have become too wet to hunt.

The author expected the reedbuck in the area to be of the common variety, but instead they were clearly East African bohor reedbuck, making this buck a welcome and unexpected prize.

Geoff Broom and the author were extremely pleased with this last-day, last-hour East African sitatunga, driven from a small reedbed and shot literally in the air. They were delighted to get him, but believe the area holds much better bulls.

Like all sitatunga, the East African variety have elongated hooves for moving across the papyrus beds. These hooves make sitatunga tracks the most distinctive of all antelope tracks.

An unfortunate aspect of safaris in the C.A.R. is the necessity for long and expensive air charters—but there are no alternatives. Depending on rainfall and river crossings, it could take ten days to drive from Bangui to this strip at Trois Rivieres!

Natural salt licks are an infrequent but consistent aspect of the C.A.R.'s topography. Virtually all the large mammals come to the mineral licks, making them ideal places to look for fresh tracks.

The author's Lord Derby eland was a huge-bodied old bull with massive bases and worn tips. The author rates it as the most impressive animal he has ever taken—and the most difficult.

After tracking all day, Joe Bishop shot his eland in the same salt lick he'd started tracking from ten hours earlier. This is a wonderful bull, completing Bishop's collection of spiral-horned antelopes.

Rudy Lubin and crew with a very nice Nigerian bohor reedbuck. These guys are wonderful trackers and a great team; all have lots of experience, and three have worked with Lubin for more than twenty years.

The author with a good sing-sing waterbuck. Just two years before these animals were incredibly abundant, but by 1994 poaching had reduced them dramatically and hard hunting was required.

The harnessed bushbuck is almost certainly the most beautiful of the bushbuck subspecies, small in size but with dramatic patterns of white stripes and spots. Too small and secretive to be worth a poacher's bullet, they were still plentiful in the thick riverine growth.

This safari was conducted in early February, the time of burning. The long grass was just drying out enough so that it could be burned off to make way for new growth.

One of Haut Chinko's *camp specialties is a whole duiker, preferably red-flanked, barbecued on a spit over a slow fire. Perfect!*

Rudy Lubin and the author with a good western kob. Once common, at this stage the kob was probably the most difficult to obtain of all the antelope species.

The purpose of the safari was to test these Rigby rifles chambered to the new .450 Rigby Rimless Magnum cartridge, so the first day was spent at the range and photographing the new rifles. By the way, this photo was shot on a tabletop in Samaras's camp!

The author's first bull was a normal Selous buffalo with a good boss and a modest spread. Shot at close range, it went less than twenty-five yards before piling up.

The veranda of Paul Roberts's tent became the camp gun room. In addition to the two .450s he had a lovely Rigby boxlock double .470 and a .300 Winchester Magnum he'd built on a Mauser action.

Patty Pugh, Luke Samaras, and Paul Roberts with a brace of good Selous buffalo. The one on the right is a pretty good buff for anywhere, with a spread of forty-two inches, good boss, and nice shape.

A good bushbuck was an unexpected bonus, encountered in relatively open bush at high noon. Considered Masai bushbuck, the bushbuck of the Selous are smaller and much more red, similar (and perhaps identical) to the Chobe bushbuck of Zambia and northern Mozambique.

The author's great prize of the trip was this spectacular East African eland, taken with a going-away shot from the big .450. The Selous holds the best eland in East Africa.

A big bull hippo encountered at midday near a tiny mudhole far out in the bush. The Selous is the only area where the author has frequently found hippo far away from lots of water.

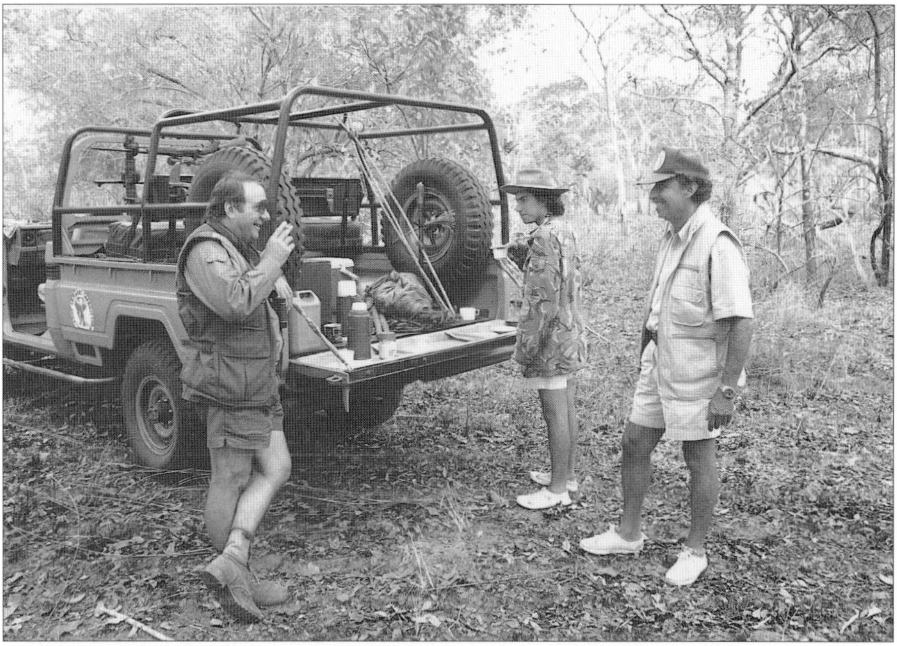

After a few buffalo were taken the group hunted together and took life easy. Paul Roberts, Jasper Samaras, and Luke Samaras take a break from wandering through the Selous thornbush.

A good Nyasa wildebeest, easily identified by the nose chevron. This bull was literally knocked off his feet by the powerful .450 Rigby Rimless Magnum.

Paul Roberts and Luke Samaras, pals of some twenty-five years, with a massive old bull wounded by the author and then tracked up on the last day of the safari. This one could have hurt somebody.

An early-morning wash at Russ Broom's camp in Zambia's Mulobezi block. Camps like this—thatched huts on cement slabs—are the most common among most of Zambia's safari companies.

Russ Broom with some of the trophies from previous safaris in the Mulobezi. The sable is huge and the kudu not far behind. This was his first season there, and he was justifiably delighted with the area.

Although black lechwe are found only near Bangweulu, shooting one isn't much of a trick once you get there. The real problem is finding a bull and keeping track of it until it steps clear for a shot.

While scouting for sitatunga haunts the hunters saw many lechwe, and some were inevitably better than the one the author shot. They're hard to judge, but the bull in the center with the radical forward flip to its horn tips may approach world-record dimensions.

This fine sitatunga was taken at first light on a very cold morning—the stocking cap is not just for show! The rifle is a .270, a good choice for light-to medium-size antelope.

Packing out the sitatunga in the early morning light. That's professional hunter Rodgers Kasela walking just behind the pole carriers, with PH Angelo Angelos bringing up the rear.

The heavy thornbush of the Save Valley is ideal for a wide range of antelope species, with greater kudu easily the most plentiful of the large antelope. This is a young bull, but there's no limit to how big kudu can grow here.

The return of the elephant is one of the newly formed Conservancy's great promises. In 1995 the population was about seven hundred, with new calves visible in all the cow herds.

Professional hunter Cuan McGeorge and the author with a very unusual buffalo: completely normal on one side, an upside-down eland horn on the other. The bull was taken with one shot from the Dakota single-shot after a perfect hunt.

This is a typical lunch that Jiros would have waiting at camp at midday. Humani Ranch's vast vegetable gardens, orchards, and poultry augmented the game meat.

Trackers Gudzira and Lymon and the author with a wonderful Limpopo bushbuck, still-hunted and shot at very close range in the Save's thick riverine bush. This is a great area for big bushbuck.

Cuan McGeorge drags the bushbuck to a spot clear enough for a photograph. Bushbuck thrive in riverine jungles like this, but hunting them in such cover is very difficult.

alwork; good express sights; and sturdy detachable mounts. The rifles were fairly heavy and had straight stocks. This was good, because you can't have that kind of power without recoil. We all shot the guns and they felt fine.

Secretly Paul and I each wanted to be first to take a buffalo with the new .450, so Jasper and I were torn between holding out for a big bull or taking the first decent animal that came along. Old habits die hard, and selectivity won out. Jasper and I worked our way along a broad, sandy, dry riverbed in the heat of the day; he expected that some bulls would come to the scattered pools for water, while others would lie down on the cool sand under overhanging branches. He was right on both counts; we saw and passed at least a dozen bachelor bulls. One heavy-horned old fellow stood under the bank for long seconds, and I'm sure it was the biggest buffalo we saw on the whole safari. But we passed it, and we passed more the second day.

So it was, that, appropriately enough, Paul took the first buffalo with his new cartridge. It worked perfectly, no surprises; shoulder-shot, the buffalo ran less than twenty yards and dropped. That same night Patty got her leopard with a single shot from a pretty little Rigby-Mauser .300. We had a double celebration that night, and Jasper and I decided we'd better get ourselves in gear.

We did. The next morning we found the tracks of a good herd, perhaps sixty or so, and we followed quickly until we could see red dust ahead, raised by the hooves of a moving herd. Then we slowed down and closed in. The herd was moving and feeding, and on first contact we thought we saw a decent bull. It was lost in the mass before we could isolate it, so we circled ahead.

We did this about four times, the wind staying steady, but the bull we'd seen–or other good bulls that may have been there–were hidden on the far side of the herd.

They had stopped by now. It was late morning and winds were getting unstable. We tried a new angle, creeping in with a big, round antheap for cover. We reached its base, took a breath, then crawled over the top under cover of a thornbush. The nearest cow was just a few yards away, with several others also close by. The rest of the herd was hidden. Then a puff of swirling breeze spooked an unseen buffalo somewhere in the herd. They all stampeded in a cloud of dust–but, as sometimes happens when they can't tell the origin of a threat, in a few seconds they all came trooping back.

We saw them coming and got ready. The black mass passed twenty-five yards from our antheap and luck was with us; a nice mature bull was on the outside of the herd, on our side. I saw it coming, pointed it out, and waited until it was just opposite. As it passed I shot it very carefully in the center of its left shoulder, a third of the way up its body.

At that distance it took the full blow from the heavy rifle, rocked, and nearly went down. Then it recovered, spinning around to go right while the rest of the herd continued to our left in high gear. I had time to work the right-handed bolt and slam a solid under the bull's tail, and then it was lost in red dust and black bodies.

We waited for the dust and hoofbeats to drift away, then waited some more. I was 99 percent sure and so was Jasper . . . but if he should ever give in to the impatience of youth with future clients, I wanted to be damned sure he didn't learn it from me. We waited. Then we moved in, finding the buffalo lying not fifty yards away. We would have seen it fall but for the dust.

This was an absolutely dead buffalo. I shot it again just to be sure, and to make a point. I don't want to hunt with anyone who doesn't insist on that insurance shot.

With two buffalo down with two shots, all follow-ups being paid-up life insurance, and with recovered bullets showing some 90 percent weight retention, Paul's cartridge was clearly a success. Now we could play.

Luke wanted to spend a few days getting Patty her first buffalo, and maybe follow some elephant tracks with Paul. Samaras has a passion for elephant hunting just as deep as

Paul Roberts's, which is undoubtedly partly why they have remained close friends for a quarter-century. Jasper and I could keep hunting buffalo, which we did. But what I really wanted was one of those big eland for which the Selous is famous.

Selous eland are classed as East African eland, which certainly works for me, but they're much larger than the typical eland of Masailand and Kenya. They are also extremely plentiful in the Selous, roaming in big herds, bachelor groups, and as single bulls. Of all the game in the Selous, the best and most consistent trophy quality is found in the eland. Of course, that doesn't mean they're easy, just present.

We tracked a couple of single bulls until the wind turned sour, and a couple of days later we tracked a pair of big bulls. After a couple of hours they led us to the top of a fairly open ridge that looked down into a big bowl. There they were, feeding on a big, leafy tree in the center of the bowl. At this stage I think they were five hundred yards away, maybe more–much too far for the .450 (or anything else), and there wasn't much cover.

I crawled on alone, closing the distance quite a bit. Or so it seemed. Then there was no cover at all. I should have waited until they fed on into the brush, then we could have resumed tracking. But I was hot and impatient. I knew I couldn't judge the range well–unfamiliar country, big animal–but I didn't think I could miss an eland. Yep, sure could! I thought the shot was three hundred yards, but it was farther. The big bullet passed just under it, and that was the end of that.

Patty shot a fine buffalo bedded on the edge of a herd, and when one of its mates got aggressive Paul shot his second buffalo. These were two more one-shot kills, and Paul's was a particularly good buffalo, by far the best of the trip. They also took exceptional Nyasa wildebeest. Jasper and I blundered into a very good bushbuck, a rare trophy for the Selous. Paul and Luke eventually tabled elephant until another safari, and we spent the last few days hunting together.

I think it was Luke who saw the eland bull first, just its head and neck sticking out of some bush down in a low watercourse. I didn't see it as an eland, but at least I saw the animal and reached for the rifle. While I was figuring out what that distant blob was, Luke was looking at horns. By the time he said, "Shoot him," and I figured out what I was supposed to shoot, the eland had swapped ends and started to go. It wasn't spooked, but it was moving off in that ground-eating trot, gaining distance fast with lots of bush in the way.

Fortunately it chose to climb up out of the streambed, exposing itself for just a few yards. Curse me if you will, but I went for the Texas heart shot that was offered. I wouldn't have tried it with a light rifle, probably not even with a .375–but with the big .450 I thought I could get away with it. I swung a bit above that broad behind and fired just as it went into some bush.

We heard the bullet slap, saw it hump, and it was gone. So were we, running at an angle to cut it off. Puffing hard, I missed it as it plowed through brush. Then it slowed, very ill, and I shot it through the shoulders with the solid that was next up in the magazine. And what a bull! It was long and thick with a wonderful cape–much bigger than the spectacular eland I had shot in Kenya many years ago . . . and probably bigger than the fine Livingstone eland I took in Zambia in 1984.

We were happy with the hunt by now, so we mostly looked around half-seriously. Paul shot a good reedbuck, and I absolutely flattened a wildebeest with the .450. And then, on the last day, I just plain screwed up on a buffalo.

We had tracked three bulls into a very thick piece of cover, and came upon them face-to-face. I took a step toward Luke to get clear, found the shoulder of a big bull, and started the squeeze. Then things went bad. The bull started to move–fast–but somehow I couldn't stop the trigger squeeze. I got the barrel moving, but it was too late. I knew exactly where the bullet had hit, and I told Luke, "At the diaphragm, angling forward. Probably got one lung." On buffalo, big guns are better than little guns, but no gun is big enough to make up for poor shot placement. One lung is never enough, and I knew it.

Four hours later, in very heavy cover, after Paul's .450, my .450, and Luke's .416 had all spoken, I had the tiny consolation of having called the first shot correctly. That bull should have gotten somebody. A half-dozen times it had waited for us in thorn far too thick to reliably stop it in, but then it had moved on. We were lucky and we got it, so it made an exciting finish to a perfect safari among friends. But I'm sure glad Jasper wasn't along that day. He still thinks I shoot buffalo pretty well.

19 KAFUE AND BANGWEULU

Russ Broom and his dad, Geoff Broom, and I had left two pieces of unfinished business in Zambia in 1984. We'd had a fabulous safari, but we'd finished up at Lake Bangweulu at the start of the rains. In fact, the rainy season started with a torrent while Geoff and I were watching a sitatunga haunt from a termite mound, deep in the swamps at about four o'clock one afternoon. The next morning we had to leave lest the dirt strip become too soft for takeoff.

I'd eventually taken a sitatunga in Botswana, but there was only one cure for the second bit of business. Through sheer stupidity I'd failed to take a black lechwe while at Bangweulu. They were there; the first morning a nice herd of bulls paraded in front of us. I don't know what I was thinking. Well, I sort of do. None of the bulls was really *black*. Of course few black lechwe really are, but it was a good excuse. We'd just come from the Kafue Flats where I'd taken a great Kafue lechwe. These were smaller and I just wasn't mad at them that day. I didn't know the rainy season was just twenty-four hours away. I was also counting pennies; we'd had a *very* successful safari and the trophy fees I already had to pay would break me. It would have been better if I'd remembered *then,* instead of later, that the black lechwe is found only at Lake Bangweulu.

Geoff and Russ and I discussed a return engagement, but after too much governmental interference they pulled out of Zambia a year or so later, and my return engagement was postponed for a decade.

Ten years–actually, eleven–is an eternity in African hunting. Things are changing so fast that an area that remains constant for three or four seasons is a bastion of stability. Zambia is a great safari country and I didn't intend to stay away for eleven years–it just happened that way. During those eleven years Kenneth Kaunda was finally voted out of power, and I'd heard things were much better under the new government. When Russ Broom told me he was going back into Zambia in 1995 I didn't hesitate. Together with Zambian partners he had formed a company separate from his Zimbabwe operation, basing out of Lusaka as African Game Conservation and Safari Company, Ltd. He and his partners had exclusive use of the Mulobezi hunting block on the southwestern edge of the Kafue National Park.

Well and good, I told him; I'd love to see the Kafue again and maybe shoot a buffalo . . . but if we hunted Zambia I wanted to go to Bangweulu. As it had been previously, Bangweulu is a "common" area, used by all the safari companies. Russ hadn't been there in a decade and needed to see it. So we agreed on a quick buffalo hunt, then an experimental trip to Bangweulu for black lechwe and sitatunga.

Mulobezi is one of the Kafue areas most distant from the capital city of Lusaka; by road it's actually much closer to Victoria Falls. After leaving Zambia I'd be going on to Zimbabwe's lowveld to hunt with Roger Whittall. Russ himself would be coming out of his Zambezi Valley area, so we agreed on Vic Falls as our meeting place.

Russ was there to greet me, but I was only half there. I'd slept wrong on the plane to Johannesburg and had badly tweaked my back and neck. I'd overnighted in Jo'burg, and after a long night I'd felt a bit better in the morning. So, pretending I was a tough Marine, I'd made the terrible mistake of going running, hoping to work out the kinks. The effect, predictably, was just the opposite. By the time I cleared customs and found Russ, I could hardly walk.

I'd expected to leave for Zambia immediately, but we were short some paperwork that Russ's wife, Amanda, was sending on a plane from Harare. We'd stay in the Falls that night, and it was just as well–I was in no shape for a long drive. Russ got me some muscle relaxers and we had dinner at the Vic Falls Hotel, catching up a bit until the pills took effect and I faded gratefully away.

I was still hurting in the morning, but greatly improved. In late morning we finally crossed the bridge over the Zambezi Gorge and drove into Zambia. The drive was long but smooth, and by late afternoon we were in camp.

Zambia had changed a lot since I'd been there. The new government is much more supportive of tourism and sport hunting, and we had no problems with customs or with the occasional police checkpoint. A new program called Admade, similar to Zimbabwe's Campfire Program, was funneling portions of license fees directly to the local areas for the first time. A downside is that, unlike back in the eighties, now you must purchase all of your licenses "up front." That makes for very difficult decisions in a country with so rich and varied a game list as Zambia.

This time it seemed easy, at least when I made my choices. My main interest was Bangweulu, but Russ insisted I also see Mulobezi; he described it as every bit as good as the hunting areas he'd had in the early eighties–which were very good indeed.

This was an exploratory trip. To keep costs down we would drive rather than use air charters. This would mean a lot of driving and limited hunting time, so there was no point in going hog-wild on licenses. I had Russ get me a buffalo license in Mulobezi because I like buffalo hunting, and also because it would be very hard to get a good magazine story out of a Zambian hunt without buffalo. Bangweulu, of course, has limited species. The rarity is black lechwe, found only in that region, while the great prize is sitatunga. I left it at that. Other Bangweulu game includes tsessebe, oribi, and reedbuck, the latter two not always on quota.

I wasn't necessarily haunted by these decisions, but it was almost amusing that, during just two days in the Mulobezi, I saw the most amazing procession of wildlife I have ever seen. Our list included kudu, sable, roan, eland, hartebeest, wildebeest, zebra, impala, warthog, bush pig, oribi, duiker, buffalo, and even chance sightings of both lion and leopard. Many animals were of superb trophy quality–and remember, all I was looking for was one buffalo bull!

I didn't particularly want to shoot any of these other animals; it was treat enough to see them. However, I'm obligated to say–as often as I can, in the hopes someone might listen–that Zambia would be better served by an open license subject to quota, as is the system in Tanzania and Zimbabwe. In an area with more than fifteen species, no one can predict what might turn up. Nor are most clients knowledgeable enough to decide, weeks before and thousands of miles away, *precisely* what trophies they're interested in.

We were in Mulobezi in July, early in the season for Kafue. It's a rolling plateau of brachystegia woodland broken by broad, grassy watercourses or *dambos*. The streams themselves had dried, but there were numerous pools and puddles. There was also much water remaining in the adjoining Kafue National Park; Russ commented that there would be much more game in the concession in another month as water dried up in the park, but there was already plenty enough to impress me.

There weren't many buffalo in the area, just a few bachelor bulls here and there while the big herds were still in the park. We drove the *dambos,* checking water holes for tracks. Each turning opened a new vista down these broad valleys, and the procession of game seemed never-ending. Herds of wildebeest and hartebeest, a scattering of zebra, perhaps a few warthog at the water holes. Common game seemed almost always in sight–and then a herd of sable or eland would add spice, or perhaps we'd see a roan or kudu slipping into the trees.

Shortly after leaving camp we drove into a big pride of lions and watched them fade away. That evening, relaxing by the fire ring in camp, I looked out across a big *dambo* and watched the sunset. My game list for the day was pretty full, but I added bush pig and impala to it. And then, at sunset, I capped it by watching a leopard drift out of the far trees and slip along the edge, exposed for just a few seconds. I doubt you could have a better–certainly not a more varied–game viewing day in any park in Africa. And the Mulobezi has never been a park; it's been a hunting area for many years.

The buffalo hunt itself was the simplest and easiest I have ever been in on. Partly, I must admit, because I had no intention of being picky. We didn't have a lot of time, and I was anxious to get on to Bangweulu. Even so, it's unheard of for things to go so smoothly.

Russ was the outfitter, but at this time he wasn't licensed as a professional hunter in Zambia. So Russ was essentially an observing outfitter, and my professional hunter was Rodgers Kasela, a big, good-humored Zambian–good company and a good hand.

Through the early morning we found a few old buffalo tracks, but it was nearly ten o'clock, alongside a tiny water hole at the edge of a big *dambo,* before we found fresh tracks. It was a single bull, and the tracks were very large.

We debated for a while. It was late to start a track, but they looked quite fresh–almost certainly made after sunrise. However, the morning had been very cold, almost frosty, so determining a precise age was difficult. Then there was the question of a single bull. In a group of three or four, which we had hoped to find, we could probably bank on at least one shootable bull. A single bull with so large a track was surely a mature old *dugga* boy–but he could have broken horns. I had Bangweulu on my mind and opted to give it a try.

The wind was steady in our faces and the tracks led straight through open woodland. My back was still killing me and I was a bit goofy from medication, but other than that it was a nice stroll through the woods on a cool, sunny morning.

After just fifty minutes, a record for me, the tracks began to meander as the bull sought a place to lie down. Ten minutes later Russ held up a hand to stop us and raised his binoculars.

I don't know how he saw it; the bull's head was just a dark spot among many dark logs and tree trunks. But he pegged it instantly at about sixty yards. It was lying down, facing away. We crept in, cutting the distance to less than forty yards, and stopped behind a double-trunked tree. The bull's body was hidden and we could see just one horn. We waited, binoculars glued, and finally it tilted its head enough to show us the other horn tip. I nodded and got ready.

Russ clapped his hands. I had expected the bull to stand, but perhaps it had played this game before. It stood, all right, but it came to its feet in one fluid motion and kept moving, exactly as it had been lying, which meant quartering strongly away from me.

I had the Dakota single-shot .375 rested and ready, and as soon as the vertical wire passed the off-front leg the rifle went off. The bull lurched, hard hit, then turned away and showed its broad behind as it cantered through the trees. This is a classic reaction to the first shot, and this is where, with a double or magazine rifle, you give it a solid through the rear. But I didn't have a double or a magazine rifle.

Dangerous game with a single-shot was an experiment for me. I've used Ruger Number Ones a lot on lesser game, and I'd practiced a lot with this rifle. I'd anticipated exactly this moment, and I had extra cartridges between the fingers of my supporting hand–I thought I was ready.

There was lots of time; I could have emptied a bolt action–possibly I could have emptied and reloaded a double. But the

Dakota single-shot, an unusually beautiful and smooth-handling rifle, doesn't eject. Eyes on the buffalo, I cleared the empty, started to stuff a fresh .375 Dakota cartridge into the chamber, and realized I'd never make it–the trees were now closing around the departing buffalo.

At my shoulder, ready, Russ said calmly, "Do you want me to shoot him?"

Unprintable affirmative. His .416 Heym went off and the bull vanished, then reappeared again through the trees. Then it slowed, stumbled in a half-circle, and went down.

My X-Bullet from the fast .375 Dakota had pierced its heart and all the rest was window dressing, but that first shot might not have been so perfect and there was nothing I could have done about it. Food for thought.

The journey from Mulobezi to Bangweulu was extremely long, but not unpleasant. Given the value of hunting days, I do not recommend driving, but it was enjoyable and scenic.

Angelo Angelos, a young Zimbabwe PH who was learning the areas for upcoming safaris, preceded us to pick up supplies. We rendezvoused with "Angie" in Lusaka. From there, both vehicles piled high with tents, bedding, and food–a full fly camp–we convoyed north toward Bangweulu.

Our intent had been to push on through to Bangweulu, but the last petrol station along the way is located at Serenje, near the Zaire border. We got there well after dark, and despite heroic efforts were unable to locate the owner. We had drums, but Russ's "worst-case" planning dictated that we needed to fill the vehicles at this point as well. We had no choice but to wait until morning, so we drove a few miles out of town and found a spot off the road that appeared safe. Throwing mattresses on the ground, we slept.

With tanks full, we continued on through another cool morning. We soon turned off the main road to Tanzania, heading straight north past the lonely monument to David Livingstone. In late morning the trees thinned and we rolled across Bangweulu's vast floodplain toward the game guard station. At Bangweulu–"Where the Water Meets the Sky"–the perpetual mirage of the floodplain marches across the horizon and elongates distant trees and animals. Fishermen walking across the plain seem many yards tall and the far tree line reaches toward the sky. This is the most unique and perhaps most beautiful place I've seen in Africa. And what it lacks in variety of game it more than makes up for in quantity. The lechwe were there to greet us, a great herd of several hundred, not a mile from the tin roofs of the lonely game guard outpost.

At the station we learned that our camping gear was unnecessary. The local chief had established a safari camp at the edge of the trees a few miles away. We checked it out and it was just fine, a neat collection of thatched sleeping huts with mosquito-netted beds encircling a dining hut and fire ring. Communications are sketchy in Zambia's backcountry; the existence of this camp was news to Russ and a great boon. It meant that to take clients into Bangweulu for a few days all he needed to do was send a PH with vehicle and food. The clients could fly in, and the local camp was fully staffed with cook, skinner, trackers, and all.

After a quick lunch we went out and shot our black lechwe. This is one of those deals that, no matter how you slice it, is a collection rather than a hunt. As Gary Williams commented a year later, "Stevie Wonder could shoot a lechwe here." But you must go to Bangweulu to make the collection. Once there it's a matter of selection. At least until the rains come there are thousands of black lechwe on the floodplains, and in big herds.

An acceptable bull is about twenty-two inches and a great bull is twenty-four or twenty-five inches. The distinction is subtle, and you study horns until your eyes grow tired. We looked at many and ultimately picked out a very fine bull. Of course, once you find the one you want you must keep your eyes on it and stay ready until it's clear of the ever-shifting herd–perhaps the most difficult part. But we got it, and I was delighted to complete this eleven-year task. The next day, while prospecting for sitatunga haunts, we found two lechwe bulls that were clearly larger, but I'm still happy with mine. Just being there and seeing the big herds is the key, and the actual shooting is so anticlimactic that it's hard to covet an extra inch or two or horn.

Now, with the lechwe secured and fresh meat in camp, we could get serious about sitatunga.

The area is called Lake Bangweulu, but the lake itself lies to the northwest across many miles of swamp. I know of no one, except perhaps Jay Mellon, who has actually hunted at the lake proper. Instead you hunt lechwe on the floodplains to the south, tsessebe and oribi in the trees and abandoned casaba plantations farther south yet, and sitatunga in the papyrus beds lining tributary rivers that cut the floodplains.

Most of these rivers are just small trickles in the dry season; you don't hunt these sitatunga from dugout *makoros* as you might in Botswana, but almost exclusively from pole *machans* overlooking clearings and breaks in the papyrus. The game guards and camp staff had several *machans* ready, and with the lechwe business finished we sat in one that evening.

We were camped in a different spot and we approached from a different direction. Also, eleven years had passed. I didn't recognize the area until we reached a small fishing village on the slight rise of an island in the swamps. There are a number of small fishing villages scattered through the area, but this one is distinctive due to a round galvanized-metal grain bin. Geoff Broom and I had hunted here briefly in 1984 and we'd seen sitatunga. Strange how little had changed.

The *machan* overlooked several alleyways between papyrus beds and was in an ideal spot. We sat there night and morning and saw a couple of females–they always remind me of mice the way they sneak and then scurry–but no bulls showed.

We reasoned that we were awfully close to both the village and the game guard station; this spot simply must be picked over. In this we were wrong. Angie took a fine sitatunga from that spot on the next safari, and I had my own moment of glory from that blind a year later. But at the time we all agreed we must move.

By eight o'clock in the morning, the fishermen have left their villages and are checking their traps and the sitatunga hunting is all over. We went back to camp, had breakfast, and went scouting. We were on the Lukuzi River, a major tributary to Bangweulu. Just a few miles up we found some big reedbeds separated by some small pools and a mud flat a couple hundred yards across. It was an ideal sitatunga haunt, and there in the mud were the splayed, space-creature tracks of big sitatunga bulls.

We left a crew to build a *machan* and continued exploring. We found no spots that looked better for sitatunga, but we saw many black lechwe, including a couple of potential world records. We also got hopelessly turned around in the deep mounds of an old casaba plantation. It took a couple of hours to inch the Land Rover out of the maze, and we had just enough time to make it to our new *machan.*

Eastern whitetail hunters would appreciate sitatunga hunting from a stand, while those who have trouble sitting still would hate it. I'm not crazy about sitting still, but it's really the only way–and this is active stand hunting, wherein you keep your binoculars going all the time. The papyrus beds are beautiful, too, in the soft light of late afternoon and early morning. The bird life is fabulous, and in the evening you can hear the swamps come to life as night approaches.

We sat through dusk and into darkness and listened to the hippos sound off and watched shorebirds and waterfowl. We saw no sitatunga at all and heard none splashing in the papyrus, but there were fishermen working their nets close by until dusk. I figured it might be a better morning spot, and we quickly discarded any notion of trying elsewhere–at least not for another day or so.

The morning was very cold and I shivered as we stood in the *machan* and awaited the dawn. Angie and Rodgers and one of the game scouts were with me, each huddled in his thoughts as we awaited the dawn.

It came with a light pink glow in the east and our limit of vision slowly expanded. Our stand looked out across the mud flat for perhaps 200 yards. At about 150 yards the flat became a narrow gap between two big papyrus beds. The gap was perhaps 75 yards across, broken by a couple of clumps of papyrus. There were tracks in the flat in front of us and more crossing that narrow gap. It was in that gap that we concentrated as the light began to grow.

Angie had never guided for sitatunga–they don't exist in Zimbabwe–but he had great eyes. He saw the bull walk into the gap from the right, but I could not. It was just too dark. Then it was behind one of the clumps, and finally I saw it. The game guard said it was a big bull. Angie was unsure, and all I could see was a black blob that probably had horns. And then it was gone behind a little screen of grass. The light was coming quickly and it must reappear . . . but long minutes passed and it never did.

Rodgers saw the second bull first, then Angie. It trotted out from the right and from the side its horns were tall. Later we discussed whether the first bull was bigger. The game scout thought so; the rest of us didn't know. But the second bull looked just fine. It stopped behind a clump of papyrus in the middle of the gap and when it stepped out it looked at us, no doubt seeing our new *machan* for the first time. Its horns came out, pinched in, then turned out in a beautiful lyre shape–a good bull.

Angie, never rattled, whispered, "Yeah, Craig, I think he's all right." I was already trading the binoculars for the Dakota .270.

Resting across the upper rail of the blind, I put my eye to the scope. The exterior of the lens was hopelessly fogged by the cold, wet air. I dabbed at it frantically and tried again. The light was pretty good, but the scope was not. The sitatunga stood broadside, head thrown back, staring at us, but through the scope it was just a dark outline. The crosshairs were almost invisible; I put the center of the scope on the middle of the front half of the dark blob and squeezed the trigger.

We clearly heard the bullet hit, but the sitatunga swapped ends and ran back the way it had come. It passed behind the same clump and stopped, just its head and shoulder exposed. I fired again with the same hold and even through the fogged scope I saw water spray from its wet hide when the bullet hit. It went down this time, and we waded across the cold mud and admired it in a beautiful sunrise.

20

THE SAVE CONSERVANCY

We packed up in Bangweulu and made Lusaka late that night. We stayed there overnight, bid Angie and Rodgers farewell, and then Russ and I drove through to Harare. There I overnighted with Russ and Amanda and marveled at how their two boys had grown, and then I proceeded onward for the next part of the trip.

More than fifteen years earlier, when Zimbabwe was still Rhodesia, I'd been one of the first clients when Roger Whittall opened his Humani Ranch to sport hunting. Humani is a big ranch down in the lowveld along the Save River, riverine growth and thick mopane woodland perfect for a wide variety of wildlife. Roger's grandfather homesteaded Humani and transformed it from virgin bush into a working cattle ranch. Over time much of the game was removed to make room for cattle–elephant, buffalo, wildebeest, zebra. Lions were not tolerated, but despite seventy-five years of warfare the leopards continued to hold their own. By the time I hunted there the once-numerous buffalo were almost gone, wiped out to control hoof-and-mouth disease. There was still plenty of game in the late 1970s–kudu in the hills, bushbuck in the riverine, thousands of impala, and scattered pockets of zebra, sable, and such. And of course there were plenty of well-educated, clever leopards.

During the ensuing years, the from an informal start on Humani, the safari operation run by Roger and his partner, Barrie Duckworth, became one of the country's largest. They obtained concessions in Matetsi and the Zambezi Valley. I hunted with Roger in Mozambique in 1989, and he outfitted in Zambia as well.

As good government concessions grew ever more scarce and expensive, Roger became convinced that the future of African wildlife rested in large private holdings like Humani. He had long since converted Humani from cattle to game and had reintroduced several long-gone species. His dream was to bring Humani back to the way it had been when his grandfather first saw it. He couldn't do that alone. As big as it is, Humani isn't big enough to bring back buffalo, elephant, and rhino. All three require lots of room and are hard on cattle fences–and buffalo would not be tolerated so long as any neighbor raised cattle.

It took years, but he finally convinced all of his neighbors to opt for game rather than cattle. The act of faith–and the iron will required–to change the generations-old economy of eight old-line cattle ranchers was unprecedented. But the cattle went.

The bulk of the Save River Valley–more than eight hundred thousand acres–was pooled into the Save Valley Conservancy, the largest private undertaking of its kind in the world. Internal cattle fences were dropped and the wire reclaimed to make several hundred miles of double perimeter fence, electrified by solar panels.

The dream started to become reality even before the fence was completed. For several years Roger had offered Humani as a haven for young elephants orphaned in culls, so the Conservancy started out with a few dozen elephants. Zimbabwe has more elephant than available habitat, so culling has remained a grim necessity. Over time it was determined that the most effective culling technique, and the one that resulted in the fewest future problem elephants and the least disturbance to the elephants' social order, was to target and eradicate entire family groups. Only very young calves were occasionally spared–a horrible but necessary business.

The Conservancy offers badly needed elephant habitat, but you can't dart and move elephant quite as readily as antelope. Clem Coetzee, a Zimbabwe elephant expert who has almost certainly shot more elephant than any of the famous old ivory hunters, worked out a plan.

An entire family group could be herded to a suitable location near a road, darted, then loaded by conveyer belt onto flatbeds and quickly moved to a waiting convoy of trailer trucks. A transfer could be made, the antidote given, and the elephant moved to their new home and unloaded. Undoubtedly not as easy as it sounds, and frightfully expensive, but possible. When I saw the Conservancy in July 1995, the elephant population was about eight hundred, with a target of a sustainable population of two thousand.

Black rhino were already present as well. Despite international treaties and bans and "shoot poachers on sight" policies, Zimbabwe has continued to lose its black rhino, especially in the vulnerable border areas like the Wankie Corridor and the Zambezi Valley. The ban on ivory has worked pretty well, but the black market price for rhino horn is just too high. For several years, quietly, Zimbabwe has been darting rhinos in such areas and removing them to suitable areas in the interior, mostly private lands. Humani had received several, so the Conservancy opened shop with a breeding herd. There is room for many more . . . but Zimbabwe's once-plentiful black rhinos are now so scarce that only scattered survivors remain for relocation.

Buffalo can be live-captured without darting, so moving herds from drought-threatened or overpopulated parks is a great deal simpler. Obtaining buffalo should have been no problem, but unlike rhino and elephant, buffalo aren't threatened in any way and have aroused no popular sympathy. Moving buffalo from government land to private is fraught with political considerations, and when I was there the going had been slow. The Conservancy's goal of ten thousand buffalo will take time, but in 1995 there were already several hundred. Even among a group that size there are already surplus bulls.

Over the years, Roger had kept me posted on the sweeping changes on Humani. We'd often discussed me coming back to see how it was progressing, and I'd intended to for years. But different horizons kept interfering and, shame on me, I never got around to it. At the 1995 SCI convention Roger told me that the Conservancy was a reality, I had to come see it, and I could be one of the first to hunt buffalo on Humani in more than fifteen years.

So I was going home to Humani, site of one of my first safaris. The timing was perfect; I was privileged to sit in on a meeting of the Conservancy, and I watched them ratify their constitution. It was fascinating. Here was a room full of old Rhodesian cattlemen who were no longer cattlemen but wildlife men. I watched them harangue over word changes, and then they unanimously approved the document.

The cattle were already gone and their ranches no longer had internal fences or boundaries, just a common perimeter. The constitution was thus just a formality, but an important one. Unlike so many similar schemes created by philanthropic preservationists to shut hunting out, wildlife utilization on a sustainable-yield basis is part of the Conservancy's charter. As Roger said, "We're still in red meat production; it just isn't cattle anymore."

I agree with Roger's concept and dream because it is based on this key principle. In the Conservancy I believe I see a chance for survival not only for wildlife, but also for African hunting as I have known it.

Right now, in the late 1990s and for some unknown period into the next century, some wild Africa remains in Tanzania, Zambia, Botswana, the Zambezi Valley, the vastness of central Africa, and a few other spots. But these wild areas are shrinking fast. Game ranching has saved wildlife in Namibia and South

Africa, and I see the concept spreading. It will save most species and ensure quality plains game hunting so long as there are hunters to support the industry. But the nature of game ranching is such that you can't track elephant and buffalo, and you can't hear lions roar on limited acreage. The Conservancy is different; it's privatization on a grand enough scale that the full range of African wildlife can coexist.

A driver from the ranch picked me up in Harare and drove me down, a matter of about three hours on good roads. I hadn't come in from this direction before, so the drive was unfamiliar. It wouldn't have mattered; after so many years I recognized nothing until we arrived at Roger and Anne Whittall's house. It was much the same, sort of, but the trees were bigger and there were more outbuildings. In the 1970s, the height of the bush war, the house, situated in a bad area, had been a fortress. Back then the clients stayed in guest rooms at the headquarters–it was the safest place, especially at night when large groups of terrorists were crossing the area into Mozambique and into tribal trust lands to the east across the Save. I had assumed that, as before, I would stay in the house, so I was confused when, after a quick visit with Roger and Anne, they introduced me to my PH, Cuan McGeorge, and asked if I was ready to go to camp.

"Sure," I said, but I was thinking, "What camp?"

Staying at the ranch was ancient history. Roger had built several satellite tent camps at scenic spots. Mine was the Save Camp, right on the banks of the Save River's broad, sandy channel–dry at this time of year. It was perfect and beautiful and exceptionally well organized. There were wall tents for clients and hunters, and a thatched lounge and dining area. A few yards away was a neat kitchen area, then staff quarters and a cement slab with a game pole for initial meat and trophy care. Water was gravity-fed from an elevated tank, with an elevated-drum hot water heater feeding into a shower. The camp was designed to be more or less self-sufficient, though just a half-hour from ranch headquarters, and it was set up to function smoothly with minimal staff. We had Jiros to cook and Mac to do laundry and camp chores, while Gudzira and Lymon were trackers and skinners. After caping and initial salting, trophies were delivered to ranch headquarters for final preparation. The ranch headquarters provided vehicle maintenance as needed, and vegetables and fruits from Humani's gardens and orchards supplied the larder. By using existing facilities Roger was able to keep the costs down, and this minimal crew did a great job. I'm sure I've never had better meals than Jiros concocted, nor have I been in a camp that was more smoothly run. The interesting thing is that Roger's prices, at least in 1995, were extremely low for the level of service and the atmosphere. His goal was to supply the experience of a tented wilderness safari at ranch safari rates, and that's exactly what he provided.

The game situation had changed dramatically, too. Roger had spent years developing Humani's game, starting long before the Conservancy was even an idea, so what I was seeing was, if all goes well, the future of the Conservancy—a bright future.

The elephant were extremely visible; we saw herds every day, and the elephant were gentle and clearly undisturbed. And of course there was lots of plains game. Kudu and impala were everywhere, and most days I would see wildebeest, zebra, warthog, bushbuck, and duiker. Other species were present, but many were in the building phase. Also, Zimbabwe's lowveld is heavy thornbush with few broad vistas. Unless a species is extremely plentiful or you go looking for it in the right spot you're unlikely to see it. Roger had introduced nyala and reintroduced waterbuck, with good breeding herds of each; we saw a few waterbuck in the riverine, but never saw (nor looked for) nyala. I know there were good eland present as well, but we never saw any. Chances are we wouldn't have seen any buffalo had we not gone looking for them, but that was our first order of business.

Cuan McGeorge is another very young Zimbabwe hunter—lean and quick, disgustingly polite, and extremely competent. He and Angie Angelos are good friends, though they hunt for different outfits. Between Jasper Samaras in Tanzania, Angie Angelos in Zambia, and now Cuan McGeorge I was starting to feel like a fossil, but if these three are at all typical of today's young PH's, then there just might be a bright future for African hunting. Cuan is himself an avid bowhunter, and his stalking skills and hunting savvy impressed me tremendously.

We had a great buffalo hunt that first day, though we didn't shoot anything. As usual it began by checking water holes for tracks. We found them at midmorning, a herd of thirty or so, and tracked them up readily. Then the fun began. The herd was resting–not bedded tight yet–in a patch of heavy brush. The wind was steady and perfect; we stalked in first one way and then another, looking for a good bull.

The herd remained exceptionally cooperative. We worked them for a long time and from several angles, closing within thirty yards of the nearest animal several times. We found a couple of bulls, but nothing fully mature. However, the thorn was very thick and the buffalo were blanketed in black shadow. We were still pretty sure we hadn't seen them all.

Cuan led us a bit farther to the right to give them our wind. That did it; the dark glade erupted with moving buffalo–more than we'd thought. They stampeded out of the cover and we ran with them, cutting back to the left to remove our scent. The herd stopped after a short run and milled in a grassy clearing, confused. Now we could see them. There was a mature bull on the right side, but its horns were flat and ugly. Ah, there was a better bull back behind it–hard boss, and the side we could see indicated a reasonable spread and good curl. It turned its head and there was something wrong; at first glance it looked like its right horn was freshly broken and hanging down alongside its forehead. Too bad.

We kept looking. There were a couple of young bulls, probably the ones we'd seen earlier, but that was it. By now the herd was moving off slowly and we kept looking in case we'd missed one. The broken-horned bull stood clear for a moment and we realized its right horn wasn't broken, but a freak. It grew straight down alongside its head like an upside-down eland horn, while the boss and left horn were completely normal. Then the herd was running again and we let them go.

That night we sat by the fire and watched the moon play its silver light on the Save's white sand. I'd been thinking about that weird buffalo, and I told Cuan, "I've shot a lot of normal buffalo, and I doubt we'll find a bigger one. I've never seen one like that droop-horn bull before. I think we'd better try to find him again."

There were just a few water holes up that way, and we found fresh tracks readily. The size of the herd was about right, likewise the location and direction; odds were it was the same bunch.

We followed, and in just an hour or so we found the herd bedded in thick mopane. We couldn't see the bulls. In fact, it was so thick we could see only a couple of animals. We started crawling in, but something gave us away and the herd thundered off, smashing branches and leaving a plume of red dust.

We sat down for twenty minutes to let them settle, then followed the tracks. Another hour, and there was a cow lying down, maybe a hundred yards away through a little lane in the mopane. We were fortunate to spot it from so far away, and now our chances were pretty good.

We slipped along on the downwind side, ticking off the cows and trying to find the bulls. They were near the head of the herd, all balled up together in patches of shade. We spotted a youngster, and a bit farther on three big animals were lying together under a clump of trees. One was visible, and it was a mature bull. Cripple-horn must be in there as well. There was a cow off to the right, but closer. The way the wind was blowing we had to crawl in past it and hope our bull was there.

This was open mopane with little underbrush, just hard-baked and very hot red earth between the trees. We crawled slowly from tree to tree on hands and knees and then, to get past that cow, we dropped to our bellies, rifles cradled in our arms. This is hard work at any time, and here the baked ground burned our bare arms and legs.

The three bulls lay very close together in that little clump and it was difficult to define black animal from black shadow. At about sixty yards–with that pesky cow bedded not forty yards to our right–we were certain the right-hand animal was old cripple-horn. But it was hopelessly masked by twigs and brush.

We crawled another ten yards and slid into a small patch of shade. Now the picture was clearer. Our bull was lying more or less broadside, head to the right, with its head turned toward us. The good horn was visible extending out to the left, and I could visualize the crippled right horn coming down alongside its chest. It was as if it had its head propped up with it, and perhaps it did. Its body was obscured by just a bit of brush, and it was still almost impossible to see its shoulder.

Slowly, slowly, ever-mindful of the cow off to our right, we shifted this way and that trying to get a clear shot. The distance was perfect, maybe fifty yards, but the setup was horrible. The best course would be to lie there in the shade and wait until it stood, but it was approaching midday and getting very hot. As soon as the wind started to swirl, that nearby cow would have us and the jig would be up.

Cuan left his rifle in the shade and crawled a few feet to the left, then took a long look through his binoculars. Taking them down, he nodded at me. I slithered out of the shade and onto the burning clay and joined him. "There, you can see his shoulder just over that forked stick."

He was right. I slid the Dakota forward and wrapped into the sling. Even at five-power the bull was still little more than a shaded mass, but with effort I could make out the head and front shoulder. The forked twig served as a perfect aiming point; all I had to do was hold low in its vee–and not hit it–and I should have a perfect heart shot. I put the crosshairs just above the bottom of the fork and squeezed the trigger.

Buffalo erupted everywhere. I had to jump to my feet to reload and Cuan had to dash to the right to retrieve his rifle.

There was no second shot, but some concern about the buffalo streaming by on both sides!

When the hoofbeats faded we started forward, casting in the direction the bull had gone. If we didn't find anything right away we'd come back to look for blood and tracks. There was no need. The bull was piled up fifty yards past its bed, dead in midstride. Cuan's forked twig had provided a perfect mark; the Barnes X-Bullet had broken the on-shoulder and destroyed the top of the heart, then penetrated the off shoulder–good work for a .375 softpoint.

The upside-down horn had apparently grown that way all of the bull's life. It was a great trophy, and of course the real trophy was to hunt buffalo in the Save Valley again. Everything went perfectly, but again I had to question the wisdom of hunting dangerous game with a single-shot rifle. It had made us extremely careful about shot placement–but I don't think I'll try it again.

I'd figured the buffalo would take a few days longer, so suddenly we had time on our hands. Of all the species present in the area, the two that exist in the highest trophy quality are probably greater kudu and bushbuck, which happen to be two of my favorite antelopes to hunt. So we decided to spend the rest of the hunt looking for truly huge examples of either.

I never shot a kudu on that trip, but I was definitely in the right place to look for one. We turned down dozens of perfectly shootable bulls–some very big–but we just never found the right one. One huge bull had one perfect horn in the mid-sixties, but the other horn was a bit shorter and mismatched. Another big bull gave us just a glimpse from the road, and we tracked it for a mile or so and caught it feeding in some heavy cover. If I had really needed a kudu, this would have been a dandy. It was heavy-horned and wide and we agreed it was about fifty-three or fifty-four inches, not less–a superb kudu. But I had the luxury of a few days to look for the bull of a lifetime, so we walked away from it.

We did see two bulls that possibly reached the magical sixty inches we'd set as our goal. Both were with cows. They gave us quick running looks only, and sharp-eyed cows kept blowing the whistle on us when we tracked them up. Both times we eventually acknowledged defeat and walked away, thinking we'd seen the kind of bull we sought, but never knowing for sure.

We had better luck with bushbuck. One morning we walked out from camp to still-hunt some thick riverine along the Save–not a bad place for big kudu and perfect for bushbuck. This was how Cuan the bowhunter liked to hunt; we moved very slowly along a series of trails, and at one point had a very nice kudu bull dead to rights at ten yards.

A little while later I saw a bushbuck run through a patch of grass just off the trail. Size was indefinite, but for sure it had horns. I thought it had gone on, but we proceeded very slowly to a thick wall of vines and thornbush at the end of the grass. A bushbuck barked, seemingly right behind the screen. I motioned to Cuan that we should stand still.

Long seconds passed while we tried to stare through that tangle of vines and thorns. A bushbuck barked again, very close, and then I saw movement behind the screen. It was just the twitch of an ear, but with that I could separate out the face, white neck markings, and outstanding horns.

The body was covered by thick branches, but it was just a matter of feet away from me. Then it took a step and vanished. That step took him into Cuan's "window." He pulled me to him, and through the fork of a double tree trunk I could see the bushbuck's white neck markings, head thrown back. I raised the .270 and fired, holding below the neck where I thought the shoulder must be. It crashed away at the shot, but we found it a few yards farther on, a lovely bushbuck with unusual lyre-shaped horns, like a miniature sitatunga.

Obviously there was much hunting that could have been done in such a place. Cuan and I shot an impala for the pot one evening, and on the last day I shot a zebra–my buddy, Joe Bishop, had asked me to collect a skin for him. Mostly, though, the great thrill was just to see Humani, and to imagine what the Conservancy would look like in a decade. Superb hunting remains in Africa at this writing–but in the Conservancy I see for the first time a promise of some real Africa in the future.

21 THE CONGO BASIN

Africa's broad forest zone is the Africa that hunters–all outsiders, for that matter–know the least. The humid equatorial forests that comprise the rainshed of the huge Congo River occupy something like a fifth of the continent, stretching west along the equator from Uganda to the Atlantic and several hundred miles north and south. Countries included in this forest belt are southern Sudan, the Central African Republic, and Cameroon; Zaire, Congo, and Gabon; and small states along the bulge of West Africa from Benin to Senegal.

The forest is not uniform throughout this vast region, but the game is remarkably constant given Africa's wonderful specialization and diversification among its ungulates. Depending on the density of the forest or the presence of clearings, familiar species such as waterbuck, bushbuck, warthog, and even lion and leopard may be encountered throughout the forest zone.

There are buffalo and elephant throughout, generally smaller subspecies adapted to the forest, but some areas are known for big tuskers. Today some forest areas undoubtedly also hold big elephant that have retreated from more vulnerable habitats. Little elephant hunting–and no hunting of big tuskers that I'm aware of–remains in the forest zone. And certainly there are better and much easier places to pursue the various thornbush and savanna species that intrude into the forest.

It's the specialized forest species that most fascinate hunters, and make penetrating the forest worth the effort. Most of the forest species seem to occupy very broad ranges, although there are exceptions. The okapi, never sport-hunted, seems confined to the Ituri Forest. Pygmy hippo seem restricted to West Africa's coastal forests. Some varieties of forest duikers seem quite localized, and it's even possible some duiker subspecies remain unidentified. But most of the forest prizes occur throughout the region, with densities varying somewhat.

The bongo, that large, blocky, burnt-orange, spiral-horned antelope, occupies a huge range across Equatorial Africa. Secretive and cover-loving, the bongo is quite plentiful in some areas. Usually much less common than bongo but sharing its wide distribution is the forest sitatunga. Then there's the big yellow-backed duiker and all the other forest duikers. And the forest pigs–the nomadic giant forest hog and the red forest adaptation of the bush pig. All game is scarce enough in the forest that most times you will see nothing, but at any time you could see any of the forest prizes. The trick is to stay alert during those long, hot days of seeing nothing.

This was my third safari with *Les Safaris du Haut Chinko;* the first two had taken me into the savanna woodlands along the Upper Chinko River in the northeastern C.A.R.. This time we would hunt the forests well to the southeast, along the Mbari River, a tributary to the great Oubangui River that divides the C.A.R. from Zaire and then Zaire from the Congo before it feeds into the mighty Congo River.

My hunting partner, Tucson businessman Sherwin Scott, is a trophy hunter's trophy hunter. He's interested in only the best, but unlike so many that profess such discipline but fail to show it, Scotty is serious–he's perfectly happy to come home empty-handed, happier than he would be had he settled for a trophy that fell short of his high standards.

After at least a couple of years of discussions, Scotty had booked with *Haut Chinko* in the eastern C.A.R. for a couple of reasons. First, while the eastern C.A.R. almost certainly lacks the concentrations of bongo found to the southwest toward southern Cameroon, the largest trophies have generally come from the east.

Second, Scotty wanted to hunt bongo by tracking, without dogs. I agreed with both of his reasons and added another: I had already hunted twice with these people, and I knew and trusted them.

Scotty and I agreed that he would hunt with Rudy Lubin, who had twice been my PH. We felt Rudy knew the area best and might give Scotty–who's pickier than I am–a slightly better chance for a big bongo. I would hunt with Jacques Lemaux, also a twenty-year veteran of hunting in the C.A.R. and, at least in my view, every bit as good a PH as Rudy.

Scotty and I joined up in Paris and made an all-night flight into Bangui. Jacques met us there; he'd just come back from a midseason break at home in northern Italy. Within the hour we were headed east by twin-engine charter, destination a dirt strip at the village of Yalinga. Rudy would be there to meet us and would whisk us to our new home, a hard five hours south along an old French road–much of which had just been reopened by Rudy.

Over the next three weeks Scotty and I spent a lot of time discussing hunting in general and bongo hunting in particular. I've already mentioned that we, by choice, were avoiding the use of dogs. Dogs, with the right training and handling, can be used to trail and bay up bongo much as they can with bear and wild hog. Use of dogs is not surefire, but it is very successful. I don't have anything against it, especially since it's one of few techniques that allows a good look at the bongo before shooting. But we elected a hunt without dogs for pure aesthetics; tracking bongo on foot is the classic way to hunt this elusive animal. Also the least successful. For it to work we needed two things: Plenty of bongo to follow and plenty of rain to keep the tracks fresh and the forest quiet.

At first it seemed we had what we needed. A hard thunderstorm pelted us as we approached camp from Yalinga, and the next morning, the first hunting day, both Scotty and I, hunting in different directions from camp, had fresh tracks to follow.

I never caught up with my bongo; its tracks eventually led into a grassy meadow and became hopelessly mixed with the tracks of a cow herd. Scotty had better luck. They caught up with a small herd in open gallery forest, saw the bull clearly, and decided to pass him. He was about twenty-six inches, a nice, mature bull I would have died for–but it seemed an auspicious beginning.

The rain became more erratic and eventually it quit altogether. By the midpoint of the safari I already knew we were in trouble. Then our campfire discussions waxed more eloquent on the pros and cons of using dogs–and the pluses and minuses of pioneering new country.

This was new country for Rudy and Jacques as well as for Scotty and me. Rudy felt meat poaching was taking its toll in his old bongo area, so he'd done some prospecting and come up with this area. It had been hunted before, by the famous French hunter Claude Vasselet, back when the C.A.R. and Chad were combined into the massive colony of Oubangui-Chari. Rudy figured no safaris had been here for twenty-five years.

A quick scouting trip had yielded bongo tracks and a couple of sightings at a nearby saline, so Rudy had opened up the road a bit and built camp in a small natural clearing near the Mbari River. Being the first safari into an area sounds wonderful, but isn't always. When things get difficult–in this case, through lack of rain–there is no corporate knowledge of game movement to fall back on. The old north-south French road was the only road, and we started the hunt with knowledge of just four salines.

These natural salt licks are a common occurrence in the Central African Republic–and perhaps throughout the forest zone, but I can't speak to that–and wherever they occur they serve as a magnet for the forest's widely dispersed game. The location of salt licks is critical knowledge, passed down through generations of local hunters. Some of Jacques's and Rudy's trackers were in this circle, so we knew four of these secret spots, but what would happen when we'd tracked the bongo at these salines?

Four places to hunt is very few for a two-by-two twenty-one day safari, and before too long Jacques and I were exploring. We would study the old French topo map and find interesting hill masses or perhaps the headwaters of a stream, then we'd plan routes and enter the latitudes and longitudes from the map into the GPS as waypoints. This was technically transition forest, with fingers of savanna here and there that were open enough to allow the GPS to "see the sky." These savannas were shown in white on the map while the forested areas were in green. Although decades old, the map proved surprisingly accurate. In large measure we could navigate from savanna to savanna, avoiding the tedious, frustrating, and strength-sapping forests unless necessary. In this fashion we covered a lot of ground, and I saw more genuine utility in the GPS than I have seen since it appeared on the scene during the Gulf War.

We also found some very interesting things. An hour's drive north and an hour's walk west, tucked down in a steep-sided ravine, was a little saline. This one we knew about, but on our visits there the only tracks were bushbuck and waterbuck. On some impulse we consulted the map and planned a cast that would take us to a watercourse a couple of miles farther west, then south, and eventually back to camp on foot–a long and typically ambitious day's hunt. We found a new salt lick pounded flat by many buffalo; there were herds living right there. Farther along we found a valley being frequented by many elephant, and there was large bull spoor among the cow tracks. But on that entire broad swing we never found a bongo track of any age, which gave us pause.

That salt lick down in the ravine never held a bongo track during our safari, although we checked it several times. The other three known salt licks all produced well. Sort of. There really weren't enough good licks to go around, so we had to trade off until each team started finding its own favorite spots. The northern lick, the one from which Jacques and I had tracked bongo the first morning, had fresh tracks every time it rained, and it held waterbuck, buffalo, duiker, and bush pig in the area as well.

The southern salt lick was a broad pan two hundred yards across and four hundred long. It held bongo tracks somewhere along its perimeter almost every day, at least until every bongo in the neighborhood had been tracked and jumped. Waterbuck and bushbuck could be seen there every morning and evening–usually the same ones. Eventually we realized one of the bushbuck ewes was actually a female sitatunga, which explained some odd tracks we'd been seeing.

Jacques and I came to think of the northern lick as ours, while the southern lick belonged to Rudy and Scotty. Naturally, each team thought the other had the better spot . . . and we poached in each other's territory on the slightest pretext.

Forest hunting is very hard, frustrating work–hard on the body, but harder on the mind. Jacques and Rudy have done many forest hunts together, and no doubt have said "never again" each time, but they're actually a very good team, proven by the fact they've hunted together for many years without once shooting each other. Scotty and I, too, have known each other the best part of twenty years, but we had never shared difficult hunting conditions.

Sherwin Scott is a great lover of the English language with all its nuances. My degree is in English, but I pick up a new word or two every day I'm around Scotty. He's also a very tough and dedicated hunter. He put up with serious heat rash, a bad back, and a covey of blisters without any whining. But–a rare thing for Scotty–he'd get awfully quiet after a particularly tough day. You get to know someone well during a hunt like this; it's probably a tribute to both of us that we're still speaking and quite willing to do it again!

One advantage was that we did have a fine camp to return to and relax in. It was a neat cluster of thatched huts, essentially a mirror image of Rudy's old camp on the Upper Chinko, simple and comfortable. It sat under a giant mango tree, one of the hallmarks of the French colonial roads. At least every few kilometers you'll find huge mango trees along these roads, planted by design or accident at least a half-century ago. Our camp mango tree was a monster, and its fruit was ripe at this time of year. Fresh mangos were a welcome treat, but every few minutes, day or night, we'd hear the *snick* of a stem breaking, then a long *swish* and *plop* as a mango fell to earth.

Between preemptive poaching and salt lick roulette, it came to pass that Scotty shot his bongo on "my" northern lick. And quite easily, as such things go. They picked up bull tracks at first light and followed slowly, slowly through the very thick forest that surrounds the lick. Then they came into interspersed belts of forest and savanna, with bull bongo tracks running ahead straight and hot like a torpedo. They found it in a little savanna, feeding on terminalia, and they had all the time in the world as it launched toward the cover it would never reach. He was a nice bull, but the real tragedy was that while I would have been delighted with it, it wasn't the bull Scotty was looking for. It had the shape of a big bull with parallel tips–but it wasn't.

Faces were long that night, and never quite recovered. The forest gets to you. Unfairly, even absurdly, Jacques and I regarded Scotty's bongo as *our* bongo, and that Scotty wasn't satisfied with it only added fuel to the fire. Physical stress, unrelenting heat, and human greed are a poor combination. All things considered, we worked our way through it pretty well.

Mind you, there was no basis for my jealousy. Scotty shot his bongo at "my" saline, while on that day Jacques and I tracked bongo at "his" saline. His saline never yielded a bongo for either of us, but it did give me a neat old buffalo.

These are "forest buffalo" in that they live in the forest, but they're a great distance removed from true dwarf forest buffalo in both geographic distance and appearance. The herds are a mix of black animals and reddish-brown individuals, with the older bulls most often being black. The horns are more the short, curved "bush cow" horns of the forest, *sans* boss, but they're larger in the body than the all-red dwarf buffalo. Technically these are northwestern buffalo, the same variety as in the savanna country where I'd hunted giant eland. But these are clearly farther along in the transition to dwarf buffalo, and in any case I hadn't shot a buffalo up in the savanna. I'd told Jacques from the start that we needed to do a buffalo whenever convenient.

We saw quite a few, always early in the morning on a day that promised bongo. Then, after tracking a bongo from Rudy's saline and jumping it several times–without actually seeing it–we broke off at midday and found our way back to the saline. There was a herd of buffalo at the far end–hardly a quarter-mile from the truck! This was not only convenient, it was too good to pass up.

We made a quick stalk and Jacques pointed out the black bull among the reddish cows and youngsters. They were across a little lagoon, in some deep grass at one end of the saline. I had to wait until the bull stepped clear of a cow, and then I shot it where the neck joins the shoulder. It was down so quickly I didn't know what had happened; only that, in the panic that followed the shot, I could see only brown and red buffalo, nothing black. It had dropped behind a bit of grass, and we were able to back the Toyota right to it and load it whole.

There was yet another salt lick we considered neutral ground. It was the very devil to get to, and I have no idea how any humans knew of its existence. Rudy had chopped a little track for a few miles along our camp river, then staged a dugout canoe. Across the river an old elephant trail wound through the dense riverine growth until the forest opened a bit. And then a series of game trails led through mixed forest for nearly an hour. Finally, in the middle of a thick grove, a big saline suddenly opened up. This one was a classic depression scooped out by eons of elephants, although in the current absence of numbers of elephant the center of the saline was now a tangle of thick bush. Rudy maintained he'd seen bongo tracks there while scouting, but we never did.

The first time we checked it the depression was full of buffalo, but we hardly needed a buffalo this side of the river and so far from the truck. Of greater interest were the fresh, rounded, and shockingly big tracks of giant forest hog.

Twenty years earlier, while hunting buffalo on Mount Kenya, Willem van Dyk and I walked into a small herd of those impressive and elusive porcine monsters. Of course I didn't have a license for one. I had even asked about them when Willem and I bought our licenses at the game department offices in Nairobi. Willem had said, quite correctly, that the chances of seeing forest hog were too slim to justify the purchase. So for twenty years I've hated African licensing systems that make you project what you might or might not run into . . . and for twenty years I'd wanted a giant forest hog.

Over the course of dozens and dozens of C.A.R. safaris, Jacques Lemaux has taken seven or eight giant forest hog, which probably qualifies him as an expert. These creatures occupy a large range, from Ethiopia and the Kenya highlands discontinuously all the way to West Africa, but they are certainly more scarce than bongo and much more difficult to hunt on purpose.

Jacques reckoned the hogs would return to this saline each day until the mud dried–the question was, at what time of day?

We hit them on the third or fourth try, at about four o'clock in the afternoon. We were ready, mainly because you must always *stalk* a saline, not just approach it. Anything from bongo on down could be standing there–at any time of the day. This time we'd seen fresh bush pig tracks on the way in and we'd heard a piglike grunt just before we reached the lip of the depression. We were ready, but not for a family group of giant forest hog. Jacques instantly pointed out the big male and I shot him just as soon as I could get the crosshairs to steady. The .375-caliber X-Bullet dropped it in its tracks, and then *another* unseen boar, one that we hadn't seen before, came up and rooted at him!

Jacques grabbed my camera and took off, saying, "Cover me!" Regrettably, he didn't know how to operate the zoom lens, but even so he took some extraordinary photos of one of Africa's most elusive animals.

Scotty tried several times to get that second boar, but to no avail. Perhaps his luck was limited to bongo. Or, more probably, he'd used up his forest hog fortune–he'd shot a huge boar two years before while hunting Derby eland with Fred Duckworth.

Jacques and I also had a lot better luck calling duikers, but we worked at it pretty hard. If we broke off a bongo track we'd make several calls on the way back, and often we'd go out in the evening just to call duikers. Jacques was a whiz at it, better than his trackers. Over the course of the hunt we called up many blue duikers and three or four yellow-backed duikers. I shot the first of these, a fine specimen that came crashing in, then stood behind a thick, brushy screen. I had to guess at the body, but I guessed close enough. The yellow-backed duiker is hardly a beautiful creature, but as the largest of the duiker group it's rightly a forest prize.

I also shot a couple of blue duikers to be barbecued whole, a great delicacy. There were many blue duikers, and we called in more than a dozen. With duiker calling, quick flashes is about all you get–just seeing them, let alone shooting, can be enormously difficult. I did not get a Weyns duiker, a midsize orange duiker found only in that general area; we saw a quick flash of one once, but that was it. Although you may call many times for each yellow-backed duiker that responds, due to their size shooting one that comes in is relatively simple, and even a deaf old shooter like me can hear them crashing in. On the other hand, although you'll call in far more blue duikers, getting a shot ranges from difficult to darn near impossible–sort of like trying to catch a fly with your hands. You hear a little scratching in the leaves, and then a tiny form darts through and is gone. Or perhaps it comes slowly and you can see an ear twitch. Then you have a chance.

I enjoyed the calling as a diversion from endless walking through the forest. Scotty wasn't crazy about it, but he's better able than I to focus his efforts, and all he really cared about was bongo. For what it's worth, the sound used to call duikers is a high-pitched mewing created by pinching the nostrils and mewing deep in the throat. Jacques's tone was deeper than the trackers', and he called in all the yellow-backs that responded. Our youngest tracker, calling at a much higher pitch, had great success with the blue duiker. Perhaps we simply didn't have the tone right for in-between-size duikers like the Weyns.

I did not get a bongo. A purist might feel I'd have done better had I foregone the duiker calling and ignored buffalo and forest hogs and such. I don't think so, but perhaps. We did no other hunting on any day until we had either failed to find fresh bongo tracks or we'd exhausted the tracks we found. The decision about what to hunt is a very personal one, and in Africa, with so much variety, not an easy one. In terms of preference, that's up to you. But in terms of hunting strategy, there's a fine line between being sidetracked to the detriment of the main pursuit, and just plain being stubborn.

In my younger days I had trouble obtaining both lion and leopard. Part of the fault was mine, because I wanted to do everything when I should have been concentrating on checking bait. On my first trip to the C.A.R., however, I had an opportunity to shoot almost every species present in the savanna, but I shot nothing because all I wanted was a Derby eland. I got no Derby eland, hence got nothing. That's well and good, but especially in my business it's hard to write stories about nothing–and there's a very limited market for stories about failure.

So I wound up without a bongo, but I got a very nice bag of forest game as a consolation prize. Mind you, we didn't shoot up the countryside, and I don't think the success we enjoyed impacted on the lack of a bongo. We could have shot more. Scotty and I each saw good bushbuck, waterbuck, and oribi, and I missed a big warthog while headed back to camp one midday. And then there were the lion.

We heard lion from camp several nights running. Judging from the sound, there were two different males, a long way off and some distance from each other. Then one morning Jacques and I drove right into them, two males, reasonably maned, definitely mature. This was an "open" area, meaning no quota established, and the C.A.R. has an open license. Whether I could have shot both lion is questionable, but for sure I could have shot *one* if I'd wished.

One ran in front of the truck and into some thick stuff; the other stood in some brush less than a hundred yards away and looked at us. It was tempting. If Mother Nature offers a gift like this, it's poor policy to kick sand in her face. But this was too much of a gift. These were nice lions, but not huge, and a chance encounter from a vehicle is a poor way to take a lion. It wasn't a lion hunt and I couldn't make it a lion hunt–so we drove on, continuing the search for bongo tracks.

The hunting was not as physically demanding as I'd expected. It was hot, but not unbearably so–especially in the forest's shade. There was plenty of walking, but the pace was slow and the terrain fairly gentle. Probably the worst part was the constant bending and twisting to get under and around the vines, and the taller you were the worse it was. Scotty is several years older than I, but also a fitness buff. Other than bouts with a chronic bad back, he also had no serious problems. Flying insects were not the problem I'd anticipated, but there are more varieties of biting ants than I'd dreamed existed. Long sleeves and long trousers are the proper dress, despite the heat.

The biggest challenge was the mental exercise of staying alert and going on, hour after hour, and day after day.

Jacques and Rudy have both been quite successful at tracking bongo–not 100 percent, but much better than the fifty-fifty they achieved with us. Both agreed it depended on the rain, which left our part of the forest right after Scotty got his bongo, only to resume the evening before we departed. Jacques amended that by saying the bongo hunt usually unfolded in stages: "First we find tracks. Then we make contact. Then we see the bongo. And then we shoot him."

Tracks were no problem. Phase two was also simple. Several times a shift in the fickle midday breeze or the noisy forest floor gave us away and we heard bongo jump from their beds and crash off through the forest. That's making contact.

We even progressed to seeing the bongo. Once. Sort of. We were tracking a lone bull with huge tracks, and I think we'd already jumped it twice. I didn't expect it to stop for a while yet. Okay, I'll admit it–I wasn't as ready as I could have and should have been. We were in a patch of reasonably open hardwood forest, with perhaps twenty yards' visibility. The bongo jumped at thirty or forty yards and quartered away across our front from left to right. I never really saw it; I saw movement and perceived an orange flash. The gun was coming up, front sight snarled in a vine, but it was much too late.

I don't think anybody could have shot that bongo–I *know* I couldn't have. That's Jacques's phase three, *seeing.* We never got to phase four. Partly that's a matter of averages and percentages. Jacques figured, honestly, that if we could track ten bulls we'd get a shot. I'm sure we tracked seven or eight, but the rains left us before the law of averages turned my way.

Oh, but we were close. After the rains quit and after we figured we'd tracked and jumped every bongo using our salt licks, Jacques and I studied the map trying to figure where some of those bongo might have gone. There was a hill mass, really a mountain, between the southern salt lick and the old French road. We did our GPS plotting and we walked to that mountain three days before the safari ended. We found a buffalo trail which took us to a little water hole. Bingo! Bongo tracks, probably a day old.

Rain is essential to keep the forest quiet enough to approach game, but fresh rain is also critical for aging tracks. Humidity and heavy dew make it very difficult even for our great trackers to tell yesterday's tracks from today's–unless it has rained. Without rain, we followed day-old tracks more than once.

This day we followed these tracks for a while, not believing they were fresh but desperate to learn what the bongo were doing. These tracks led to a bongo cathedral. For a hundred yards along an old elephant trail the ground was torn up–it was a saline, but a bongo saline, undisturbed by elephant and buffalo, pounded and pawed by bongo alone.

As soon as we found it, we left it, hoping for rain that never came. Those last few days of the safari the skies tormented us, building through sweltering afternoons to towering thunderheads on one horizon or another. Then it rained–somewhere–but never where we were. On the last day, with nothing to lose, we returned to our bongo cathedral. But of course they hadn't returned. Just like us, they were waiting for the rain.

After forty-odd years of building it and watching it grow, Robert E. "Pete" Petersen decided to sell Petersen Publishing Company, the company that owns the magazines I've worked for these last eighteen years. Everybody knew it would happen sooner or later, and the event itself was painless, bloodless, and nearly transparent–at least at my level. But it was a traumatic time for all concerned. It probably escaped those of us who envisioned our rice bowls breaking, but 1996 was a particularly tense year for Petersen himself. It's probably no coincidence that he planned to be in Africa during two major milestones in his life: his seventieth birthday and the final days before Petersen Publishing Company passed to new owners.

A couple of years earlier I'd arranged for us to print several thousand copies of a Zambian-government-sponsored booklet on game management areas, regulations, and wildlife distribution; in exchange, Pete was to receive some license and concession fees. At that time I didn't know whom to recommend in Zambia, so after making the initial introductions I stayed out of it.

22

BANGWEULU AND KAFUE

Pete wasn't able to go that year, but in 1995 I made a brief reconnaissance safari with Russ Broom to his Mulobezi concession in Zambia's Kafue region, and then to Lake Bangweulu. I knew Russ's organization would be just fine, and it was, but I was tremendously impressed by the country and the amount of game. This time I had an answer when Pete asked about Zambia.

Pete, Ken Elliott, and I met with Russ at the Safari Club convention and worked out the details. Somewhere in there Pete invited me to go along, a surprise but hardly an unwelcome one! We would essentially reverse my '95 safari, starting at Bangweulu and staying for a few days, then going to Mulobezi for the bulk of the safari. Pete would hunt with Russ and Rodgers Kasela; Ken would hunt with veteran Zambian PH Austin Wienand; I would hunt with Angelo Angelos. Artist Doug Van Howd came along to video and photograph the trip and see Zambia for the first time. At some point fairly late in the planning cycle Mrs. Petersen decided not to come, so Pete invited his ranch manager, Gary Williams, to join us. He probably debated about as long as I did.

This made for a most interesting group. I alone had been to Zambia before, but Pete, Ken, and Doug all had extensive African experience–in Pete's case, back to Uganda in the mid-sixties. Pete and Ken both have hunted Africa more or less continuously–every other year or so–for the past twenty years and more. Doug Van Howd spent a tremendous amount of time in East Africa in the 1970s and was even a part-owner of a safari company, but he hadn't returned to Africa in some fifteen years. Gary Williams was experiencing Africa for the first time.

The trip over was like a fairy tale. We took Pete's new Gulfstream IV from Van Nuys, California, to Puerto Rico, overnighted there, then fueled at Recife on the bulge of Brazil. From there it was a quick hop across the Atlantic, landing at Lusaka at daybreak. Austin Wienand was there to greet us, and customs went smoothly.

At this point things started to break down a bit and I was worried. The charter planes to take us to Bangweulu couldn't depart until midday, but we were ready to go *now.* Ministers had changed, so of course the Zambian government was reneging on promised licenses. Dale Lewis, the American director of the Admade program and the guy who had set up the swap, was in Lusaka but apparently lacked the nerve to face us. Lusaka was hot and we were tired. And Russ wasn't there, leaving Austin holding the bag.

Nothing was insurmountable. We relaxed at Austin's house for a few hours while license negotiations continued. Dale Lewis never did show his face, but ultimately all parties compromised and everything worked out. But for several long hours that morning I was seriously regretting helping plan the boss's safari–something I had studiously avoided during the past eighteen years.

In due course we returned to the airport and loaded the planes for Bangweulu. The journey took little more than an hour, stark contrast to the interesting but exceedingly long drive we'd made a year earlier! Austin flew in with us while Angie met us at the strip. Russ had figured two PH's and two vehicles more than adequate for our few Bangweulu licenses, which is why he hadn't been in Lusaka; he planned to meet us in Mulobezi for the rest of the safari. He was right, but it made for a rocky start.

Finally we were there, and a big herd of lechwe awaited us just off the end of the strip. We piled in the trucks and headed for the distant tree line and camp. Externally the camp had changed little, but Angie and crew had been busy: There were now flush toilets and battery-powered electric lights. Russ's last fax had warned, "This camp isn't up to our standards"–but it looked and felt wonderful to our group of tired hunters.

Midafternoon had come and gone; there was little time for unpacking if we were to catch an evening hunt. Ken and Gary went one way with a game scout while Pete, Austin, Angie, and I headed for sitatunga *machans.* En route we stopped to check zero. Pete's Ken Jarrett .300 Winchester Magnum was perfect, as always. My "light rifle" was an experimental 8mm Remington Magnum, put together by Geoff Miller and Norm Bridge at Rogue River Rifleworks as our concept of a long-range elk rifle. At this stage the rifle wasn't quite finished; the stock was about 90 percent completed, the metal was unblued, and the scope only roughly collimated. It took a few shots, but it seemed to respond well.

Pete and I had sitatunga licenses, and that was my only Bangweulu license. Pete and Ken had black lechwe licenses, while Pete and Gary had tsessebe licenses. The lechwe and tsessebe would be no problem, but sitatunga are always a potential problem–especially with just three days allocated to Bangweulu. Austin wanted to start right away, regardless of how tired we were.

There were two *machans* ready, Austin told us, about five hundred yards apart and overlooking different portions of the same maze of papyrus beds. It was September, late in the season, and both Austin and Angie had hunted here within the past month. They had seen big sitatunga from each of these stands. One was easily reached from the road, while the other, though just a quarter-mile away and visible, required a circuitous walk of some three-quarters of an hour. Pete had a knee that was swollen like a balloon and very painful. We were all worried about it, so there wasn't much question about who went to which stand. Turned out to be a great deal for me, not so great for the boss.

The channels of the Lukuzi had changed yet again–perhaps they change every year–so once again I didn't recognize the place until we came to the little fishing village with its round grain bin. Angie said, "It must feel strange to keep coming back to this place." Indeed it did, but surely this would be the last time.

The *machan* was in the same place, although rebuilt for the present season. A year ago we'd written it off as being too close to the village. Then, two weeks later, on the insistence of the game scouts, Angie tried it again and shot a huge sitatunga. In this season several shootable sitatunga and a couple of big ones had been seen, and at least one had been missed, from these stands.

The evening was cool and pleasant, and I doubt we'd been there ten minutes before the first sitatunga appeared. It was a mousey-brown female about halfway between Pete's blind and mine. After it vanished into the papyrus I took some more readings with the Leica rangefinder–I wanted to know how far it was to every clump of papyrus in sight. Angie commented that virtually all the sitatunga that had been seen were crossing some openings between the two blinds; we probably didn't need to worry about the smaller papyrus beds to the rear.

We saw a couple more females, then all was still for a long time. There was plenty of light, but sundown was fast approaching when the bull stepped out. Despite Angie's disclaimer, it came out of a little finger of papyrus behind us; no doubt it had been bedded there all day. It stepped to the edge of the papyrus and stopped, looking out across two hundred yards of clearing. It was sort of broadside but facing away. I think we all saw it at about the same time, and I think we all recognized it. Angie, dead calm as always, just said, "He's good." That it was–very wide tips, thick horns, and a body that looked heavy and powerful. It was the best sitatunga I had ever seen.

I almost had the rifle on it when it started to run. At first I was sure it would stop–the breeze was blowing in our favor, and it had never even looked up. Perhaps it didn't like the open ground or, more likely, it had heard us climb into the blind and was nervous. Whatever, it wanted to reach the safety of the next big papyrus bed. The rifle tracked it while I waited for it to stop. Then I realized it wasn't going to stop, and it *was* getting farther away all the time!

Mild panic set in. The long, heavy barrel got a bit ahead and stayed there and the rifle went off. It went down hard but tried to rise, so I shot it again and yet again. I knew I'd catch grief from Pete over the number of shots, but this sitatunga was worth it!

We had plenty of daylight to find the sitatunga and barely enough to take photos, but it was long past black dark when we staggered into the yellow glow of Austin's headlights with our prize. There stood Robert E. Petersen, the Chairman–grinning from ear to ear with camera in hand. "Turn him a bit. More! That's it!" he said as he snapped flash pictures in the headlights.

The next day was Pete's birthday. I hoped for a sitatunga for him to celebrate with, but it didn't happen, not that day and not during our stay in Bangweulu. He and Austin saw at least a half-dozen bulls, a lot of sitatunga to see in three hunting days. Two or three were perfectly shootable by most standards, but Pete had shot a nice sitatunga in Botswana and wanted a visibly better one. No bulls sighted quite made the grade.

He did celebrate his birthday in fine fashion, though. I went out with him and Austin that day and we looked at several hundred black lechwe before Pete shot a really fine bull. Then we went over to the tree line and repeated the process on tsessebe.

Selecting a black lechwe is a painstaking and frustrating process, but tsessebe are actually worse. Both males and females have horns, and in Bangweulu the herds can run into the hundreds. Eventually a good bull stood clear for just an instant and Pete nailed him. That night the cook made a small and tasty birthday cake, and the presents included a bronze belt buckle from Van Howd in the form of a wide, well-curved buffalo skull and horns. "That's the kind of buffalo I want," said Petersen. But we weren't quite done with Bangweulu.

Next day, while Petersen maximized his time in the swamps, I went out with Angie, Ken, and Gary. Ken had been extremely picky and by now had looked at several thousand black lechwe bulls. That's good, because there are world record heads somewhere in Bangweulu. If you hold out you might find one. Chances are, however, that you'll just get confused, for most black lechwe bulls are of a type, from twenty-two to twenty-four inches. To find one with an extra inch can take a great deal of looking.

We found Ken's bull in a huge herd, finally sorting him out for a clean shot. He was a very fine lechwe, about the same as Pete's, and probably not much bigger, if bigger at all, than any number of bulls Ken had passed. Lechwe are easy to hunt, but very hard to judge. That same day Gary Williams shot a fine tsessebe at a measured 260 yards. It was his first African animal and a very difficult shot in a shifting herd. We all felt bad about the Chief's sitatunga–or lack thereof–especially me, since I'd shot one. But we were all in good spirits and ready when the planes returned to take us to Mulobezi. Even Pete's knee was cooperating, with the swelling seeming a bit less, and certainly no worse.

As mentioned earlier, Zambia requires purchase of specific licenses before the safari. This was easy in Bangweulu with so few species, but it's a nightmare in an area like the Mulobezi. The problem is compounded by simple economics–few of the licenses are inexpensive enough to buy on pure speculation. We had long since made all our decisions. Everyone wanted buffalo. Pete and Ken both wanted sable, Pete had a lion license, and Ken wanted a leopard. Both Pete and I had roan on our list. For common game and baits there were zebra, impala, wildebeest, and warthog tags in some mix, and Pete asked for oribi and duiker so he could use his beloved .22 Hornet.

The only saving grace to Zambia's system is that an unused license can be forwarded to clients on subsequent safaris. (Unused licenses receive a partial refund at the end of the safari, and the ultimate user must still pay the fee.) Since the end of the season was nearing, some of our common game licenses came from this source, and also some good stuff. For instance, Ken had greater kudu on his list, but Russ had a kudu license on hand, giving us an extra kudu which Gary eventually took. I was also supposed to have a leopard license, but my leopard was one of the things that got lost in the game department shuffle. Russ had not one but two eland licenses, so he kept one for Pete and offered me the other, saying, "Why don't you shoot one of our big eland?" Why not?

In general, between our previous decisions and leftover licenses we had a good selection. Mostly we'd chosen wisely, but there were gaps and inconsistencies. For instance, for bait and camp meat we had impala tags. Impala are scarce in Mulobezi and the quality is poor. We got them, but we should have had hartebeest licenses instead. They are plentiful, and I was the only one who had shot one of these Lichtenstein hartebeest. Both Pete and Ken would have shot one, but we had no licenses. We also had no licenses for Crawshay waterbuck, and they were everywhere. Nobody was collector enough to care about mediocre waterbuck, but we actually saw some big ones and couldn't do anything about it. Likewise there were some huge common reedbuck, but no licenses. We didn't do badly, but we should have asked a few more questions. And I should have known better, since I'd hunted the Kafue twice before.

Too late now. We had the licenses we were going to have, and the charter planes were dropping us at a strip deep in Kafue National Park. The drive south to camp was a two-hour mixture of national park and the Mulobezi concession. It was late afternoon and we saw a ton of game, mostly sable, before we showed up at camp at last light.

This was a new camp, built for the season under Austin's direction. The thatched sleeping huts had cement floors, with showers and flush toilets twenty yards behind. We had a long discussion with Russ about which was better–private attached toilets and showers, as he had in his camps in the Zambezi Valley, or separated as he'd done it here. Opinion was split, but this was a super camp for sure. I'd been in enough of Russ's camps that I wasn't surprised, but everyone else was duly impressed. The heat from our initial problems was dissipating quickly now.

Russ had said "go shoot a big eland" as if there was nothing to it. So we did. That first morning we went far to the south looking for buffalo tracks. We found very little sign and saw relatively little game, but at eleven o'clock or so we darn near drove into a herd of eland. Somehow an alert tracker saw them through a break in the brush and stopped us before they heard, saw, or smelled us–a minor miracle with eland. It was a midsize herd moving at an angle across our front, so we bailed out and made a quick approach. This time we bumped them slightly, so we had to back off and let them settle, but from an antheap, too far to shoot, we got a good look as they drifted into thick cover.

There were perhaps fifteen eland and there were three good bulls. One was incredibly long, but it was the youngest of the three and slender in the horn. Another was very massive with a distinctively wide spread, but it wasn't as long. The third was long *and* heavy, though not quite so long as the young bull nor so heavy as the wide one. It was probably the best of the three, but no sane hunter would have turned any of them down.

As they moved off we stayed with them, not really tracking but maintaining loose contact. They were just drifting along, obviously not spooked, and it was late enough in the day that they should lie down soon. Then we could move in.

They fed along slowly for just an hour or so, covering little ground, and then they seemed stationary in a thick brachystegia grove. We maneuvered a bit and finally could make out the thick, wide-horned bull. It was huge in the body, dwarfing the cow it stood next to–and then it lay down. It was facing away at three hundred yards, just visible through a lane in the trees. Only its neck was clearly visible, and I lack the nerve to try a shot like that. So we left the trackers and started crawling. The problem was that, in using cover for our stalk, we lost our window and shooting lane. At about two hundred yards we knew where the bull must be, but we could no longer see it. We crawled a few yards farther and tucked in behind a fallen log. We were discussing where it should be when it suddenly appeared, rising to its feet and walking deeper into the trees.

Now there was a jumble of eland and tree trunks. A second big bull walked in from the right, and I'd lose and regain the gray bulls among the brown cows. Then both bulls stood together, almost invisible, behind a small clump of trees. I dropped the binoculars, rested the rifle over the log, and turned the scope up. I could make out a back line and some legs behind the trees–one of the bulls was facing left, and I felt certain it would step out at any moment. I kept the scope trained on the right-hand edge of the trees, waiting.

There was a nose, then a forehead, and the forehead had the dark skullcap of a rutting bull. Then came the horns–it was the taller of the two old bulls. A huge gray neck with massive dewlap followed, then a big shoulder. I slid the crosshairs to the shoulder, then remembered this was an 8mm, not a .375. I moved back a few inches for a center lung shot and squeezed the trigger.

Instantly there were eland everywhere and there was no chance for a backup shot. Through the chaos I was aware of our bull running right, as it was facing, then reversing and running with the herd. Then I lost it, but Angie didn't. "Jesus, he's down," he said, and that's as close as I ever heard Angie get to excitement.

Indeed it was, down and out in thirty yards from a lung shot. I was starting to like this new 8mm!

Now I had a problem. A huge sitatunga the first day in Bangweulu was one thing. A huge eland the first day in Mulobezi was another. An inside legend at Petersen Publishing–and longtime vice president Tom Siatos's favorite story–was that *nobody* shot bigger animals than Bob Petersen. And remained employed, that is. The legend continued that Tom had gone to great lengths to keep his job. I never really believed this. But, on the other hand, I hadn't hunted with the Chief a great deal. . . .

Well, I still can't tell you whether the legend is true. After all, maybe Pete somehow forgot about the sitatunga. And the eland wasn't much of an issue at all, because when we got back to camp Pete was already there with the damnedest sable I've ever seen. High forties, pushing forty-eight inches, but incredibly thick and carrying the mass throughout, with a beautiful curve. The eland became even less of a potential issue a few days later when Pete shot, no kidding, an even bigger eland bull. Russ hadn't been exaggerating about the area having big eland.

After a day or two we were into the routine, everybody hunting generally but concentrating on his main trophies. Pete was mainly involved with baiting and calling for a lion. Ken shot a lovely sable on the second day, so he turned his efforts to baiting for a leopard. Angie and I spent most of our mornings looking for buffalo tracks and our afternoons looking for roan. Gary traded off hunting with me or with Ken, and was having a ball seeing Africa and stalking zebra and impala. My main thing was roan, and that's not a focused hunt; you just have to cover ground in likely areas, which, for roan, means almost anywhere. So one morning I suggested to Angie that we go get Gary a buffalo.

It turned into one of those picture-perfect hunts you'd hope everyone's first buffalo hunt would be. The big herds were mostly in the park, but there were a couple of good herds watering at one edge of the concession. We checked this way and that, finally finding tracks near a big *dambo.* We circled again to cut the distance and actually ran into the herd with the truck, a rarity in my experience. We backed off quickly, but it was too late; of course the herd ran–but there was certainly no question about the age of the tracks.

There were more than a hundred buffalo, so the tracking was simple. We just walked fast in their scented wake. They ran for a few hundred yards, then slowed to a walk, and in about an hour we had the rear of the herd in sight.

They were walking fast, not feeding much, and they were headed back to the park so we couldn't wait them out. Angie spotted a good bull at the rear of the herd, but they were moving fast enough that we had a hard time getting out to the side without spooking them. On each of a half-dozen looping approaches the bull was covered by cows or moving straight away.

Gary's a heck of a hunter and a fine shot, but he'd never done this before. You wouldn't have known it. On about the seventh try the bull quartered away for just an instant and offered some shoulder. Gary was ready and shot it beautifully, a quartering shot from the last rib to the off-shoulder.

The shot looked perfect, but that isn't much of a shot with the .375, and I'd never seen the new Winchester Fail Safe .375 bullet on buffalo. We waited until the herd cleared, then moved forward. We found the deadest buffalo I've ever seen, no reaction whatsoever to the insurance shot. I suppose Gary was cheated in not having at least a small war, if not a full-blown charge. But a dead buffalo is what is supposed to happen when a bullet that good is placed that well.

We were in an inadvertent game of one-upmanship, caused by us all hunting different directions for different animals and enjoying stunning success. Pete had his share of glory with that huge sable and, later, an incredible eland. Gary should have been in the winner's circle with the first buffalo brought to camp, but Ken upstaged him. He and Austin tracked and shot a truly fabulous buffalo, forty-three inches wide and with massive seventeen-inch bosses–a great buffalo for anywhere and, to my eye, the best of the four buffalo we shot.

However, I'll take my small share of the glory. Gary went out with Angie and me the day I got my buffalo. There really weren't a lot of buffalo in Mulobezi yet, mostly scattered groups of bachelor bulls. A day earlier, after a tracking job that left switched-on buffalo in impossible cover, I even commented to Angie that we might not get a buffalo. He snorted.

That morning we picked up tracks of what we thought were seven or eight (there were actually nine) bulls not far from the site of Austin's old camp, where I'd stayed the year before. We followed, and they took us a very long distance–it was nearly eleven o'clock when a tracker finally spotted a black form up ahead. We circled a bit to get the untrustworthy midday breeze as good as it could be, then started to crawl in.

The buffalo were mostly hidden behind a thick termite mound; we could see one heavy-horned, narrow bull at its base and, on beyond, just glimpses of a couple more bulls. We were maybe 150 yards out. And then the closest bull lay down in plain view. We were hopelessly pinned.

We sat and waited, willing the bull to move before the wind changed. It took an hour, but it finally got up and fed away. Angie and I moved almost immediately, crawling on hands and knees toward a big tree that we figured should cut the distance in half.

We got there and cautiously rose to our knees. We could see bits and pieces of various buffalo feeding in a grassy swale behind the antheap. They seemed to be feeding away, so all we needed to do was wait a few minutes, then slip out to the side and close in. Then something happened, probably a stray eddy of our scent. All the buffalo spooked and dashed away out of sight. Then, before we even had time to discuss it, they came galloping back–right at us.

They were nine bulls running straight at us in echelon, the forward bull on our right, the rear bull on our left, and the other seven strung out in between. All nine were good, mature bulls. In twenty years of being obsessed with buffalo it was the most awesome sight I have ever seen.

The lead bull was exceptional and it had my full attention. It was heavy and wide and had a good curl, and it was also the easiest by far to shoot. Angie and I stood up, then stepped forward from behind our tree to meet them. Then I heard a very calm, very polite, and very commanding voice at my right shoulder say, simply, "Shoot the second one."

He broke my concentration on the lead bull and he was right. I should have seen it myself. The second bull was incredibly wide, with deep hooks and a perfect curl, and the bosses were fine. It was a classic Masailand bull many hundreds of miles from East Africa, and I owe it to Angie's quick eyes and calm voice.

The phalanx of bulls was still 50 yards away, but they seemed to be closing very fast. There was lots of time–except the trailing bulls were gaining and that big boy would be masked in split seconds. The Rogue River .470 came up like a good quail gun, and I focused on the second bull. With the gun swinging, I held just under the curve of the horn where the neck joins the shoulder, just as Russ's dad, Geoff Broom, taught me.

It folded at the shot. Gary, a few steps behind me, swears all four feet were in the air when the bullet hit. I saw the head snap back and the body crash down hard, and then I shot it again with the second barrel, ignoring the other eight bulls that thundered by at ten to twenty yards. It was the most spectacular finish to a buffalo hunt that I've ever had–and at forty-six inches wide with everything else to match, it's at least the second-best buffalo I've ever shot.

Even that blaze of glory didn't last long. That very evening Ken and Austin came in with a very fine tom leopard, and that's kind of hard to top.

I think Gary did it the next afternoon. We had a kudu license for him, and we'd tracked and stalked several bulls without getting a decent shot. Ken had the other kudu license, but he'd shot greater kudu before and was looking for something exceptional or nothing. Gary was easier to please.

Ken had described a narrow-horned kudu with very deep curls that he and Austin had stalked. They'd closed to shooting distance, but despite the obvious length Ken had passed it as being narrow, atypical, and ugly. Angie also knew where this bull was hanging out, and on the next-to-last afternoon we saw it feeding far off across a *dambo* with five other bulls. Gary took my rifle and he and Angie closed to a measured 350 yards. Then, over shooting sticks, Gary broke both shoulders and destroyed the top of the heart of a bull that measured almost fifty-seven inches–a wonderful kudu even if its horns were unusually parallel.

Pete Petersen, the Chief, had his moments in the sun with a spectacular sable and his eland, but in between he was keeping the skinner busy and enjoying life. Zebra, wildebeest, oribi, duiker, impala–but he passed on a reasonable lion because he'd shot better in other years. His greatest personal triumph was probably a one-shot kill on an average-sized impala at 150 yards–*with his .22 Hornet.* When all is said and done, it's really a bullet placement game.

I think it was the next-to-last day that Pete got his buffalo. By then his knee, though still painful, had improved almost miraculously. He and Russ tracked a herd and picked out a very fine bull with a dramatic curl–sort of like the buffalo on the Van Howd belt buckle. He shot it well at 60 yards–then rolled it at 120 yards as it tried to run off with the herd. The rifle was Pete's famous old .460 G&A on a Remington 30-S action, conceived by Tom Siatos and developed by Jack Lott.

With a day or so left we could reflect on a stunning run of success. In Chapter Eighteen I described the Selous Reserve as one of the best general bag areas I know of today. This is the other one. Undoubtedly there are many good areas remaining in Africa. No one person will see and know them all, and I certainly don't claim to, but this area was incredible in this snapshot of time. Due to the ongoing sale of the company, from which Pete couldn't be totally free, we had reduced the hunting days significantly from what was originally planned. We had a night, two days, and a morning in Bangweulu, then just six days and a morning in Mulobezi. In that time, excepting oddities like bush pig and hyena, four hunters working in three directions filled every license available to them, and with very fine trophies. Or, in three cases, we passed up acceptable specimens. Pete didn't get his lion or his sitatunga, but he saw reasonable males of each. Ken didn't get his kudu, but he saw many. In just thirty collective hunting days we finished with four fine buffalo, two big sable, two huge Livingstone eland, a good leopard, an enormous kudu, a very big sitatunga, two big black lechwe, and a host of lesser game. We couldn't have done much better. Oh, yes, we got two roan antelope as well.

The Mulobezi is an odd area. It always has some quantities of most game resident in the area, but it starts to come to life late in the season as the water dries in the park. The time varies from year to year, but I think we were watching it happen in mid-September of 1996. As the hunt progressed there were visibly more sable and more buffalo in the area. And more roan. Zambia is the last place native Angolan roan can be hunted; these big, short-horned relatives of the sable seem to adapt poorly to people and pressure, and their range has shrunk dramatically. Zambia's Kafue still has many, but they're widely scattered and concentrations are hard to find. We saw roan every day, but we never saw even a marginal bull. Until the last day.

On the last morning, for the first time, we saw several bull roan, more than during the entire rest of the hunt. That's partly because that's all we were looking for. But it's also due to the fact the roan were just coming in. In the late morning we saw a lone bull at five hundred yards, then tracked it into some freshly burned forest when it ran. We caught it, dead to rights at one hundred yards–but it wasn't quite there in the horn department. Fill the license or walk away? We walked away.

That afternoon we left camp a bit late, planning to hunt some big *dambos* not far from camp. We'd been seeing cow herds there, and perhaps an older bull had moved in. Maybe Angie's hunch was right, or maybe we just got lucky. We left the road, and there stood a lone bull at the end of a long *dambo.* It seemed in no hurry, so we debated for some minutes. It was not huge, but it was mature and acceptable.

We closed the distance to about 250 yards, and with a dead steady rest over the shooting sticks I just plain missed it. Later I figured out that the scope was shifting slightly under recoil, which at least makes a good excuse. But right then I was sick; I'd blown a picture-perfect end to a great safari.

We checked for blood, and of course there was none. Then we took the tracks, hoping that just maybe the bull didn't know what had happened and wouldn't go far. That's all we could hope for, because by then little light remained.

We tracked it through a thick spot and its running tracks slowed to a walk. Better–but time was running out. Then Angie did a very smart thing. He knew there was another *dambo* ahead, so he left the trackers on the spoor and we forged straight ahead, hoping to catch it standing on the far edge of the next *dambo.* It worked, almost.

The bull jumped in some tall grass on the near edge of the clearing, right under our feet. I'd remembered to turn the scope down and I was reasonably ready. I hit brush with the first shot at thirty yards, then hit it far back, but hard, with the second shot as it flew through grass and saplings. Reloading as we ran, we found it standing in tall grass just ahead. We finished it there, and as dusk gathered around us my second decade of African hunting came to an end.

That, however, was not the end of the safari. Not quite. While the rest of us packed up and took pictures around camp, Pete went out and got his own roan. He shot it at a measured 450 yards with his Jarrett .300 and made it back to camp in time to pack up and head for the airstrip–not that we'd have left without him! And yes, his roan was bigger than mine, which is the way a safari, a story, and even a book should end.

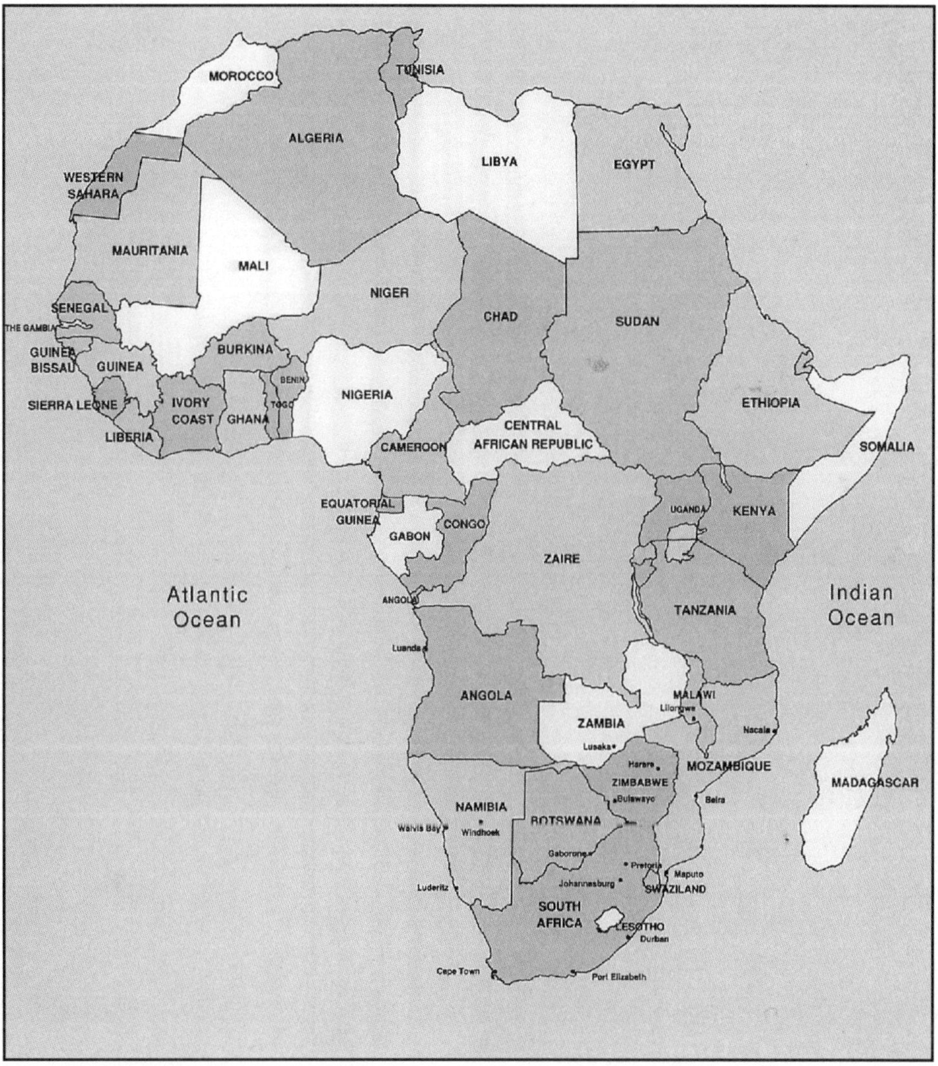
MOROCCO
TUNISIA
ALGERIA
LIBYA
EGYPT
WESTERN SAHARA
MAURITANIA
MALI
NIGER
CHAD
SUDAN
SENEGAL
THE GAMBIA
GUINEA BISSAU
GUINEA
BURKINA
BENIN
SIERRA LEONE
IVORY COAST
GHANA
TOGO
NIGERIA
LIBERIA
ETHIOPIA
CENTRAL AFRICAN REPUBLIC
CAMEROON
SOMALIA
EQUATORIAL GUINEA
GABON
CONGO
UGANDA
KENYA
ZAIRE
Atlantic Ocean
Indian Ocean
ANGOLA
TANZANIA
Luanda
ANGOLA
MALAWI
Lilongwe
ZAMBIA
Nacala
Lusaka
MOZAMBIQUE
MADAGASCAR
Harare
ZIMBABWE
Bulawayo
Beira
NAMIBIA
Walvis Bay
Windhoek
BOTSWANA
Gaborone
Pretoria
Johannesburg
Maputo
Luderitz
SWAZILAND
SOUTH AFRICA
LESOTHO
Durban
Cape Town
Port Elizabeth

Southeastern C.A.R. is a transitional zone, with fingers of savanna intruding into the forest.

Rudy Lubin and Sherwin Scott relax after a long morning of tracking. Lubin's camp was extremely comfortable, and, although very remote, amazingly well-supplied. The hunting was hard, but the living was pretty good..

The yellow-backed duiker is the largest of the duiker group. It isn't exactly beautiful, but it's an interesting and desirable forest prize. This one was called in by Jacques Lemaux.

Although the C.A.R. is very hot country, it's surprisingly cool in the shade of the forest. This is a swampy area kept open by numerous elephant. Big bull spoor was evident here.

Sherwin Scott's bongo. This bull wasn't the size Scotty had hoped to find, but it's a fully mature and very respectable animal—and altogether beautiful.

After the author's giant forest hog went down, Lemaux grabbed his camera and ran forward, getting some very unusual photographs of live giant forest hogs. The one on the left is a boar almost as big as the one they shot.

You never know what you might see when you approach a saline. This is a classic salt lick, a depression made and kept open by game. These are typical buffalo for the area, with some individuals black and some brown.

The buffalo in this area aren't true dwarf forest buffalo, but they're much smaller than Cape buffalo and their horns lack the heavy boss. This bull was black, but all the cows and younger bulls in this herd were reddish-brown.

This giant forest hog was an extremely satisfactory consolation prize in lieu of a bongo. A unique and interesting trophy, the giant forest hog is easily as hard to come by as a bongo, and this is a superb boar.

One of the salines could be reached only by driving for an hour along a track Lubin had cut, then crossing a river by canoe, and then walking for another hour. That anyone knew of it is amazing.

This is the answer to the perennial question of how horned animals go through dense trees. The hunters were tracking a couple of buffalo bulls when the wind shifted and they spooked. The scars on opposing trees near Angelo Angelos's hands show exactly how wide this bull was!

Gary Williams and Angie Angelos approach Williams's buffalo, a perfect one-shot kill with a 270-grain Winchester Fail Safe from a .375 H&H.

When a safari starts off with a sitatunga like this, anything else is pure gravy. This is a very large-bodied and heavy-horned bull, easily the best sitatunga the author has seen after six sitatunga hunts in three countries.

The herds of black lechwe must be seen to be believed. Some herds stretch to both horizons, and you look at lechwe until your eyes grow tired.

The hunters really didn't have enough time for proper cat hunting, but our luck was so good it didn't matter. Hunting with professional hunter Austin Wienand, Ken Elliott took a nice leopard on the first evening in a blind.

The author and Angie Angelos with a wonderful buffalo, taken on the dead run with a Trophy Bonded Bearclaw from a Rogue River double .470. This is the author's second-best-ever buffalo—but the greatest thrill he's ever had hunting them.

Angelos and Gary Williams with a fine kudu, taken at 350 yards with the author's Rogue River 8mm. The horns are deceptive; due to the unusually wide spirals it measures nearly fifty-seven inches.

After missing it at medium range, the author shot his roan on the run at close range in heavy cover . . . on the last night of the safari.

Gary Williams, Ken Elliott, and the author seem pleased with themselves. Well they should; this is an incredible array of fine trophies for a short safari. Bob Petersen's huge sable is in the foreground. Petersen himself is missing because on this, the morning of departure, he was still afield shooting a lovely roan!

The first-day sitatunga couldn't be topped, but this magnificent eland on the first day in Mulobezi certainly comes close. A giant bull in both body and horn, he traveled thirty yards after taking a single bullet from the author's 8mm Remington Magnum.

The author preparing to depart for a twenty-one-day C.A.R. safari. This is about as light as you can go: one rifle in a light Kolpin case, a midsize duffel bag, and a daypack carry-on.

African camps vary tremendously; you can find just about any accommodation you want. Tent camps or thatched huts are the most traditional and are very comfortable.

Most outfitters maintain a radio link with a base camp or headquarters, so emergency messages can be passed and, if necessary, a charter plane can be summoned.

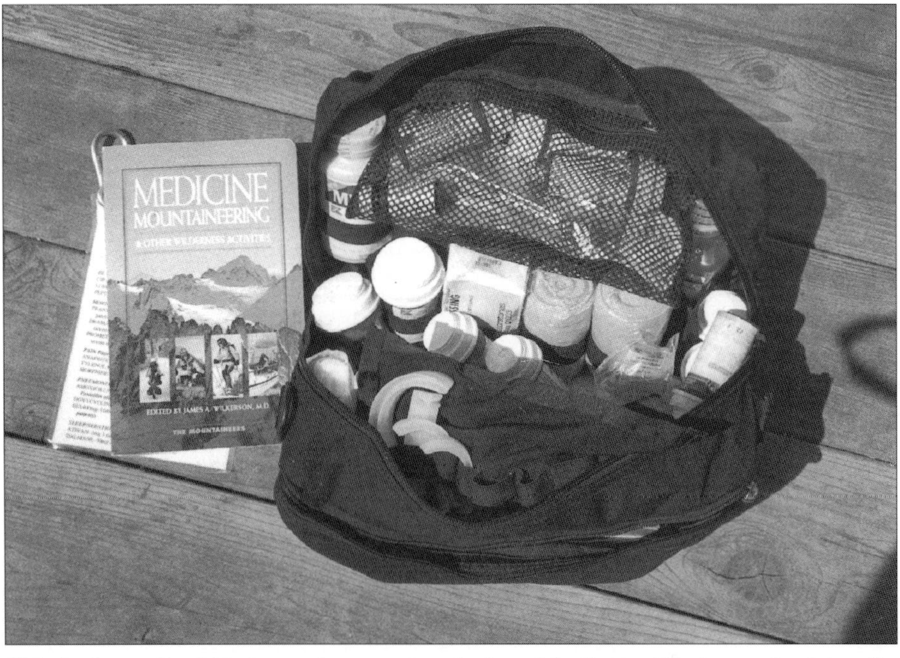

This is the medical kit the author carries, designed by Butte, Montana, physician Dr. Gilbert Preston. Most outfitters have more and better emergency equipment, but having it on hand is still good insurance and reassurance.

One of few major changes since the author wrote Safari Rifles *is the proliferation of .416s. Left to right are the .416 Remington, .416 Rigby, and .416 Weatherby Magnum. An "over .40" is not mandatory, but the .416s are wonderful medicine for the big stuff.*

Artist Douglas Van Howd and Ken Elliott with a black lechwe taken with a 7mm Remington Magnum. Choice of rifles and calibers depends on the country as well as the game; in some areas you may need quite a lot of reach.

Here's one argument against a one-rifle safari. Ken Elliott looks with dismay on the shattered stock of his Ruger rechambered to .450 G&A Short. Fortunately this wasn't his only rifle.

This is a new Rogue River double .470. Many more doubles are being built today than just a decade ago. There is absolutely a place and need for such rifles . . . but keep in mind that an open-sighted big bore is a special-purpose short-range arm.

This a .470 Capstick in full recoil. Big rifles do kick, and if you're going to use them you simply must take the time to learn how to shoot them. Big animals call for big cartridges, but you can't hunt with a rifle you're afraid of. Depending on your own recoil threshold, you *might do better work with a .375.*

Rudy Lubin in his "gun room." Lubin carries a Heym .416 Rigby, a fine and expensive rifle. He's pathological about wiping it down and cleaning it, and even after several grueling seasons in the C.A.R. the rifle still looks new.

Don't overlook scope mounts. The greater the recoil, the more critical the mount becomes. This is a Talley mount, one of very few truly repeatable detachable mounts.

Here are three Woodleigh softpoints and one Woodleigh solid, all recovered from buffalo. The Woodleigh is a bonded-core bullet, and this is the kind of performance good bullets give today.

APPENDIX 1

SAFARI PLANNING TIPS

SAFARI PLANNING

Unlike hunting on some continents, including my own North America, it's relatively difficult to plan a bad safari in Africa. You can do it, but you have to work at it. Game densities and varieties, generally ideal weather, availability of camp staff, and the overall ambiance combine to make most safaris wonderful experiences. Too, professional hunter licensing procedures in most countries are more stringent than anyplace else in the world. Obviously, the more difficult or specialized the undertaking the less the chances for success; likewise, the higher your trophy expectations.

A plains game hunt should be successful for several species. Nobody will ever fill the entire game list, so don't be bemused by "rate cards" that list twenty or more species. Depending on how picky you are and how much time you devote to the more difficult common antelopes, such as kudu and bushbuck, you can expect about an animal every other day or so. Of course, that depends on how hard you work, how well you shoot, and (again) how realistic your trophy size expectations are.

When you get into the specialized hunts, whether for cats, elephant, or the great prizes, such as bongo and mountain nyala, research becomes ever more critical–and no matter how well you do your homework there are no more sure things.

The basic sequence is to first decide *where* or *what* you wish to hunt. If you want to hunt Cape buffalo there are lots of places, but if you want to experience the Okavango Delta or perhaps the Serengeti type of savanna, then your choices are limited. Of course, the more specialized the game the more limited your choices. Again, good buffalo are found in many places, but if you want a good sable you've narrowed the playing field. You've narrowed it further if you're looking for certain combinations of game–and some combinations simply aren't possible, at least not without hunting two different countries. For example, kudu are plentiful throughout southern Africa and can be combined with nearly anything from Zambia southward. However, I'm often asked how to combine gemsbok with sable. You can't do it, possibly excepting the few (and expensive) ranched sable found in South Africa.

If you aren't certain *what* or where you wish to hunt, start with some serious reading. This book and my previous work *From Mt. Kenya to the Cape* give a good overview of the game and conditions in various areas, but neither is intended as a definitive work. You also need James Mellon's *African Hunter*, and you'll find the "country" sections of the Safari Club International record book an invaluable reference.

With basic decisions made, you can start researching a good outfitter who offers the game you want or operates in the area you want to visit. Talk to booking agents, friends, *lots of references;* read books and magazine articles, and make notes. Remember that agents and outfitters you meet at shows want to sell you a hunt. That isn't bad, just fact. Always double-check with *recent* references. Note emphasis. Get recent info before making a decision. Any magazine article–or any chapter in this or any other book–is a snapshot in time. Africa can change quickly. A few areas I've written about herein are better now than when I visited them, but some don't even exist as hunting areas. Get current information.

First and foremost in your search for a great hunt should be a great area, especially if you want quality or difficult trophies. Second–and this I learned from Jack Atcheson, Jr.–is to seek out a great PH. That isn't the same as the outfitter.

The professional hunter is the one who will conduct *your* hunt, and you may not even see the outfitter. As you check references, get a handle on which PH you should ask for. Some few are especially good at cats, others produce lots of big buffalo, and a very few today are good at big elephant–but no PH is equally good at everything! Again, check recent references, for even the great professional hunters are just people. Health problems, marital problems, burnout, substance abuse–professional hunters are no more immune than anyone else.

A hunter's youth is not a negative, nor is age. Enthusiasm counts, and you're always better off with an enthusiastic and eager youngster than a burned-out veteran who is just going through the motions. On the other hand, never discount experience–a PH in his sixties may not hunt harder, but he is extremely likely to hunt smarter!

A couple of personal notes: Due to rapid changes in Africa, many of the younger PH's did not grow up shooting leopards out of the chicken coop and elephants out of the cornfields. If you are inexperienced yourself, give some thought to getting your feet wet with an extremely experienced PH. My strong preference is for a professional hunter who was born in Africa, or at least has spent most of his life there. I go partly to learn, and I think I can learn more from hunters hunting their own turf. However, enthusiasm and initiative do count. Some American and European hunters have done and are doing very well in Africa.

Time of year is important in some areas for some game, but it's uneven. As you gather your "snapshot in time" notes always keep track of the time of season that person was writing or telling about. Some areas need rain to bring in game, while other areas are best when it's dry.

One great rule: Regardless of how your research directs you, *always* talk to your outfitter and make sure he knows what you're looking for and what your expectations are. If possible, talk to your PH as well. If that means investing a couple hundred bucks in overseas calls, don't sweat it–that's the best investment you can make.

PAPERWORK

The red tape is relatively minor, but it does vary with the area and generally increases with an area's remoteness. The more remote the area, the longer the lead time to get it all done. Outfitters would like to collect all the deposits a year in advance, and indeed the best dates with the best PH's may be booked up two years in advance. But to secure gun permits, shots, good airline reservations, etc., you really need a minimum of ninety days' lead time. You can do it in less, but you'll be jumping through hoops and you may run into problems.

I don't want to date this book by providing information that might change, so I will not provide a list of the countries that require visas and gun permits in advance. At this writing Zimbabwe, South Africa, and Namibia are the easiest countries to gain entry into. The most difficult "commonly hunted" country at this writing is Mozambique; getting visas has been convoluted and time-consuming. Somewhere in between are Tanzania, Botswana, the C.A.R., Zambia, and so forth. The best way to handle things is as follows:

1. Start early.

2. Insist on your booking agent/outfitter's assistance and *follow their advice.*

3. Use a travel agent who specializes in or has experience in the continent and region you're going to.

4. Use a visa service.

5. Call the International Red Cross for latest immunization requirements for the area you're going to. Consult your doctor, and plan early–some immunizations, such as yellow fever, may not be readily available.

6. Get all the data and plan your itinerary–in conjunction with your agent or outfitter–before you make travel arrangements. Avoid last-minute changes. Above all, think through your firearms choices before applying for gun permits (if needed). *Do not* attempt to switch serial numbers on gun permits once the permits are issued.

HEALTH CONCERNS

During the winter, when most safaris are conducted, Africa is actually a very healthy place–less so during the rainy season and in forest regions. Always consult your doctor about *your* health, and check with the International Red Cross for the latest immunization guidelines. Follow their advice. And *be honest* with your outfitter and PH about any health problems or physical limitations you might have. Some African hunting is quite suitable for older hunters, or hunters with even severe disabilities (including wheelchair-bound hunters)–but some is not.

Malaria is a very remote concern during the African winter, although a genuine threat during the rains and in the forests. However, *always* insist on a malaria prophylaxis as a precaution. Medications are changing rapidly, so check with your doctor. Note that a North American doctor is unlikely to be an expert on malaria, but he can find out, so go see him early in the planning stages.

In all of my safaris the only time I've been ill was when I gnawed on a piece of elderly biltong in Botswana (one of the healthiest of African countries). Camp food and camp *drinking water* will almost certainly be safe. Absolutely avoid ingesting any water in the shower, etc.–that's what nearly did in Joe Bishop in Ethiopia. In African towns, drink bottled water only and be careful what you eat.

HIV is, regrettably, at least as widespread as you've heard. I'm certainly not qualified to give advice in this area, but you do need to be aware of its presence, especially as you sustain cuts and abrasions from thorns and such. The primary risk, to me, would be the availability of HIV-free blood should the unthinkable happen and you are in a vehicle crash or a wreck with a wounded animal. If your hunting partner has a compatible blood type, that's great. If not, my own plan has been to get to Johannesburg if I were in southern Africa, or to Europe if I'm near the equator. AIDS and our knowledge about it is expanding rapidly, so get current advice from your doctor.

Most camps will have a very complete medical kit, but I carry my own as well. Developed and marketed by Butte, Montana, physician Dr. Gilbert Preston, mine carries a full range of prescription medications, prescribed to me, that would cover most potential emergencies. Of course, these are precautionary. If you require medication, make sure you take an adequate supply–and keep it in your carry-on bag. Likewise take extra eyeglasses if you wear them.

PACKING TIPS

Americans are terrible overpackers, and I'm one of the worst. You need what you need, but the less you can get by with the better. That includes guns; more than two are a real hassle to carry around and look after.

What you *need* includes: rain gear; a warm jacket (and probably a warm cap and gloves) for early mornings in open vehicles; a couple of changes of clothes; comfortable, quiet shoes–and not much more. Emphasize *quiet* with both clothes and shoes, and also choose fabric that will dry quickly. Laundry will be done daily, but heavy fabric like blue jeans may take more than one day to dry. Cotton is generally best, and in most areas green is better than khaki. Camouflage is a "no-no" in some southern African countries, so if you have any designs of taking camouflage clothing, ask before you pack. You should be able to get by with a midsize duffel bag, gun case, and carry-on. Ah, the carry-on.

Imagine–and always assume–that neither your gun case nor your duffel bag is going to arrive with you. Pack your carry-on accordingly. What can't you get along without–or readily borrow or temporarily replace? Medicine, extra glasses, a camera, binoculars, change of underwear and socks, shoes you can walk in, a jacket, shaving gear–think it through. If you're en route to Alaska you may be truly crippled by loss of your gear, but in Africa you don't need much. You should be able to borrow a rifle and carry on.

I've been pretty lucky with bags; the only one that ever got really lost was my duffel bag going into Mozambique. It doesn't happen often, but when you travel far and change planes several times anything can happen. A lost bag shouldn't be a show-stopper.

While packing light's primary advantage is simplified travel, there are also serious restrictions on baggage weight on smaller airlines, plus practical restrictions on charter flights. Getting heavy baggage in can range from frightfully expensive to impossible. In the C.A.R., for instance, you just about have to limit yourself to one rifle. Increasingly, international airlines are limiting passengers to twenty kilograms, or forty-four pounds of baggage. With a two-gun case this is a hard limit to meet. In areas where you need cold weather gear and a sleeping bag you probably can't do it, but in Africa you can if you work at it.

APPENDIX 2

AFRICAN BATTERIES TODAY

Some seven years have passed since I finished writing *Safari Rifles.* Not a lot has changed since then, so I'll take the liberty of referring you to that work for an in-depth treatment of this subject. Some subtle changes do include the proliferation of .416-caliber cartridges, plus a general fascination for big bores in general. There are also many more proprietary cartridges today–the whole Dakota lineup; the Lazzeroni cartridges; the .450 Rigby Rimless Magnum; and new cartridges from A-Square, including their behemoth .577 Tyrannosaur. There are also a great many more doubles being built today, mostly around large-caliber cartridges. There are also some new and better bullets.

One of these days there will be enough new material to warrant a revision of that earlier work. However, the basics of safari batteries have changed very little since the days of Roosevelt (1909), Hemingway (1935), and Ruark (1952): The safari battery, regardless of how many rifles it includes, must cover all the bases, from very small to very large plains game, plus the dangerous game. A big difference is that today's safaris are shorter and more specialized, bag limits are smaller, and although modern transportation is much faster and more efficient, baggage limitations are far more restrictive. Our purpose here is to discuss how modern safaris impact the choice of an African battery.

First off, although I've done it myself and surely will do it again, I cannot recommend any battery of more than two rifles. The only exception would be the lengthy (three weeks or more) classic safari involving several buffalo, both cats, perhaps elephant, and a full range of plains game. Even on such a hunt you could get by with two rifles, or even one, but on a "cost is no object" safari the classic three-rifle battery of a true heavy, a medium, and a light rifle remains valid, if allowed. Zambia, for instance, now restricts hunters to two rifles, regardless of length of safari.

Lengthy safaris are rare today. Far more common, in fact dominating the safari market, are shorter plains game safaris that include *no* dangerous game; and plains game safaris that include buffalo. For the former, you must consider (based on the game list and the rifles you have available) whether you need even a .375–and you certainly don't need anything heavier. For the latter, you obviously need something adequate for buffalo, plus you must be prepared to handle a diversity of plains game at a variety of ranges.

For a plains game safari there's certainly nothing wrong with a .375, especially if eland are on the list. But even if eland is to be hunted, something along the lines of a .33 or .35 magnum will do just as well. And if the largest game is, say, kudu or zebra or sable or wildebeest, then a .300 magnum is perfectly adequate. Then you should consider whether you really need a second rifle at all. Something on the order of a .270 would be very useful for the smaller antelope, but truly isn't essential.

Still, most hunters will be most comfortable with two rifles. The trick is to pick two rifles that compliment each other and will be used, and that also will offer some backup for each other should one rifle fail. The most common failure is probably scope failure, and that's more sensibly cured by backup iron sights or, better, a spare scope set in rings, than by an extra rifle. However, I've seen rifle stocks broken at least six times on safaris, and this will generally put a rifle out of action for the duration. I've also had two mechanical breakdowns that simply couldn't be fixed.

This is why I don't like to see specialization in a two-rifle battery. If you have a scoped .375 or .338 as your "heavy" or "main" rifle, then you could have a wonderful time with a .243 or even a .22 centerfire on the smaller antelopes. But supposing the stock splits on your heavier rifle? Better to go a bit heavy on your lighter rifle so you've got some redundancy between the two, just in case.

The ultimate redundancy would be two rifles of versatile and identical caliber–a pair of .338s or .375s, with the second rifle purely a spare. I wouldn't go that far, but I would recommend the second rifle be large enough in caliber to handle, at least in a pinch, *the largest game you intend to hunt.* Of course, this can be tempered by your knowledge of what rifle or rifles your professional hunter will have in camp. For most situations, something between .270 and .30 caliber will offer the versatility you may need in a second rifle.

The country makes a difference, too. Shooting is likely to be longer in South Africa, Namibia, and East Africa's savannas than in thornbush like Zimbabwe. A .35 Whelen would be a great plains game rifle in Zimbabwe but lacks the range for open plains.

Now add buffalo and things change dramatically. You must up your heavier rifle to at least a .375, perhaps a .416. Should you also increase the lighter rifle? Perhaps. It depends on what you're hunting, but never forget you can shoot light game with a heavy rifle, but not vice versa. If you have a .375 you have one rifle that will do everything, so you can be flexible in your lighter rifle. Optimally, especially if you're hunting open country, you might want something with a bit more reach, perhaps a .300. But if you prefer to bring your pet deer rifle in .270, 7mm magnum, .30-06, or whatever, you're in good shape, unless something happens to your .375. You should know what rifle or rifles your PH will have in camp, and this might be considered when choosing your battery.

A two-gun battery including a .416 is much the same, except for this: The .416s (all of them) are *absolutely* better for buffalo than the .375, but the .416s are not as versatile. You probably want to match up a .416 with a lighter rifle that has both power and reach, perhaps a .300 magnum at a minimum or, better, a hot .33 or .35.

Far and away the most convenient battery is just one rifle–and sometimes baggage restrictions are so tight or the bag so limited that one rifle makes the most sense. On a short plains game safari anything from .270 Winchester to .340 Weatherby Magnum might be ideal, depending on the largest species you plan to hunt. For instance, I took just a .340 Weatherby Magnum to Ethiopia. For safaris that include buffalo, there are really just two choices: .375 or .416. I consider the .375 a better one-rifle battery than the .416, but it depends on the game and the country. In forest or thornbush you could make a good case for the .416, but on all three of my C.A.R. hunts I've taken just a .375 and I've been perfectly happy. I'm considering taking a .416 Rigby when I make another try for bongo six months from now–but I might well stick with the .375. By the way, in the forest you do want to carry a .375 at a minimum, since close encounters with elephant are always possible.

The other thing about one-rifle batteries is that one rifle must be completely reliable. You can't necessarily guard against a broken stock in baggage handling; all you can do is check carefully for incipient cracks before you pack, and make sure you've got a well-padded gun case that won't let the rifle shift. Baggage handling has been responsible for half the broken stocks I've seen. The other half, well: A Land Rover hit a bad bump and the stock snapped at the wrist; *another* vehicle backed over a rifle left lying where it shouldn't have been; and a buffalo half was loaded atop a rifle propped against the inside wheel well. The first one probably couldn't have been predicted, but the last two were pure stupidity. Hang on to your rifle–especially if it's the only one you've got. And along with that one rifle, bring an extra scope set in rings, good screwdrivers, and some duct tape and Super Glue. It's amazing what you can fix when you have to.

Specialized rifles do have a place in Africa, but if your tastes run in that direction, you have to be very careful in selecting the second rifle in a two-gun battery. For instance, you may wish to use a true big bore, be it double or magazine, on your buffalo (or elephant, for that matter). There's nothing wrong with that. In fact, there's everything right with it; there's a big difference between shooting a buffalo with a .375 or .416 and shooting one with a .470 or .500, but you must accept that the big gun will be used *only* for thick-skinned dangerous game, and just possibly a lion if the circumstances are right. Your second rifle will be used for everything else, so it must have a lot of versatility. If you want to take an open-sighted double or big-bore magazine rifle on a buffalo or general bag safari, by all means do so. That's what such rifles are for. But you should back it up with something between a .338 and a .375, with a scope. And if lion is on the agenda, make it a .375.

Now, taking the other end of the spectrum, supposing you just have to take your pet .22 Hornet or .223 for dassies, spring hares, and small antelope. You'll have a perfect rifle for such game, but it won't be good for much else. There's nothing wrong with taking a little gun–Bob Petersen almost always takes his .22 Hornet. But if you go ultralight on the light rifle, you'd best go very versatile and pretty heavy on the second rifle.

To some extent it depends on how much of a gun nut you are. If an important part of the adventure is selecting and using the perfect tool for the job, go for it, but be prepared for extra hassle and expense. On a Tanzanian safari in 1988 I took a double .470, a .416 Rigby, a .375 H&H, and a 7mm Remington Magnum. I used and enjoyed them all, but I'll never burden myself like that again.

On many other occasions I've taken a double .470 for just one animal of several, and I'll do it again, but an open-sighted big bore is so limited in range that great care must be taken in choosing the second rifle. On his Zambian hunt in 1996 Bob Petersen used a second gun permit so he could take four rifles. His .22 Hornet was for birds and small antelope; his .460 G&A was for buffalo; his .375 H&H was for lion and eland; and his Jarrett .300 Winchester Magnum was for everything else. In this age of specialization it's great fun to fantasize about the perfect rifle for every species of game you'll hunt, but it just isn't very practical. The opportunity to take four or a half-dozen rifles is shrinking rapidly.

Too, the opportunity to use a lot of rifles on safari is shrinking as well. These days six or eight trophies is a pretty good bag on the average ten- to fourteen-day safari. The days of "free" or "extra" animals for bait or camp meat are just about over, and few safari bags will hit the double digits.

On the other hand, with diminished bags each trophy taken on a safari has a greater significance. The purist in each of us wants things done just so, and having the right rifle is part of the package. Today, when very few safaris include more than one buffalo, there are more double rifles being made and used than when most safaris included three or four buffalo and a couple of elephant.

The ultimate simplicity for a safari battery is not to bring one, but to borrow or rent guns from the safari company. Chances are they'll be sound arms, since your success will depend on them. Perhaps this would be the best course, especially for short safaris with limited objectives. However, I don't recommend going this route. Selection of the right rifle and the proper bullet is important, and for most of us putting our own choices to the test is part of the memories we'll carry forever.

So my recommendation is this: Take two rifles at the most, and choose them wisely based on the game you plan to hunt and the country you will encounter. You don't need cannons for African plains game, but you do need reliability, versatility, and good bullets.

Bullet technology has advanced tremendously in the last decade, and today's bullets are so good that they actually make a difference in the calibers you can and should use. The problem with African hunting is you never know exactly what you might encounter next, but today we have bullets so good that you can do some amazing things with light rifles if you have to. Given the tremendous size variance among African antelope, this is the place for the "super premium" bullets. Depending on what your rifle shoots best, and (if you don't handload) what is available in your chosen cartridge, take a look at Winchester's Fail Safe, Trophy Bonded Bearclaw, Barnes X, and Swift A-Frame bullets. I can't pick the best among them, but with any of these the .375 H&H is much more gun on buffalo than it used to be. And your garden variety .270-7mm-.30-06-.300 is much more gun on the larger, tougher plains game. These same bullets are also wonderful in the big bores, but unless your cartridge runs to extreme velocities, bullet selection is less critical in the over-.40 calibers. I've had wonderful success with Woodleigh Weldcore, A-Square Dead Tough, and Speer African Grand Slam, all bonded-core bullets–but I've also had great results with plain old Hornady softpoints.

As a final thought on bullets, I do believe in softpoints–*good* softpoints–for the first shot on buffalo, and for all soft-skinned game. The only sensible uses for solids are: backup on buffalo, elephant, hippo, and rhino. If your safari includes any of these animals, include ten solids for the heavy rifle in your mix of ammunition. There are a number of good solids today, just as there are many good softpoints. The homogenous-alloy solids–so-called "brass bullets"–are absolutely wonderful, but because of different pressures and regulation, I don't fire them in my doubles. In the doubles I stick with Woodleigh because the profile and bearing surface are similar to those of the old Kynoch solids, but depending on caliber availability other very fine choices are the Hornady, Speer African Grand Slam, and Trophy Bonded Sledgehammer.

You don't need a solid very often, but when you need one you need it bad, so don't forget 'em!

We'll finish with a few lines on gun care. On average, African hunting is fairly gentle on guns–certainly when compared with hunting in Canada, Alaska, or the Rocky Mountains. The African winter, when most safaris are conducted, is mild and rain is very unlikely. Crawling around through thorns and over antheaps will cause some wear and tear on good walnut, but generally nothing that can't be easily repaired. In other words, the typical African safari is a perfectly acceptable place to take nice guns, if you have nice guns and you want to use them. The two greatest problems are dust, made worse by too much lubricant, and rust caused by contact with sweaty hands. Both problems can be held at bay by a few minutes of care each evening. Take a toothbrush, silicone rag, cleaning rod, solvent, and oil. And while you're swabbing away the dust, *always* look down the barrel. Not infrequently you'll find ants or wasps trying to set up shop in your rifle barrel, creating potentially explosive obstructions. If your rifle is so prized or so valuable that you're going to worry about it, don't bring it–you've got other things to worry about when you're closing on animals that can hurt you. But in general, safari life is kind to firearms.

There are exceptions. Generally speaking, these are: swamp hunts (usually for sitatunga, but sometimes for buffalo, crocodile, hippo, etc.); forest hunts for anything; and rainy season safaris, again for anything. On the forest hunt discussed in Chapter Twenty-One I took my beat-up old left-hand-converted Winchester Model 70 .375. I had shot out the barrel and replaced it the year before, so this rifle started the safari with a new blue job. Despite wiping down every day and cleaning the barrel after a rain, it ended the safari with virtually no bluing, a stock white from being rained on, and all kinds of rust in little nooks and crannies. I didn't mind; the rifle is an old friend, but it's been used and abused for years. Sherwin Scott, on the other hand, took a David Miller .375, a beautiful and valuable rifle. Mind you, none of the abuse it took couldn't be fixed, but I felt sorry for him and sorrier for that beautiful rifle. Likewise, I had a double rifle on a rainy season elephant hunt in the Selous in 1988, and during every daily shower I cried a bit as rain sluiced down over the action.

I like African rifles to look like African rifles, so I much prefer wooden stocks and traditional lines. But there is a place in Africa for synthetic stocks and rustproof finishes, and it's the swamps, the forests, and during the rains.

ALTERNATIVE EQUIPMENT

Rules on both archery equipment and handguns are changing so rapidly that it's impossible to give accurate information. At this writing Zimbabwe, South Africa, the C.A.R., and Tanzania offer the simplest importation of handguns, with the best and most strictly legal hunting opportunities on private land in Zimbabwe and South Africa. Bow hunting is, again at this writing, legal for plains game on private land in Zimbabwe and South Africa. Elsewhere bow hunting may not be specifically addressed in the game regulations, so it may be conducted in the absence of regulation rather than with its blessing. This is essentially the situation in Zambia and the C.A.R., and undoubtedly a few other places.

If you're contemplating a handgun or bow safari, the best course is to check with Safari Club International for current regulations, and *absolutely* discuss it with your outfitter. I've done quite a bit of handgun hunting in Africa, and I just may take a bow one of these years. Philosophically, and at the risk of taking an unpopular stand, I think both handgun hunting and bow hunting are just great . . . for plains game. Very skilled hunters have taken the entire Big Five with both archery tackle and handguns. Of course it can be done. But I regard it as a dangerous stunt, and unfortunately it's the unarmed, courageous, and altogether too trusting trackers who take the risks.

For the full range of plains game and perhaps leopard, there's no problem. However, if you plan such a safari be realistic in your expectations. By choosing alternative equipment you are drastically reducing your opportunities for success. We seem to accept this if we go on a bow hunt for whitetail in North America, but have trouble swallowing it in Africa. It's no different, and might even be worse. Water hole hunting on well-managed private land is very successful, but in more remote country where poacher-educated game must be stalked it's very difficult to get within bow range. If you accept the challenge for its own sake, God bless you, but reduce your expectations accordingly.

CALIBER RESTRICTIONS

Back in the days when the East African Professional Hunters Association ruled the roost, everyone knew the rules: .40 caliber or greater for thick-skinned dangerous game, .375 for lion. Today things are generally less structured, and it can be difficult to determine if there are rules, let alone what those rules are. Botswana has a firm rule of .375 minimum for dangerous game. Zimbabwe's rules–on government concessions–are a complex system of minimum kilojoules (a European measurement) of energy for various classes of game. Consider it .375 H&H-equivalent for lion, buffalo, and elephant and you're on target.

Some countries haven't addressed the issue, and others apply little enforcement. However, the decades-old rule of the .375 H&H as a minimum for dangerous game remains sensible, regardless of what the local laws say or don't say. It's unlikely you'll find game wardens wandering around checking calibers in the African bush, and we can split hairs all day long about caliber and bullet weight versus velocity and energy. Some hunters seem to have a burning desire to ignore both local game laws and common sense, but recalling that local Botswana hunter whose guts were hanging out after tackling buffalo with a .30-06, I think I'll go on record as recommending the .375 H&H as a good minimum for thick-skinned game. I won't argue that a .375 is needed for either a 350-pound lion or a 150-pound leopard. Any .30 caliber with a good bullet is fine for unwounded lion, and a .270 is probably ideal for leopard. But I reckon we should support their game laws–we expect visitors to obey ours. Just as a matter of course, check with your agent and your outfitter regarding current local caliber restrictions, and let them know what rifles you plan to bring when you're in the initial planning stages. African game laws are pretty basic, but you'll run into occasional stumbling blocks, such as .22s being illegal (Botswana) or a two-rifle limitation (Zambia).

APPENDIX 3

THE FUTURE OF AFRICAN HUNTING

I don't know who started it, but it's been fashionable for many years to predict an imminent end to African hunting. I have tried to avoid this trap these last twenty years. Africa has been extremely good to me, and it is still capable of presenting pleasant surprises. For instance, I saw much more game in Zambia in 1995 and 1996 than I saw in Kenya twenty years ago.

Despite all the doom and gloom that generations of writers have predicted, the late 1990s are not a bad time to hunt in Africa. There have been serious and regrettable casualties since the "good old days"–whenever they were. The wonderful hunting for scimitar oryx and addax on the southern fringes of the Sahara is gone forever. Despite various rumors, it's unlikely the giant sable has survived Angola's long bush war. The black rhino are virtually finished, gone to make dagger handles and to be ground up into aphrodisiacs. I believe the black rhino can be saved from extinction on its native continent, but just barely. It's even possible that a very few surplus black rhino bulls will be hunted in Zimbabwe and South Africa in years to come, but I'm quite certain I won't ever have that experience.

However, the bright side is pretty bright. The ivory ban has dramatically slowed elephant poaching, and the great pachyderms are increasing in many parts of Africa. I see more opportunities to hunt elephant, not fewer, over the next few years. Right now all of the principal spiral-horned antelopes are huntable, and with the exception of the Sahara Desert, some countries are huntable in all regions and habitats of the great continent.

The roll call of nations currently open to hunting is different than it was twenty years ago, but the list is extensive. Gone are Somalia, Angola, and Uganda, probably never to return. I believe Kenya will reopen, perhaps by the time these lines see the light of day, and the reopening of southern Chad is almost a certainty. Countries like Gabon and Liberia will come and go as politics dictate. There is great potential in giant Zaire, and some possibilities in Malawi. There is some hunting currently in Senegal, Burkina Faso, Benin, Morocco, and a few other out-of-the-way places. Sudan's Red Sea Hills are currently being hunted, and somewhere in the southern part of that war-torn land there must be pockets of game remaining. Parts of Mozambique and Congo are open, with much potential for more. What I consider the "core" of African hunting currently resides in South Africa, Namibia, Botswana, Zimbabwe, Zambia, Tanzania, Ethiopia, C.A.R., and Cameroon. Collectively, the list of countries open, partially open, or likely to open is impressive. The hunting programs in some of these countries are well-institutionalized and profitable enough to maintain governmental interest and approval. In other cases the situation is more fragile, making this a fluid roll call that will certainly change, but it's extensive enough that one can safely predict a wealth and variety of African hunting well into the next century.

And yet I feel the noose tightening, at least for African hunting in the traditional sense. The concentrations of game I've seen recently in Zambia's Kafue and the Selous Reserve give me optimism for a few more decades of wild Africa, but such spots are shrinking in numbers. The widespread meat poaching I saw happen in the eastern C.A.R. is just a microcosm of what has happened across thousands of miles of once-game-rich Africa: Chad, Sudan, Uganda, Angola, and much of Mozambique are all wastelands now, and it has happened in the last twenty-five years. C.A.R. is going fast, and many once-prime blocks in Zambia, Tanzania, and even Botswana are gone as well.

It's often said that the only real hope for wildlife in Third World countries is for adequate value to be placed upon it. Safari hunting does that, and as distasteful as the idea is to preservationists, many of the most rabid among them have started to support controlled hunting as a means of preservation. But the countries just mentioned *are* hunting countries, and hunting brings in important revenues. Even they have been unable to stem the tide of meat poaching and greed for grazing and farming land by hungry people. If it can happen in countries that support and rely upon hunting, what must be happening in the hinterlands where there is no game management at all?

Privatization of wildlife has proven effective, and I believe game ranching will preserve African wildlife so long as there are hunters to support the industry. Game ranching has brought back South Africa's rich wildlife, and is preserving it in Namibia and Zimbabwe. The concept is spreading north; there are viable game ranches in Zambia and Botswana today, and should Kenya reopen some of the greatest potential lies on private land. Game ranching is effective, economical for hunters, and profitable for landowners. Provided there are still hunters in the societies of the world that can afford safaris, I expect superb plains game hunting to remain well beyond my lifetime. In suitable habitat there will remain plenty of leopards as well.

Unfortunately, game ranching can rarely be done where elephants can roam free, where herds of buffalo can follow the best grazing, and where prides of lions can follow those buffalo. Perhaps a few places like the Selous Reserve can be preserved, and privatization on a grand scale, such as the Save Conservancy and some of the huge estates along the Kruger Park will preserve slices of wild Africa–but over the next decade or two I see the Africa where you can still hear lions roar shrinking rapidly.

There is no reason to panic; the noose is closing slowly and gradually. There remains and will remain some very fine hunting. If current trends continue I see better elephant hunting in ten years than exists at this writing. Certainly there will be superb buffalo hunting for many years to come. White rhino will remain as they are today–available but very expensive. If Zimbabwe and South Africa get their way and can buck the worldwide eco-politics, there may even be a few black rhino permits. The argument is sound; surplus bulls do exist, and their value to hunters would fund enormous conservation efforts.

If I were starting out now, and were looking ahead to the African hunting I should do now before it's too late, I'd look to the country where lions still roar. The great cats will not be tolerated where cattle are grazed–and more and more of Africa will be grazed in years to come. Lions are prolific breeders and are hardly endangered in any way, but it takes two things to grow the heavily-maned lions that hunters crave: genetics and time. Right now there are few areas producing well-maned lions, and they will grow fewer. Among the Big Five, excluding black rhino, a good lion is far and away the most difficult prize. And they will get more difficult. When the great hue and cry erupted about saving the "endangered" African elephant there were still at least six hundred thousand wild elephants in Africa. They're locally threatened, yes, but have never been endangered. There are not, and perhaps never have been, six hundred thousand wild lions . . . .

Among the exceptionally desirable antelopes, opportunities are shrinking fast for both roan and sable antelope. For roan, there is central and western Tanzania, Zambia, northern C.A.R., northern Cameroon, and a bit of country farther west. For sable, there's southern and western Tanzania, Zambia's Kafue, Zimbabwe's Matetsi, and Botswana's Chobe.

Just a few places for each animal. Lesser kudu, failing a reopening of Kenya, are huntable just in northern Tanzania and Ethiopia. Among the prized antelope, perhaps the two most restricted right now are Lord Derby eland and mountain nyala. Both exist only in dwindling and vulnerable ranges, the former in the the northern C.A.R. and northern Cameroon and perhaps southern Chad; the latter only in central Ethiopia's mountains.

We already know the beautiful desert antelope are gone, or nearly so. At this writing we don't know for sure the status of the giant sable, the Nile lechwe, the Hunter hartebeest, and so many other localized species that had the misfortune to make their habitat in bad neighborhoods–but we can guess. If I were starting out now to build a collection of African game and safari memories, I'd look first to those animals that exist in Africa's vanishing wilderness, for, regrettably, it will continue to vanish.

That's provided, of course, that I could afford such safaris–and recognizing that many of you reading these lines cannot. If I could have afforded to hunt big elephant in Sudan or the C.A.R. fifteen or twenty years ago I would have; likewise, if I could have afforded to hunt black rhino in Kenya or Zambia during those last years they were on license, I would have. No one can do it all, regardless of resources.

If you can go where the lions roar, you should. But if you can't, take heart at the good news: Much African hunting is more affordable now than it ever was. While it may change and become ever more specialized and more privatized, much of Africa and much African hunting will remain for many, many years to come. And it's all wonderful.

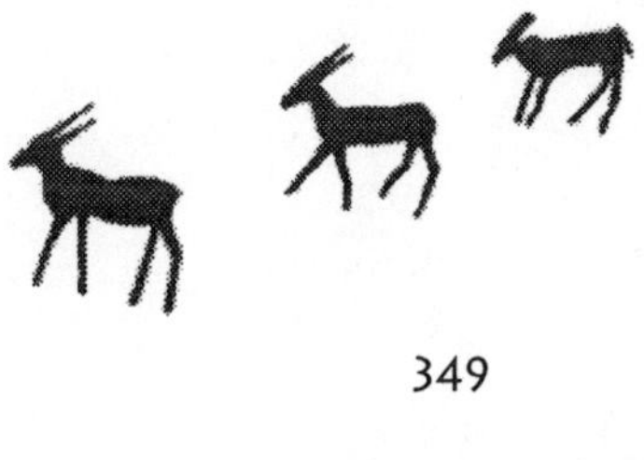

SAFARI PRESS